DATE DUE

APR 1 1998	
APR 29 1998	

GAYLORD   PRINTED IN U.S.A.

PERGAMON GENERAL PSYCHOLOGY SERIES

Editors: Arnold P. Goldstein, *Syracuse University*
Leonard Krasner, *SUNY, Stony Brook*

Creating Change in Mental Health Organizations

PGPS-42

CREATING CHANGE

IN MENTAL HEALTH ORGANIZATIONS

Drawing by Paul Brown

Creating Change in
Mental Health Organizations

GEORGE W. FAIRWEATHER
Michigan State University

DAVID H. SANDERS
Assistant Commissioner of Health
Cincinnati, Ohio

LOUIS G. TORNATZKY
Michigan State University

with

ROBERT N. HARRIS, Jr.
Rock Island, Illinois

PERGAMON PRESS INC.

New York · Toronto · Oxford · Sydney

PERGAMON PRESS INC.
Maxwell House, Fairview Park, Elmsford, N.Y. 10523

PERGAMON OF CANADA LTD.
207 Queen's Quay West, Toronto 117, Ontario

PERGAMON PRESS LTD.
Headington Hill Hall, Oxford

PERGAMON PRESS (AUST.) PTY. LTD.
Rushcutters Bay, Sydney, N.S.W.

Library of Congress Cataloging in Publication Data

Main entry under title:

Creating change in mental health organizations.
  (Pergamon general psychology series 42)
  1.   Community mental health services--
Administration.   2.   Organizational change.
I.   Fairweather, George William, 1921–
[DNLM: 1.   Hospitals, Psychiatric--U.S.
2.   Mental health services--U.S.   WM30 F172c
1974].
RC439.C816   1974   362.2   73-13833
ISBN 0-08-017832-4   (S)
ISBN 0-08 017833-2   (H)

\

Printed in the United States of America

Contents

Preface

This book presents the results of a national experiment aimed at finding the parameters of social change in mental health organizations. While the experiment involves most mental hospitals in the nation, it is the hope of the experimenters that the groundwork has been laid for innovation utilization experiments that transcend the mental health area. For it is the firm conviction of the authors that the major survival issue man will have to solve in the latter part of the 20th century and in the 21st century involves changing his institutional practices, behaviors, and values in more innovative directions.

In order to complete this experiment it was necessary to involve 255 mental hospitals throughout the nation in various ways in an attempt to persuade them to adopt an innovative treatment method, the community lodge, which was established in previous research as a valid and helpful mental health program. This book presents the results of the study from a variety of perspectives: from the perspective of the experimenters themselves, from the perspective of the persons within the hospital who gave information about their involvement in the change processes, and from the perspective of others in certain hospitals who succeeded in finally establishing the lodge society. The problems faced by all the individuals on the research team and in the hospitals who attempted to establish the lodge society—some of whom failed and some of whom succeeded—cannot be overemphasized. Although the sorrow and happiness of people who failed and succeeded may not be clearly defined in the book, it is hoped that this background of emotion will be felt by the reader.

All research material has been edited to preserve anonymity. Fictitious names have been used throughout with some attempts to add humor to the descriptions of the various research activities. Identifying dates and the names of professional persons have been altered.

The authors have attempted to present the events that occurred in this major social change experiment in a longitudinal way. Thus, each successive step toward completion of the experiment is elaborated in terms of the sequential nature in which it occurred. The authors have described the background for the experiment in Chapters 1 and 2. They have attempted to capture the flavor of the experiment, particularly in Chapters 3 and 5. In Chapters 4, 6, and 7 the quantitative results are given. Finally, a summary of the results in the form of operating principles or guidelines for social change is presented in Chapter 8 while Chapter 9 offers a broadened view of social policy decision making.

No longitudinal, naturalistic field experiment of this kind could be carried out without the involvement and dedication of a large number of people. We cannot name all of those who have made a significant contribution to this study, nor can we adequately recognize all those who have had a meaningful involvement in it. But to all of them we are deeply indebted and express our gratitude. Some persons and organizations contributed so much to the total project that, despite the injustices imposed by the brevity of the recognition, their names deserve special mention. We are indebted to NIMH which funded the project under Grant No. 7 R12 MN17888-01 that provided the financial support. The late Dr. Thomas Kennelly aided the project in its initial stages by engaging in many discussions about the manner in which social changes might occur in large mental health organizations. To Helen Pearson and Dorothy Bleck, two of the early researchers, we express our deepest gratitude for their help in getting the project off the ground. Drs. Roger Jennings, David L. Cressler, Hugo Maynard, as well as Larry Gerstenhaber, Jeffrey Taylor, and Ladd McDonald traveled extensively throughout the nation in their attempts to help implement the lodge program. Their careful attention to research details and their devotion to the research cannot be overvalued. Without their help this project could not have been completed.

For the usual daily hard work, other persons have made an equal but different contribution. We are especially indebted to Sharon Doolittle who helped manage the early part of the research study when a great deal of traveling was done. Difficulties in making arrangements and last-minute changes in itinerary were commonplace. She effectively handled all aspects of the job and to her we are deeply grateful. We are also grateful to

Mrs. Gudrun Gale who helped manage the research study in its latter phases and was responsible along with Mrs. Marjorie Curtis for the typing of this manuscript. We applaud Mrs. Gale and Mrs. Curtis for their admirable handling of the problems faced by Mrs. Doolittle, for their tolerance of the incessant chatter of researchers and for their ability to survive the difficult hours as victims of their search for perfection.

But among those who are most deserving of our gratitude are the ex-patients and staffs who marched out the hospital gates to establish residence in new community lodges. Their hard work and willingness to engage in this adventurous activity was an integral and essential part of the study. Most of all we were inspired by the willingness of these small groups of motivated and humane individuals to withstand the pressures from their peers to conform and by their ability to slice through bureaucratic redtape that is one of the keys to essential social change.

G. W. F.

D. H. S.

L. G. T.

About the Authors...

George W. Fairweather (Ph.D., University of Illinois) is Professor of Psychology and also of Urban Affairs and is Director of the Ecological Psychology Program at Michigan State University. He has been Principal Investigator of NIMH research projects co-sponsored by Stanford University and the Veterans Administration, 1963–67; by Portland State University, 1967–69; and Michigan State University, 1969–71. Dr. Fairweather has also worked as a research psychologist at VA Hospitals in Palo Alto, California; Perry Point, Maryland; and Houston, Texas and is the author or co-author of many professional journal articles and books. He is a member of Phi Kappa Phi and the American Psychological Association.

David H. Sanders (Ph.D., Adelphi University) is Assistant Commissioner of Health, Division of Mental Health, Cincinnati, Ohio. He has been a clinical and counseling psychologist at the VA Hospital in Palo Alto, California, Research Associate, Stanford University, and Associate Professor in the Departments of Psychiatry, Psychology, and Community Medicine at Michigan State University, and from 1967 to 1969 has worked with Dr. Fairweather as Project Director, NIMH-Portland State University Research Utilization Project. He has contributed many articles and books to the psychological literature and is a member of numerous psychological associations.

Louis G. Tornatzky, Jr. (Ph.D., Stanford University) is Associate Professor in the Departments of Urban & Metropolitan Studies and Psychology at Michigan State University. He is involved in research exploring interorganizational relations, organizational change, and the evaluation of social programs. From 1969 to 1971 he has worked with Dr. Fairweather as Project Manager, Michigan State University-NIMH Research Utilization Study. He has authored or co-authored many important professional papers.

CHAPTER 1

The Need for Social Change in Treating Mental Illness

Man's unchanging patterns of behavior have created an ever-increasing number of crises in contemporary societies. Environmental degradation continues to worsen, population grows at a rate that almost insures a reduction in the quality of man's life, racial tensions routinely explode into violence in the urban centers and, yet, man continues to behave in ways that tend to perpetuate these problems. It appears daily more obvious that for man's survival and an improvement of his quality of life, continuing change is required in his daily patterns of living. But when change is needed, even when his survival depends upon it, man appears increasingly unable to act in constructive ways. It seems that his patterns of behavior have become so very difficult to change because they are continuously reinforced by the mores and folkways of large and unchanging social institutions. Through their social roles and statuses these organizations maintain a consistency of attitudes, values, and behaviors whose main *raison d'être* is to preserve the status quo (LaPiere, 1965).

Unfortunately, man has given little thought to how he might change his institutions. He typically responds to crises by postponing constructive actions or by implementing *ad hoc* solutions. The practice in democratic societies of constituting a committee as an alternative to constructive action is well known to every concerned citizen. The Kerner Report, The Report of Violence in America, The President's Commission Report on Nutrition, and the recent Report on Campus Unrest in the American University—all attest to the emergence of committees at the time of crises. Most such committee reports are found gathering dust within several months after they have been written, and *ad hoc* solutions to survival

1

crises abound. Arrived at by debate and rule of the majority, the assumption is made that these verbally arranged solutions, when placed in action, will actually solve the problem for which they were intended as solutions. Unfortunately, a history of failures—the 18th Amendment did not stop drinking, the Job Corps did not erase unemployment, the 1964 Civil Rights Act did not dispel racism—teaches the lesson that meaningful social change must be based upon evidence that the accepted societal action will actually solve the problems it is intended to ameliorate.

Such ineffective ways of producing change have been followed in the field of mental health as well as in the aforementioned human problem areas. Historically, most of the changes that have occurred in the mental health field can be most accurately described as social movements. The invention of the large mental hospital, the various forms of shock therapy, psychoanalysis and other forms of psychotherapy, and even the contemporary community mental health programs have usually occurred as changes without appropriate experimental validation. Even today their outcomes remain unknown. Generally, these movements are begun by a person endowed by his peers with a special "expertise" which serves as the basis for validating the outcomes of his own inventions. New mental health programs have more often than not been instituted on the basis of the authority of the advocate for that program rather than upon any careful longitudinal exploration of the outcomes of the new technique, particularly as it is contrasted with other treatment programs. Thus, even in the infrequent case when new valid treatment programs have been found through experimentation, no adequate mechanism for implementing these new programs has been available in the mental health field.

Implementation of new programs, including those experimentally validated, is difficult to achieve because one must overcome the resistance to change existing in mental health organizations. There are many barriers to change inherent in the organizational structure of mental health services, but two are of paramount significance in preventing change. First, there is the barrier of *professional groupings*. Generally, groups are united either by their task, their theoretical position, or their professional organization. Often, for persons in the mental health field, there is a specific task orientation, such as chemotherapy, psychotherapy, occupational therapy, and so on. Task similarity serves as one factor that unites groups of mental health workers. Common experiences serve to create groups whose power positions are jealously guarded. There are, however, other bonds of group formation that also help create groups with special interests and limited membership. One of these is the theoretical position about personality development and treatment. Schools of traditional psychoanalysis, neoanalysis, behavior therapy, and the like serve as rallying cries for the "true believers" and very often determine the relationships such individuals will have with patients, the treatment methods that are used, and the bonds established with other professional persons or groups. Membership is usually restricted to those who have a particular training and who espouse a specific theoretical position. Thus, theory is another basis for the formation of tightly knit mental health groupings. It has existed since the early days of psychoanalysis and it continues to be seen today in such new groups as the behavior therapists as well as others.

Finally, a third force contributing to the grouping of mental health workers is the professional organization. Certain professional organizations, such as the American Psychiatric Association, the American Psychological Association, the National Association of Social Workers, etc., attract persons who are identified with the group through education and training. Many identify with the goals of the parent organization. Enhancing the economic position of its members is usually a function of these professional organizations and a strong acceptance of their policies carries with it a sense of belonging. When a new program is perceived by any of these groups as diminishing their political or economic power it can readily become unacceptable to those members whose own goals are directly related to the parent organization. Often the power aspect of these memberships take the form of defining roles and, accordingly, some of the essential questions for such professional organizations are: Who can do psychotherapy? Who can do occupational therapy? Who can hand out pills? It is at the juncture of prescribing role behaviors that the political and economic power of the organization becomes most pronounced. Unions have operated in this way for years. That jurisdictional disputes have economic power as their main consideration has long been recognized by industry and labor alike.

The aforementioned factors (task similarity, theory, and professional organizations) have served as the basis for the emergence of special interest mental health groups. Many have become cohesive units. The boundary lines around such groups are often almost impenetrable and communication flow to persons with other persuasions and new notions is frequently pushed aside at the group boundary lines. Their members share a common language, a common experience, and frequently accept a common belief system. Since new evidence must fit into existing theory and practice, they do not readily accept new information as a means of modifying existing treatment practices when it requires a deviation from accepted social status structure or institutionalized practice. Thus, contemporary mental health treatment programs many times have been uncritically accepted by treatment planners because these traditional programs are promoted by special interest groups who perceive their own interests as involving the maintenance of institutionalized practices.

In addition to the barriers established by such cohesive groups, the *hierarchical structure* of mental health organizations is a second factor in the prevention of change. The organizational structure typically places decision making in the hands of a few management and professional personnel. Ordinarily, the flexibility that can be brought about by more loosely organized, democratic groups where decisions are made by group concensus and discussion is absent in the organizational structure of the mental health system. This is true whether the system is the large mental hospital defined by Goffman (1962) as a total institution, or in the more recently established community mental health centers where the same hierarchical social status arrangements often exist. In many cases, these "new" community organizations parallel administratively and organizationally the parent mental hospital.

An essential characteristic of this vertical social organization is the rigidity of the power positions in the system. Recent studies (Fairweather, 1964; Fairweather *et al.*, 1969) show that mental hospital personnel clearly perceive hospitals as organized by professional rank with authority distributed in the following descending order: psychiatrists, psychologists, social workers, nurses, aides, and patients. Persons within each of these positions also are permitted decision-making power in descending order—much at the top, little at the bottom. This status structure lends itself to decision making generally emanating from the top and, hopefully, seeping down to those in subordinate status positions. This is another aspect of the organization of mental health services which makes treatment programs so difficult to change. For major change in the area of mental health, services may require a change in the behaviors usually associated with these superordinate and subordinate social statuses. Thus, the vertical organization and rigidity of mental health social statuses and roles are coupled with the special interest groups just mentioned to create the central barriers to the adoption of new mental health practices in America.

Essentially, then, the acceptance of any new mental health program requires overcoming rather severe organizational rigidity. It seems quite clear that to the extent that any new mental health program requires change in the social status structure of the organization or a perceived loss in power by its special interest groups, to that extent will the new program be resisted and will its adoption be less likely to occur. However, for continued improvement in mental health practices these obstacles must be overcome because the key to improving mental health treatment programs often lies in changing these social roles and statuses. It is toward a resolution of this problem that our attention is now directed.

Since the adoption of most new treatment programs requires organizational change that is so difficult for persons to make, any advocate for a new program should be relatively certain that the adoption of the new program he is promoting will improve treatment outcomes. For this reason, considerable time and effort must be spent in discovering and validating new programs and an equally strong effort must be made to develop change strategies through which these experimentally validated programs can be assimilated into existing practice.

Historically, research in the mental health field has often not been used by mental health administrators to alter their existing programs; research and service usually proceed along parallel lines, neither one affecting the other very much. And few, if any, consistent promotional efforts are usually made by the researchers to implement their own newly discovered programs regardless of how valid they might be. Unused research material accumulates at an ever-increasing rate because there is no direct relationship between the inventors and users of mental health programs (Glaser and Wrenn, 1966). It is this linkage between the researcher or discoverer and the users of mental health services that so clearly needs to be understood and expanded. It was with this thought in mind that the researchers began the study reported in this book.

The opportunity for a definitive study in the area of social change in mental health practices presented itself as the result of a recent research into the community living of formerly chronically hospitalized mental patients. This study clearly established the value of a particular community treatment program—the lodge—in rehabilitating chronic mental patients. For some understanding of the tedious longitudinal research process leading to the creation of this new mental health treatment model that needed to be adopted nationally, one must understand the sequence of experiments leading to its discovery and validation.

The lodge program was the outgrowth of several years of innovative model building and evaluating experiments. These sequential studies are summarized elsewhere in the following manner (Fairweather, 1972):

The first of a series of such model building and evaluative studies was conducted in 1955. Its results appeared in three publications (Fairweather *et al.*, 1960; Fairweather and Simon, 1963; and Forsyth and Fairweather, 1961). At that time three very basic questions about mental hospital treatments were asked. They were:

1. Are any of the currently used mental hospital treatment programs more beneficial than others?
2. Is behavior in the hospital related to community behavior?
3. Are some treatment programs more effective with certain types of patients than with others?

The results of these studies showed that patients who participated in the three most common hospital treatment programs [(1) individual psychotherapy, (2) group psychotherapy, and (3) living and working together as groups] do no better or worse in community adjustment 18 months after release from the hospital than those patients who had simply worked in the hospital setting (a fourth condition). Neurotics, acute and chronic psychotic patients showed the same rate of recovery in each of these treatment programs—the acute psychotics responded better to all treatments than the chronic psychotic or neurotic patients. Finally, very little relationship was found between improvement in the hospital settings and the person's subsequent adjustment to community living. Thus, patients who showed improved behavior in the hospital did no better or worse when they were released than those whose behavior did not improve. And regardless of treatment, 72% of the chronic psychotic patients returned to the hospital along with 55% of the neurotics within 18 months after their release. The results clearly indicated that hospital treatment programs were not as beneficial as they might be, at least for these two patient groups. It was, therefore, decided that a new treatment program should be devised for the neurotic and psychotic patients who were spending most of their lives in the mental hospital.

In 1958 a second research was begun to see what kind of treatment programs could be created for them (Fairweather, 1964). The idea had begun to take shape among the researchers, from information given to them by the returning patients, that a vehicle was needed to bridge the gap between hospital and community living. It seemed logical that patients might be organized into problem-solving groups who could then be moved in their own reference groups from the hospital to a citizen's role in community settings. Such reference groups were known to have a stabilizing effect on their members in other situations. If this should be the case with mental patients, the small group itself might help maintain the released patient in the community setting. The first model that needed to be created and evaluated, therefore, was one aimed at discovering whether small groups of patients could take care of each other and adequately solve their daily living problems. A hospital ward comprised of patients organized into small groups who planned their own futures was established. It was compared with a traditional ward. The most significant findings of this study were that small groups of patients whose daily activities were organized around solving their own problems could be formed by even the most chronic patients. The degree of autonomy that the patients assumed surprised the staff. Morale of both patients and staff increased when contrasted with the traditional ward. But, despite these improvements, once a patient left the hospital and his reference group, he returned to the hospital as quickly as a person who had participated in the traditional program. And one result stood out above all others. There was a very high relationship, a correlation of .86 between a patient's remaining in the community and the support he received from the people with whom he lived at the time. It now seemed evident that supportive community living situations needed to be created for such patients. If the group itself could be moved into a community as a unit, it might provide such a supportive situation.

As time passed, this idea seemed more and more relevant to the problem. Accordingly, a model designed to test this hypothesis was created in 1963 and a study to evaluate the model was completed in 1969 (Fairweather, Sanders, Maynard, and Cressler).* For this study, chronic mental patients were again divided into two groups. Both groups participated in the small-group hospital treatment program just described, but when the time came to leave the hospital, some left for a community dormitory

*Special recognition is due to the National Institute of Mental Health (NIMH), which provided the funds for this study (Grant No. 5 R11 MH 01259 and No. 7 R01 MH 14690).

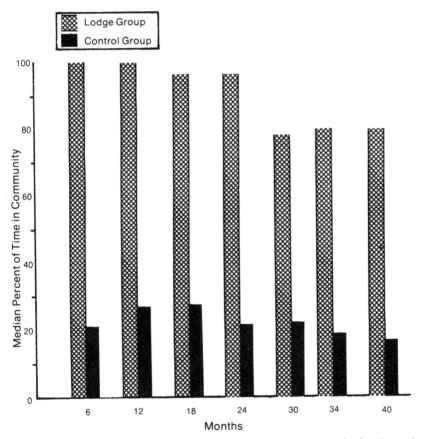

Fig. 1.1 Comparison of lodge and control groups on time in the community for 40 months of follow-up.

(lodge) where a work and living situation was provided for them while others left the hospital independently and used the treatment facilities available to the typical patient in the community, such as outpatient clinics.

Initially, those in the dormitory needed considerable supervision, but they eventually were able to handle all of their problems themselves. Medical care was provided by a private physician in the community. All of the customary daily needs of the former patients, such as food preparation, were managed by the group itself. Eventually, these ex-mental patients became entirely autonomous and self-supporting. Some of the results can be seen in Figure 1.1. It shows that during the first six months of follow-up, the lodge group's median time spent in the community was 100% contrasted with 20% for those receiving traditional community services. Figure 1.1 also shows that similar results obtained for the entire 40 month follow-up period of the project.

Figure 1.2 shows the rather dramatic results when the community lodge and the traditional treatment programs are compared on employment for the same period of follow-up. The median percent of time employed for lodge members was 72% for six months but 0% for those receiving the usual community treatment. These differences

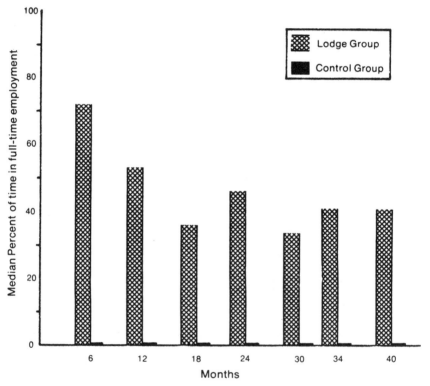

Fig. 1.2 Comparison of lodge and control groups on employment for 40 months of follow-up.

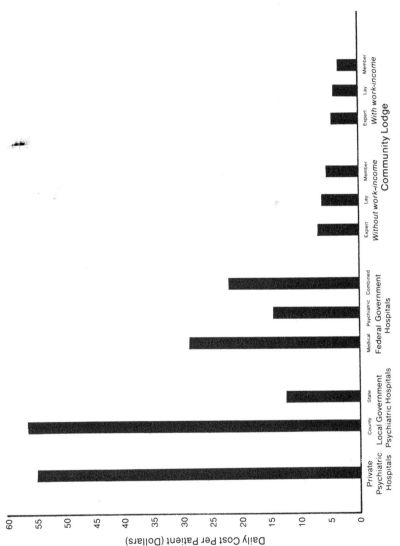

Fig. 1.3 Mean daily cost per person for alternative treatment settings.

for the first six months were not transitory. Figure 1.2 shows that similar differences continued throughout the entire 40 month follow-up period of the project.

And the reduction in cost was dramatic. Figure 1.3 shows that the community treatment program cost less than half that of hospital care. In fact, those living in the dormitory eventually became self-supporting. But these figures fail to capture the high morale of the dormitory members and their general improved perception of themselves and others. The improvement in the ex-mental patients' perception of themselves and their world was very heartening for all mental health workers associated with the project.

The lodge program also resulted in beneficial effects to the community in which it was implanted. It was accepted by the neighborhood where it was located as a place where industrious and reliable working men lived and worked. The neighbors themselves believed that the members of the lodge were more desirable neighbors than those persons who had lived in the same house before them. Lodge members were accepted in the business community as well. Thus, the relationship of the lodge and its membership to the surrounding community was a positive one in which the members contributed to the community as first-class citizens and the community treated them with the respect and dignity given such citizens everywhere. These results clearly show that movement into the appropriate community setting can replace most mental hospitals.

A new community treatment program had been discovered through continuous longitudinal research which not only enhanced the ex-mental patient's perception of himself, lengthened the time he remained in the community, increased the satisfaction of professional personnel, but also could be carried out at one-third the cost of keeping a patient in the mental hospital. It seemed inevitable that most mental hospitals would be pleased to implement such a new program. And so it was with this in mind that the administration of the hospital where the research project had been initiated was approached about instituting the lodge program as a permanent part of the hospital's community treatment program to be made available to persons treated by that hospital.

It was a matter of some surprise to the researchers who had created and evaluated the lodge program to find that though the hospital management was sympathetic to the new program and readily perceived its merits, it was unable or unwilling to establish the lodge project as an integral part of the hospital treatment program. *Apparently, experimenting with a new social treatment program is one process; incorporating it into ongoing treatment programs is quite another.* The sequence of events that occurred in an attempt to get agency support for the lodge treatment program was described elsewhere as follows (Fairweather *et al.*, 1969):

A few months prior to termination of research-project support for the lodge operation, the research director tried to interest several federal, state, and county agencies in financing the lodge as a permanent community program for discharged mental patients. This action was consistent with his responsibility for the welfare of lodge members. The response from each of the various agencies was remarkably similar. None disagreed about the need for such a community treatment program but each of these positive expressions was followed invariably by arguments demonstrating why the particular agency involved could not implement such a program. Agencies most frequently gave the following reasons for this inability: they would need additional funds for such a new program (despite the cost reduction shown in the results); such a unique program would not fit into the agency's practices; professional staffs would not accept a program which would allow more autonomy for mental patients, since granting such autonomy would require unwelcome changes in professional roles. During this period, the research director also contacted the board of directors of the rehabilitative corporation for whom the members worked. This nonprofit corporation was the only organization that expressed an interest in continuing the lodge as a treatment program for mentally ill persons. However, it was completely unable to provide the necessary funds.

The director of the psychology services at the hospital from which the lodge members came believed that the hospital itself might be able to use some hospital funds to support new members in the community. He thought it might also be possible to get special funds for continuing the lodge. This seemed reasonable because patients could be taken from the hospital to live in community residences at less than one-half the cost this very hospital would otherwise expend to continue them as patients. Accordingly, the psychology director made this proposal to the director of the hospital, who informed him that authority for the allocation of such funds would be required from the agency that supported the hospital. The agency's central administration was contacted by means of an official communication from the hospital director which presented the results of the investigation in detail. The document concluded by stressing the urgency of the situation, in view of the opportunity not only to provide for the continuation of the lodge at reduced expense to the hospital but also to avoid the financial and human costs of hospital reentry and reinstitution of the program at a later date. At nearly the same time, the research director made a personal presentation of the research results to the central administrative staff of the agency. Despite such attempts to convey this information and its urgency, the agency did not provide the action necessary to continue the lodge program.*

After the lodge had been rejected by the sponsoring hospital, the research team who created the prototype lodge was contacted by a Dr. Brown from a hospital located in another state. The psychiatrist had just finished reading the book, *Social Psychology in Treating Mental Illness* (Fairweather, 1964), which demonstrated that autonomous groups of patients could be created who would be mainly responsible for their own

*After the members of the lodge society received the information that the hospital would no longer support their cooperative society, they leased their own home in the community where they continued the operation of the business they had developed while in the lodge. A complete description of this move toward self-sufficiency is given in the book *Community Life for the Mentally Ill*, Fairweather et al., 1969, pp. 101–126.

treatment program. The young psychiatrist was excited about the possibility of establishing such autonomous groups in his own hospital since
there were few professional persons to help the patients there. He expressed the belief that a program where patients could be more responsible for
their own treatment would be acceptable to him and the other staff. He
was then informed of the recent lodge project where such autonomous
groups had been functioning in the community. As the lodge project was
described to him over the telephone he became even more interested and
asked that one of the research staff members make a visit to his state
hospital so that the program could be explained in detail to the staff there.

From this initial telephone call a consultant's visit to the hospital was
arranged. It was decided that the consultant would advise the hospital
staff to follow the procedures used in establishing the prototype lodge itself. The procedure consisted of two phases:

1. Creating autonomous problem-solving groups of patients in the hospital.

2. Moving the functioning groups into community residences as units.

The consultant's experiences in aiding this first hospital to complete successfully these two phases are presented in this verbatim account of his
activity from the research journal.

> I brought with me on the consultation visit a set of procedures that needed to be
> followed in creating small groups. The three-day consultation had the following pattern:
> meeting for seven to eight hours a day very intensively with the ward staff or a subgroup
> of the ward staff continuously going over the small group program and discussing the
> problems involved in starting such a program; describing the principles of establishing
> peer groups and allowing them to be as autonomous as possible with the staff playing
> the role of shaping their behavior and decision-making ability through feedback from
> staff evaluations (Fairweather, 1964). Prior to the termination of the first three-day
> meeting with the ward staff, I agreed to return in the near future providing they met
> certain criteria which they would have to meet before the program could actually start.
> Such things as selecting the groups of people, setting aside meeting rooms for the
> groups, establishing employment situations for the patients in the hospital and so on.
>
> Approximately three months later I received a call from the head nurse indicating that
> they had reached these objectives. The nurse stated that the staff would be ready to
> start on November 1 which happened to be a Monday. I questioned whether they were
> really ready to initiate the program and made her review for me once again how they
> had met all the criteria to establish the groups that we had agreed upon earlier. When I
> was satisfied that the criteria had been met, I indicated that I could return to the hospital
> for one week's time. She felt that it would be preferable for me to be there when the
> program began. At this point I gave her an alternative, namely, that I would either come
> out for the first week of the program or for the second week of the program to help

evaluate the first week's performance by the autonomous patient groups. She was quite anxious to start the program but apparently she had considerably more anxiety about how the staff would go about evaluating the small groups than she had about initiating the program. Consequently, we decided that I would go there for the second week of the program and allow the staff to initiate the program by themselves, making whatever errors they might happen to make.

The major purpose of the week's visit in November was to give the staff group emotional support and information about how to conduct the staff evaluation of the patient group so that the staff's feedback to the patient group would begin shaping the group's behavior. After arriving on the scene and reviewing the program the staff had created, it was clear they had done a surprisingly good job in following the guidelines to establish the program, almost to the letter. They were very happy—some even ecstatic—about the fact that the program started well—with a bang at six o'clock in the morning on the first Monday—and went through the first week with hardly any difficulty. This week's time was spent mainly in reviewing notes sent to the patient group and reviewing their responses in terms of action the peer groups took regarding their members' behaviors. I spent most of my time helping the staff conduct evaluation and feedback meetings of the patient group since everything else was running quite smoothly. Approximately six months later I received a call from the head nurse indicating that the groups were now functioning well, were able to solve their members' problems, and were ready to move out of the hospital into four lodges in a community which was approximately forty miles from the hospital. Arrangements were not made to visit at that time because the staff felt they had the situation under control. However, we agreed that a visit would be made in a few months to check on just how well the community lodge program was developing.

The next visit was made for a period of three days about three months after the establishment of the lodges. During this time I visited the four lodges that had recently been established—two for men and two for women. The greatest problem observed was that the staff coordinators for the lodges were not permitting the lodge members to develop sufficient autonomy to run the lodges themselves. A simple example of this was that the staff coordinators would go with the ex-patients to shop for the food. During these trips they did not allow the lodge members to select the food freely because they were frightened that the members would make the wrong choices or that they would spend large sums of money rather than staying within the budget. This procedure that prevented member autonomy was easily corrected by pointing out this controlling behavior to the coordinators, even though there was some resistance from them. By the time I left, they had agreed to adopt a procedure that allowed the members to do their own shopping and to make their own errors as a learning procedure.

Upon reviewing the newly established lodges and contrasting them to the prototype lodge, it was apparent that the major principles for the establishment, development, and operation of the lodges were the same. However, it was equally clear that certain minor modifications in the operation of the lodges had been made because of the local conditions and the environment where the lodges were located. In essence, what happened with the program was that the hospital borrowed major pieces of the program and utilized them because they appeared to fit in with their needs and desires. Clearly the staff that initiated the new lodges needed to feel that it was their new program. Even slightly modifying a program to which a staff can then attach its name seems important.

Examples of some local changes are: in the prototype lodge the maximum membership was thirty-five persons living under one roof, however, in the new location four
smaller lodges accommodated from ten to twelve persons each; in the prototype lodge
there was one coordinator whereas in the lodges in the new location they had one
coordinator for each of two lodges who spent somewhat less time at the lodge than the
coordinator had spent at the prototype lodge. Another aspect that was modified because
of the local environment was the work situation—in the prototype lodge an independent
business was established which was run by the patients and through which new employment was created. The new lodges were in no position to establish their own business;
rather, they developed crews or teams of workers who were employed in several already established job situations. For example, the men worked as teams of grounds
keepers at the local golf course and as janitors for some of the local motels while the
women worked as teams of nurses aides in the local nursing homes. Consequently, the
patients did not run their own business as they had done in the prototype lodge. However, all money earned or receipts obtained from the separate teams working for other
employers went into a general fund for the operation of the new lodge, just as had been
done in the prototype lodge. The lodge members then received salaries from their peers
based upon their value to the entire lodge situation, considering their contributions to
both the living and working situations of the lodge society. Approximately nine months
after my last visit to these new lodges, several members of their staff visited our
research team in order to discuss their new program with us and to look at the prototype
lodge. The most interesting observation from their visit involved the clear impression
that they had adopted the lodge system as their own—in fact they stated that their lodge
was operating considerably better and "more autonomously" than ours (the prototype).
Apparently, the corrections that were made in the system from my previous visit had
worked and worked so well that they had now completely adopted the system as their
own.

Concurrent with the establishment of this first lodge replication, consultation visits by members of the staff were made to other mental health
programs. As a consequence of these visits, it became apparent that the
urban or rural geographical setting of a hospital might be a factor that
would influence the acceptance of a lodge. Two illustrative cases (one
rural and one urban) exemplify some organizational differences between
rural and urban hospitals. When the *rural* state hospital was visited two
major factors appeared to influence its decision-making processes: (1) the
hospital had a grant from NIMH and needed to establish some kind of
community rehabilitation program for chronic patients as part of it; and
(2) there was a lack of special interest groupings among the staff and the
rigid hierarchical structure so common in mental health organizations was
not apparent in the staff's daily operations. The superordinate decision-
making model was not used there. The psychiatrist on the ward was there
only part time and the nurse was usually in charge of the ward. Psychiatric aides had a fairly high social status in the program. They were given
far more decision-making responsibility than their counterparts in an

urban hospital visited later. The hospital was affiliated with a major university. There the hierarchical system did not allow psychiatric aides to take any responsibility in decision making. This hierarchical and non-participative organizational structure seemed impervious to new ideas. The staff evidenced no interest in establishing the lodge program despite considerable evidence that it was needed. The personnel, at least on the surface, seemed content with the program they had.

The failure of the parent hospital to adopt the lodge program its own staff had created and these further attempts to implement it with urban and rural hospitals raised a question about what constituted the facilitating conditions for implementing change in mental health organizations. Although the beneficial effects of the lodge mental health innovation had been experimentally verified, the researchers' experiences made it clear that the adoption of this innovation by existing mental health organizations would not occur automatically. Even though, logically, such a successfully demonstrated community treatment innovation as the lodge should immediately be incorporated into community mental health practices as an extension of mental hospital treatment programs everywhere, no such automatic processes occurred. The researchers were now faced with the serious problem of deciding to what extent they were responsible for diffusing the new program they had created and evaluated. Should they adopt the traditional scientific position that the research was ended with a publication of its already accomplished results, or should they assume a more active position and become advocates of the lodge? Essentially, the issue was: to what extent were they, the innovators, responsible to mental health workers and mental patients for making the new treatment program available to them? After much soul-searching the team concluded that they should assume the responsibility for implementing the lodge on a national scale. But how was this to be accomplished? What techniques could they use to implement the lodge? The central issue now facing the researchers was: how can existing organizations be persuaded to incorporate new programs into their current practices? Since no ready answers were available, the research group decided to explore experimentally how mental hospital practices could be changed. It is with an evaluation of this active effort to discover the parameters of social change that this book is concerned. But in order to put these experiences in perspective, it is necessary to view them in the framework of the organizational change experiment, to which the discussion now turns.

CHAPTER 2

The National Experiment: Organizational Change Background and Research Plan

ORGANIZATIONAL CHANGE BACKGROUND

Changing the structure and function of complex organizations to meet contemporary needs is one of the paramount issues facing society today and is the generic issue with which this research is concerned. The initial difficulties in promoting the adoption of the lodge treatment program described in the previous chapter are only one example of the larger societal problem created by institutionalized forms of behavior which have become virtually unchangeable, though in many instances they are inhumane and unjust. And while it is true that rapid social change must continue to occur if man is to solve the survival issues he is facing today, the techniques through which western technological societies can accomplish these changes are not at all clear. This chapter reflects the design of a search for those change "handles" that will make institutions responsive to human needs. This study of the change process in mental health organizations may also yield information about change strategies that could have direct applicability to other institutions, and possibly other societies. The development of change strategies that "work" and are "free" to be used by others is desperately needed in American society to significantly reduce the level of conflict, coercion, and discord in this country.

Historically, man has developed various means of attempting to change unchanging institutions, and they have often been violent. This is not the place to present a thorough review of the role of revolutions, riots, guerrilla warfare, and other violent techniques of change adequately presented elsewhere (Bienen, 1968; Fairweather, 1972), but it can be noted that they are not very helpful means of producing the types of changes currently needed to solve the survival issues of our time, such as the need for new health delivery systems, family planning, etc. Such problems require social cooperation for their solution and often demand the survival of a delicate and sometimes vulnerable social innovation. Even though man frequently has attempted to solve problems of oppression and powerlessness by violent activity, the tactics of violence have more often than not resulted in the destruction or polarizing of the institutions of a society with no guarantee that new and more beneficial institutions will be established.

But are nonviolent protest and traditional political activity equal to the task? The answer here seems clear. The more often used nonviolent techniques have not demonstrated themselves to be effective in creating the type of organizational change now necessary in contemporary society. Marches, strikes, boycotts, and other forms of civil disobedience have not often created the utopian society hoped for by their proponents. Although such techniques may provide the atmosphere for social change, they do not themselves prescribe what changes will yield what outcomes. In short, the politics of nonviolent confrontation have extremely limited impact on what an organization does in its day-to-day activities. They can produce changes in hiring, allocation of budgets, etc., but they seem to have limited effect on changing the social roles within the target institution. Traditional political activity has similar limitations. The control of elective office has resulted in little meaningful and continuous change in public and private institutions. And since laws typically reflect status-quo opinion they appear to have little direct effect in producing solutions for survival problems like environmental degradation, racism, and population regulation.

The problem is very clear. How does a society change the structure and function of complex organizations in an orderly way so that needed problem-solving social change continuously occurs? In this chapter we will examine some conceptualizations of how this problem might be solved, what the relevant variables are in creating social change, and what is an appropriate change strategy for industrialized societies. A review of the organizational change process could point to the directions for this task.

Change Variables Emanating from the Organizational Change Literature

In this section we will rely heavily on the social change categories proposed by Ronald G. Havelock (1969) as a basis for an evaluation of the organizational change literature as it pertains to the process of social change itself. Havelock has examined nearly 4000 studies dealing with "the processes of innovation, dissemination, and knowledge utilization." He has grouped discussion of dissemination and utilization activities into three "perspectives": (1) "research, development, and diffusion," (2) "social interaction," and (3) "problem solving." These categories are particularly appropriate for considering the problem of how organizations can be persuaded to adopt innovations that require changes in their institutional practices.

Variables from the "Research, Development, and Diffusion" (R, D, & D) Perspective   This model is the one that is explicitly, or implicitly, used in much of American industry. It is descriptive of an essentially orderly and rational process that begins with a marginally related idea and ends with a widely used product. Though there is considerable variance within the literature (Clark and Guba, 1965; Clark and Hopkins, 1966; Havelock and Benne, 1967; and Miles, 1964) the stages usually include research, development, diffusion, and adoption. Research is generally viewed as basic in nature, and somewhat separated from the applied product. In other words, research in this mode is a general knowledge-seeking activity. The development phase occurs when applied research (if any) takes place, and the activities typically described are the creation of a package or model related to the concepts generated in the course of the pure research. Evaluation, or pilot testing, of the model is mentioned by some, but not all, writers as a precursor to diffusion. Diffusion (or dissemination) of the model is viewed within this perspective as an activity of the R, D, & D group oriented toward a generally *passive*, but *rational*, audience. The process of the diffusion effort is usually construed as a communication endeavor: making people aware of the new information available. Adoption of the new model is not generally considered as a separate, or definable, process.

Taken as a whole, the R, D, & D perspective is descriptive, but not predictive. It is generally better at giving one an overview of successful product creation and diffusion than of explaining the social change process in public institutions and organizations that deal with more complex social issues. A specific criticism of the model is its unclear relationship to a data and research base. There is a lack of clarity about the extent to which applied research, program evaluation, and research related to the diffusion and adoption process are either emphasized or acknowledged. As a source of potential variables for study in the diffusion-adoption process this perspective is somewhat barren. There is, however, one paramount message that can be translated into manipulatable variables. There is a belief in the efficacy of a rationalistic information-dissemination process of diffusion. If we—as external innovators—want to set in motion a process that results in the organization doing something different, we should merely present our information to those at the policy-making and higher administrative levels; they, being rational men in a rational organization will, of course, respond positively to this outside educative source. Needless to say, there is reason to believe that such a change strategy might be naïve, although it should be systematically tested.

Variables from the "Problem-Solver Perspective"   This approach is closely linked to issues within the field of organizational theory, and it might be useful to briefly consider these. The initial bureaucratic model as formulated by Max Weber was essentially a mechanistic one, which considered an ideal type of organization as one in which very definite structures, rules, and modes of operation determined the social interaction (Weber, 1958). The traditional writings have described the bureaucracy as a rationally designed social organization with processes oriented toward accomplishing stated goals in the most efficient manner possible. Theoretically, the strength of the formal organization is its ability to focus knowledge and expertise on attaining its stated goals. Specialization in work activity, rules delineating areas of specialization, and the use of hierarchical decision making to minimize interpersonal conflict are essential characteristics of this model.

The problem-solver perspective itself emerged from an alternative model of organizational functioning—the human relations school. This movement evolved almost accidentally from research undertaken within the *zeitgeist* of the formal organization model. The Hawthorne studies (Roethlisberger and Dickson, 1964) were some of the initial findings showing the importance of interpersonal relations and peer group pressure in the manner in which ostensibly formal organizations functioned. A body of literature developed (Selznick, 1964; Whyte, 1964) which indicated that informal work groups existed with their own normative structures regarding productivity and job expectations; that interpersonal conflicts could affect intraorganizational communications and effectiveness; that "irrational" factors often influenced what was done and how much was accomplished in organizations; and that policy decisions were often not imposed from above but agreed upon below. This view of organizational functioning does not represent a rational, efficient, goal-directed mechanism envisioned by Weber but a social-psychological labyrinth of intra- and interpersonal needs and interactions.

From this conceptual and empirical background an entire theory and practice of organizational intervention has evolved. Examples include the T-group approach pioneered by National Training Laboratories, the managerial grid of Blake and Mouton (1969), the organizational survey technique of Mann (1957), and the strategies of intervention proposed by leaders of this group such as Argyris (1970) and Bennis (1966). While it is somewhat unfair to categorize this diversity together, there are many common threads. The focus of intervention is on solving the client organization's problems, which is done primarily by a self-examination of personal style, communications patterns, and the like, and with an emphasis on the process of organizational functioning rather than the context of organizational tasks and goals. Although not explicitly stated, the intervention implicitly assumes that some modification of the hierarchical structure is the way organizations should and do function. From this point of view, most change agent efforts should be focused on management rather than lower level personnel. It should also be clear that this theory of interventive practice bends over backward to avoid prescribing what the organization should be doing in a moral or ethical sense. As Argyris states it:

> A second implication states that change is not a primary task of the interventionist. To repeat, the interventionist's primary tasks are to generate valid information, to help the client system make informed and responsible choices, and to develop internal commitment to these choices. One choice that the clients may make is to change aspects of their system. If this choice is made responsibly, the interventionist may help the client to change. (p. 21)

In sum, the logic seems to be that by making inter- and intrapersonal relations more positive and mature the whole organization becomes more responsive to change of a general and unspecified nature. But there is only limited help here in indicating the specifics of "what to do" to implement a specific change in an institution when an advocate is entering from the outside with a *new* practice he believes should be adopted. Virtually all of this literature has as its vantage point, the internal organization, and its goals, how to make it more efficient, effective, or humane. In a sense, all of this literature implicitly is supportive of the status quo in organizations. The change agent following the prescriptions of this literature might, indeed, help create an organization with better communication, higher morale, a better differentiation and integration of subunits, but the organization might still be engaging in processes that are either wrong, immoral, or ineffective.

However, the problem-solver perspective does provide some clues regarding variables to be manipulated and measured in an experiment that probably would have a direct bearing on effecting change. For one, there is a clear emphasis and elaboration of the concept of a change agent who must actively intervene from the outside. This is clearly different from the more passive and rationalistic approach of the R, D, & D perspective, and also begins to clarify at least one of the important procedures that ought to be a central feature of any social change experiment.

Variables from the "Social Interaction Perspective" This body of literature has been more explicitly concerned with the spread of innovation, albeit often in a non-organizational context. Much of the literature is concerned with the spread of technical and agricultural innovations. Research has focused on tracing the diffusion of innovation, on the forms of communication used in spreading innovation, on the match or mismatch between old norms, values, and scales *vis-à-vis* the innovation, etc.

The recent work of Rogers and Shoemaker (1971) is the most complete. They outline the diffusion of innovation as a process, which has several stages (knowledge—persuasion—decision—confirmation) with different channels of communication, playing more or less important roles at the different stages. (Formal communications, important early on; informal communication with peers in later phases.) Similarly, they delineate the characteristics (education, non-authoritarianism, cosmopolitanism) that discriminate early from late adopters. The literature has also outlined the difficulty that diffusion will encounter if the innovation demands changes in norms or roles, or if the change agent (sender) has different norms or values from the potential adopter.

From an organizational change point of view, it is unfortunate that the bulk of work within the social interaction perspective has been concerned with the adoption of innovations by individuals. Although there is some literature pertaining to the adoption of innovations within formal organizations, it is incomplete on at least two counts. More often than not, it is concerned with an internally generated innovation. For example, the problem sometimes evolves around how an industrial manager can get his subordinates to change. Also, there is little literature on the innovation-diffusion process where the innovation itself demands some degree of organizational change.

Despite these shortcomings, the Rogers' model of innovation diffusion in formal organizations is as highly instructive as it is with a person's adoption of an innovation, but in organizations the participants in the process change over time. Due to the hierarchical structure of organizations the decision-making phase is controlled by persons high in power and status. Thus, after knowledge of an innovation is gained by such an individual or individuals, a persuasion process, or evaluation of the innovation, is undertaken by the decision unit, and a decision is reached concerning acceptance or rejection of the innovation. Then the decision unit must engage in communication with subordinate adoption units in the organization (directing, ordering), and action is undertaken by these units to implement the innovation.

What role do Rogers and Shoemaker (1971) assign to participating subordinates in this decision-making process? They argue that participation in the decision to adopt or not adopt by subordinates (eventual responsibility of the adopting unit) is extremely important:

> Thus, *attitude toward* an innovation and *satisfaction with* the decision are two important dependent variables; the adoption unit's participation in the decision stages is a predictor of both acceptance and satisfaction. (p. 309)

They go on to mention that non-participation by subordinates may result in temporary overt implementation, and eventual discontinuance.

A point they make is relevant to the previous discussion of the organizational literature. They argue that authority decisions are often impeded by the restraints of the social structure (that communication within the organization is often distorted, that sensitivity to the environment is often poor). They point out that in addition to decentralized restructuring and management styles that emphasize participation and management visability, an organization can create an "adopting unit." This unit's function is to be sensitive to the social environment, to evaluate potential innovations, and to have well-developed intraorganizational ties to get new programs moving.

Finally, some comments on the role of the change agent as perceived by them: There is a clearly different conceptualization as contrasted with the problem-solver perspective. The change agent is seen as definitely trying to change things in a specific direction, and to implement a specific innovation. Although the change agent must be aware of client needs, client value systems, and their problems, he should also develop a need for his innovation, influence its acceptance, and translate this acceptance into action. Rogers and Shoemaker also suggest—much in keeping with the organizational change writers—a "client-organization," programming "compatible with client ends," "empathy with clients," and a high degree of credibility.

Reflecting the weight on social interaction and communication, they advise that change agents should be homophilous with their clients (e.g., be alike in background, language, etc.), and should work with opinion leaders. However, these comments are not presented as prescriptions for intervention in an organization, but more as general principles of change agentry. It is unclear how these principles would be specifically realized in interaction with a complex organization with an ostensible high degree of "authority decision making."

Basic Problems that Emerge from the Literature

There are some points of agreement in the views presented thus far. In this section we would like to integrate the views from the three perspectives presented in terms of common problems they may propose in effecting organizational adoption of an innovation. The problems themselves may serve as experimental variables to be manipulated and evaluated in order to assess their impact upon creating organizational change.

The Decision-Making Problem   Both the human relations model of organization theory and the problem-solver perspective stress the importance of informal groups and their potential positive impact on organizational functioning. Similarly, Rogers and Shoemaker argue that involvement of individuals and groups of a subordinate status in the decision making relevant to the success of an innovation will result in a more consistent adoption. Although there is a clear appreciation of subordinate task peer groups, this is not clearly reflected in strategies for effecting change. All of the writers seem to assume implicitly a hierarchical decision-making pattern that interventions must work through. Rogers mentions that the basic decisions are made by "authority," which will hopefully "involve" subordinates in decision-making evaluations. The change strategies of Argyris (1970) and Blake and Mouton (1969)—while not directly focused on innovation diffusion—are similarly directed at the management level. It appears that though there is an acknowledgment that organizations do, in fact, deviate from the "machine" model (Katz and Kahn, 1966), those higher in the social structure are still determining the intervention strategy. However, this is a moot question empirically. The question that needs to be experimentally answered appears to be: is it essential to get decision making and participation at a subordinate social status level in an organization before an intervention strategy can be effective? One way to attempt an experimental answer would be to enter the organization at different levels in the authority hierarchy and compare the results.

The Communication Problem   Another question to be asked when making an intervention in an organization is what mode of communication is to be used. There are a number of variables to be considered. Communications can vary in the scope of their impact; mass media can reach a large number of people while face-to-face interaction can only reach a limited number of people. Similarly, the intensity of effect can vary with different media. While a pamphlet mailed to individuals in an organization might produce some discussion, social interaction, and affect, an informative group discussion might produce a considerably different impact. Intensity can also be increased through task orientation. Some modes of communication can be considerably more task-specific than others. For example, a consultation session with a single ward group trying to improve its treatment program might be much more action-oriented than a lecture session to a large staff gathering. The three change perspectives we have reviewed deal with the communication issue mainly by implication. Nonetheless, communication is central to all three and the effect of different forms of media in creating change still remains an open question to be experimentally evaluated.

Given the potential differential effect of the scope and intensity of communication, it seems essential to integrate them into a change effort as viable experimental conditions. For example, the size of the adopting unit and the role change necessary to adopt the innovation would have implications for the mode of communication to be used in intervening with a particular type of audience. If an innovation is to be adopted by individuals, and it involves little change in role specification and normative behavior, a communication having wide scope but limited intensity or persuasive power might be the method of choice (a memo or a pamphlet). However, if the innovation is one in which radical changes in role behavior are called for and in which the adopting unit is a cohesive social group within the organization, a communication of limited scope but of high intensity to overcome existing peer group norms and make specific action recommendations (a task-oriented consulting session) might be needed. Thus, the mode of communication-intervention selected for a given task will depend upon how many people will need to know about the innovation, what degree of intensive interaction and decision making needs to evolve, and, by extension, what degree of self-persuasion and norm change is required to implement change. Communication intervention is clearly a relevant dimension for experimental study of the change process.

The Receptivity Problem   One of the arguments forcefully offered by the organizational theorists is that complex organizations can have differing degrees of receptiveness and responsiveness to external reality, based on their structure and bureaucratic restraints. For example, some organizations may be relatively free and autonomous in their capability of responding to environmental inputs (i.e., externally prescribed innovations) and many, in fact, develop specialized units to deal with such inputs. Others may be constrained by a more restrictive bureaucratic style of functioning. They would be predicted to be less responsive to the uncertainty of innovation because of its incongruence with their roles, structured mode of operation, etc.

Another variable affecting receptivity to innovation might be labeled the social or cultural milieu in which the organization and its members are located. Rogers and Shoemaker have pointed out that personal characteristics of cosmopoliteness and education, and norms favoring innovation and change will be related to innovation diffusion. If such social climate variables can be identified *vis-à-vis* an organization, they should have some influence on its receptiveness to innovation.

An Experimental Strategy Aimed at Finding Answers to These Organizational Change Problems

While the aforementioned review of the three perspectives presented elsewhere in great detail by Havelock (1969) has led to the isolation of some essential questions about organizational change, a close inspection of the literature indicates that there is a dearth of supportive data about the relative importance of these variables in achieving organizational change. It is of special importance to discover what different variables enter into the social change formula for mental health organizations if a strategy that will permit the adoption of new mental health practices is to be developed. One way to determine the degree to which selected variables influence innovation and dissemination is through an experimental approach. This strategy is essentially a field experimental one and follows the methodology initially outlined by Fairweather in 1967, and later in 1972, under the rubric of Experimental Social Innovation (ESI). In this strategy, each phase of the innovation process is defined operationally and exposed to experimentation to find the relevant determining variables. The strategy provides a way of choosing through true experimentation among the variables explicitly and implicitly mentioned in the three problems already discussed. Experimentation is thus used as a feedback mechanism to identify the key social change variables that can be used to create the desired change.

The ESI approach first requires the creation and evaluation of a model or models that meet the needs of the problem population. In this instance, the lodge model* was arrived at through the mutual cooperation of the patients, the institution (mental hospital), and the researchers. This cooperative effort combined research, problem solving, and a commitment to problem solution on the part of all the individuals involved. From this approach, the lodge model described in the last chapter emerged. It met the needs of the patient population and institutional management. An evaluation of this model showed that on all criteria of success it was more beneficial than traditional models.

Accordingly, the next experimental step, with which this book is concerned, involves a research approach to the problem of implementation. This successful model needs to be promoted to other mental health institutions so that they will adopt and diffuse it. The experimental approach to the spread of an innovation requires obtaining valid information about how to carry out the four operational processes of implementation: approaching the target organizations, persuading them to adopt the innovation, activating the adoption, and diffusing the innovation to non-adopting organizations. This research approach provides the experimenters with feedback about the success or failure of their tactics in these four stages so that such information can be used in further attempts at promoting adoption. A graphic example of the similarities and differences between the ESI approach and the three previous approaches to organizational change is presented in Table 2.1.

It is now important to place the information about change presented in the R, D, & D, problem-solver, and social interaction perspectives into the experimental social innovative framework. From the brief review of the three approaches presented in this chapter, it seems clear that certain change processes need to be operationally defined and experimentally explored for their effects on implementing the lodge society. Implementation efforts must strive to persuade authority figures and lower-status per-

*Henceforth, the innovative lodge rehabilitative society will be referred to as the lodge.

Table 2.1 Four Approaches to Effecting Innovation in Organizations.

	Experimental Social Innovation	Research, Development and Diffusion	Problem-Solver	Social-Interaction
Phase I Model Creation & Development	Model is created by ESI team using research, client population, feedback, and target organization in planning. Model is implemented on a pilot basis in a formal longitudinal experiment. Evaluation determines subsequent dissemination.	Using basic research data, a model is packaged or engineered. Little input from client population or target organization. Limited emphasis on formal evaluation of the model.	Change agent focuses on organization's needs and desires. Works to improve greater communication, empathy, role clarity, articulation of goals, and the like.	Unspecified
Phase II Model Adoption & Dissemination	Alternative ways of approaching, persuading, activating, and diffusing adoption of the validated model are compared experimentally. Any technique is legitimate providing it is ethical, is nonviolent, and works.	Rational information about the model is disseminated to an interested target audience.	Unspecified	Adoption-dissemination proceeds through channels of formal and informal social interaction and communication.

sons to become aware of and convinced of the decision to adopt the lodge program as well as to become involved to assure its success. Important variables to consider include the channel of the intervention message (which will also have different scopes, intensity, and influence of intraorganizational interaction), the social status level in the organizational hierarchy on which to concentrate the messages, and an awareness of the social and bureaucratic constraints in which the organization is operating. To explore how these organizational variables can be placed in an experimental framework is the burden of the next section.

EXPERIMENTAL PLAN

The first concern of the research team was to obtain the funds to carry out a national implementation study. They soon discovered that the National Institute of Mental Health was itself deeply concerned about implementation because they were aware that newly discovered treatment procedures, often established and validated through painstaking longitudinal research, were frequently not adopted by the mental health installations for which they were intended. The problem of the utilization of scientific information to solve the problems of society was also an increasingly important issue confronting many governmental agencies beyond the area of mental health. A specific example is a recent study about the transfer of technical knowledge to industry from NASA which shows this lack quite clearly:

> Of the 21,000 companies which NASA thought could use the inventions, 30 companies
> .... adopted or seemed to have a good prognosis for adoption. (Wright, 1966)

Because of experiences like these, including the unwillingness of the sponsoring hospital to adopt the lodge treatment program despite its experimentally validated beneficial effects, the National Institute of Mental Health entered into a contract to support a national lodge implementation experiment.*

Designing the Experiment

It was obvious from the outset that this experiment would differ from the usual studies of organizational change and diffusion for many reasons but, particularly, because most of the former studies had been attempts to

*Special recognition is due the National Institute of Mental Health (NIMH), which provided the funds for this study (Grant No. 5 R12 MH 09251 and Grant No. 7 R12 17888).

understand the processes that create change from an inactive, usually a survey, perspective rather than from becoming actively involved in changing the organizations as an integral part of their studies (Havelock, 1969; Rogers and Shoemaker, 1971). In viewing organizational change from an action perspective as proposed in experimental social innovation, an attempt is made to create actual change in the concerned institutions. The experimenters would have to go through the four sequential activities required by an implementation effort for any innovation. Thus, the advocates of the lodge would have to: (1) *approach* the selected organizations to make them aware of the new mental health program; (2) *persuade* persons who could create the change within the institution that the new program was more desirable than their current treatment programs; (3) *aid* the institution in *adopting* the program it had been persuaded to accept; and, finally, (4) *discover* what *diffusion* occurred within and outside the organizations that had initially been approached about adopting the lodge. Information about how to best accomplish these four sequential tasks might be not only instrumental in helping to diffuse the lodge to other institutions but also helpful in understanding organizational change generally.

The four implementation activities were divided into three phases. The research attempted to find techniques that would be effective in approaching and persuading institutions to adopt the lodge, to find avenues that would aid those mental hospitals that had decided to establish the lodge in actually activating it, and to trace the diffusion of the lodge to hospitals that did not initially adopt it.

The Approaching-Persuading Phase

Action–Inaction   In order to evaluate the effects of different techniques of persuasion it is first necessary that the participating hospitals agree to permit the person advocating the change to communicate his message to their personnel. Accordingly, various persons who had considerable knowledge about how organizations could best be approached were interviewed. It was the consensus of such individuals that the best single way to approach persons within institutions was through person-to-person telephone calls. For this reason, it was decided that telephone calls would be made to all selected institutions in an attempt to "get a foot in the door" so that persuading them to accept the lodge could be attempted.

But even if the advocate could gain entry to the hospital, what technique of persuasion would he use? What mode of presenting the lodge program would be most effective? The literature about social change gives few, if any, definitive answers to these questions. It seemed obvious, from the different points of view expressed in the first section of this chapter, that even though little is known about the effectiveness of different ways of attempting to persuade institutions to adopt new practices, three modes of persuasion are most often used. They are: the written word, face-to-face meetings, and actual demonstrations. Written information is usually presented through books, brochures, and other types of written material which advocate the new practice. Because of the frequency of its use, a written approach was created to explore the effects of this persuasion condition. The creation of a readable and eye-catching brochure was developed for this purpose. It is described below.

A second technique often used, particularly by those proponents of groups methods such as T-groups, and the like, was the workshop method. In this technique, a presentation of all the material concerning the advantages of the lodge treatment program in contrast to traditional programs was presented verbally in a face-to-face situation with the concerned hospital personnel. Illustrative slides, large and small group discussions, and question-and-answer periods were the central features of the workshop technique. The detailed manner in which the workshop was conducted in an attempt to persuade hospital personnel to accept the lodge program is fully described elsewhere.

Finally, a third technique, called the action technique was developed. This involved the creation of a miniature model within the hospital setting at the ward level which had the autonomous decision-making features and group processes central to the lodge society itself. It was believed that staff members who participated in this kind of behavior demonstration would take part in the change process itself and, having personally experienced the effects of such change, would be more likely to be persuaded that a patient-run small society, which was the paramount feature of the lodge program, would not only be possible but desirable. The process of establishing these demonstration models is fully discussed in another section of this book.

These three persuasion techniques needed to be compared to explore their effectiveness in persuading others to adopt the lodge society. Taken together they created a continuum from inaction to action establishing three points on that continuum: the written word, the verbal workshop, and a demonstration technique. The question raised about these three techniques was whether or not any of the three would yield higher persuasion results than the other two.

Urban–Rural   After the lodge program had been discovered and validated, and even though the hospital in which it was initially tried did not accept it as its own program, some inquiries began filtering into the experimental group requesting information about how such a lodge could be established. One inquiry was from a group located in a major metropolitan area and another was from a group located in a relatively rural community in a state whose main industry was agriculture. The same consultants traveled to these two institutions and observed an extreme difference in the way in which the organizations responded to information about the lodge. The hospital in the urban community showed a general concern about the effects an adoption of the lodge society would have on professional statuses and roles. Even though the clientele it served were mainly the black and poor, it became a matter of record that the complaints of the patients about their living situations and environs were often interpreted in typical psychotherapeutic fashion—that they were the result of misperceptions and improper concerns of the clients rather than that they were indeed accurate statements of the conditions under which poor people live. But what seemed more important to the advocates of the new program was that the social structure of the hospital was very rigid. Each person had a well-defined role he felt compelled to carry out. Few seemed willing to explore and deviate from it.

On the other hand, the rural hospital presented an opposite picture. Few professional personnel were employed by the hospital and the leader of the program that was to transcend the hospital boundaries into the community was a nurse. Little attention was paid to the professional discipline from which the team member came. It was pointed out repeatedly to the consultant that a large number of persons in the hospital needed new experiences and any innovation that might help them would be appreciated, particularly any innovation that might reduce costs and the need for large numbers of professional persons. Accordingly, the lodge program had considerable meaning for them. From these and other similar experiences, the idea that rural institutions might be more flexible and willing to change than urban institutions gradually began to take shape because large urban centers demanded a rigid and well-structured social organization so that individuals could belong to a group and thus maintain a protected position in the labor market. It has long been a documented fact that labor unions, specifically, attempt to spell out their own job descriptions to prevent others from doing work they consider their own. Such organizations are most frequently found in industrial centers located near or in large cities. Because of this perceived difference between rural and urban hospitals, it was decided to compare urban with rural hospitals.

Social Status   A third experimental condition that needed exploration in the judgment of the experimenters was whom to approach within the organization about adoption of an innovation. Much of the work that had been done in industrial organizations where change was desired was initiated through contacts with management personnel. The central idea here, as pointed out in the first section of this chapter, is that changes in these persons' perceptions and behaviors will filter down to those in lower-status positions and affect the total organization. However, it is not at all clear that persons high in the social organizational hierarchy would or could become agents for change. Therefore, it seemed essential to learn what results would obtain if persons at different social status levels within an organization were contacted. The mental hospital provided an excellent opportunity to do this since it is so well stratified in the perceptions of professional personnel (Mishler and Tropp, 1956). The superintendent or manager of a mental hospital is perceived as having the highest status; psychiatrists are second; psychologists, third; social workers, fourth; and nurses, fifth in the status scale. It was decided to contact persons holding different social statuses in different hospitals so that the experimenters could evaluate whether the social status of the person contacted would significantly affect the degree to which a hospital was persuaded to adopt the new innovation. Therefore, the third dimension of the experimental design was social status, on which there were five points representing the five key personnel groups mentioned above. In order that the persons contacted in each professional group held equivalent positions, the chief of each of these divisions (superintendent, psychiatry, psychology, social work, and nursing) would be contacted in an experimentally arranged order so that the effect on persuasion of each hospital status could be evaluated.

State–Federal   Finally, a fourth dimension was included in the experimental design. This involved state and federal hospitals. An indirect attempt to measure the variable of bureaucracy was made by comparing the effectiveness of persuasion on them. It was well known that most Veterans Administration hospitals often had to receive approval from their central administrative staff in Washington, D.C. before new programs could be established. On the other hand, the experimenters knew that many state hospitals had much more autonomy in determining their programs. For this reason, the variable included in the design was that of state contrasted with federal mental hospital installations.

These four dimensions (active versus inactive persuasion, social status of the persuader, urban–rural geographical location, and state or federal organizations) constitute the central dimensions of this experiment. These dimensions and the number of hospitals in each are presented in Fig. 2.1. However, it was obvious that many other variables might have a significant effect upon whether or not a particular institution was persuaded to change. Therefore, it was decided to measure additional areas

SOCIAL STATUS

		1 SUPT.		2 PSYCHIATRY		3 PSYCHOLOGY		4 SOC. WORK		5 NURSING		N
BROCHURE	STATE	8	7	8	7	8	7	8	7	8	7	75
												85
	FED.	I	I	I	I	I	I	I	I	I	I	IO
ACTION WORKSHOP	STATE	8	7	8	7	8	7	8	7	8	7	75
												85
	FED.	I	I	I	I	I	I	I	I	I	I	IO
DEMON-STRATION	STATE	8	7	8	7	8	7	8	7	8	7	75
												85
	FED.	I	I	I	I	I	I	I	I	I	I	IO

	URBAN	RURAL	URBAN	RURAL	URBAN	RURAL	URBAN	RURAL	URBAN	RURAL	
N	51		51		51		51		51		255

Fig. 2.1 Experimental design showing the social status, action, urban–rural, and state–federal variables.

to discover their contributions to social change. These areas included information about the processes within the hospital, such as decision making, communication, etc., descriptive information about the decision makers, the hospital advocate, etc., and demographic characteristics of the hospital and geographic area where it is located. A list of the areas of measurement can be seen in Table 2.2

The Adopting Phase

Manual–Action Consultants   While an analysis of the aforementioned variables concerned with persuading hospitals to adopt the lodge would yield information about the value of such techniques in positive decisions to adopt new programs, it would not tell us anything about how a

Table 2.2   Areas of Measurement.

Processes of:
    decision making
    communication (interpersonal and intraorganizational)
    advocacy
    activating
    diffusing
    approaching
    persuading

Description of:
    the decision makers
    the person contacted in the hospital
    the advocates
    the diffusers

Demographic Characteristics of:
    the hospital
    the geographical area where hospital is located

hospital can best place in action those new programs it decided to adopt. The literature about the need for change agents raises a serious question about whether organizations can activate new programs without the aid of outside consultants. Visits by the experimenters had indicated that an outside consultant served as a source of support for individuals within the institution who were attempting to change it, and the consultant also served to provide the needed information for the actual movement into the community that was necessary when a new lodge was created. The consultant was an experienced person who could help hospital personnel make such a move. Since this perception had been gained by the experimenters from two previous consultations and was often mentioned in the literature, it seemed most important to test the hypothesis about the need for action consultants in a more systematic manner. Therefore, it was decided that those hospitals that had been persuaded to establish the lodge would be divided into matched pairs on the basis of their previous experimental exposure, and then randomly assigned to either a written or action consultant approach to implementation. One group of hospitals would receive a written manual that clearly described each step in the movement from the hospital into the community, while a second group would receive periodic visits from an action consultant who would aid them in carrying out the move into the community. By comparing the progress made in movement toward adoption by those hospitals receiving the manual with those having active consultation one could clearly evaluate whether an action consultant was necessary and what the processes of these different forms of consultation happened to be. The effect of the other variables presented in Table 2.2 upon implementation could also be ascertained. This, then, was an attempt to gain experimental evidence about the value of action consultation and other variables upon the physical implementation of a new social innovation—the community lodge. These two conditions (written and action consultation) constituted the major dimensions of the Adopting Phase of the experiment. They are described in Chapter 7.

The Diffusing Phase

It was believed that after certain institutions had implemented the lodge society there might be a diffusion of the lodge program to other mental health organizations with whom these adopting hospitals became involved. Accordingly, a study of this diffusion process was established as part of the design. This study was initiated after the last lodge had been placed in the community—with the exception of one lodge which was late in starting. Each hospital was followed up for a period of about twenty-four months after the hospital's decision to implement, or not to implement, the lodge had been made. Hopefully, we could discover the ingredients of the diffusion process itself. Several questions had been posed by Havelock (1969) and Rodgers and Shoemaker (1971) concerning the diffusion process. They included such concerns as the degree to which institutions in close proximity to the innovation accepted the innovation as their own; how the process of diffusion itself worked through the various stages of the adoption process in an organization generally described by Rogers as knowledge, persuasion, decision, communication, and actions. The diffusion phase of this experiment is fully discussed in Chapter 8.

The approaching-persuading, adopting, and diffusing phases of this experiment are presented in different chapters. Figure 2.2 presents a graphic portrayal of the experiment showing its sequential nature, with each phase occurring after the preceding phase is completed. Table 2.3 shows the sequence of experimental events as they occurred for each phase.

Sampling Procedures

All mental hospitals in the United States constituted the population of hospitals with which this study is concerned. All but eight of such hospitals were incorporated in the design so the total number of hospitals in the

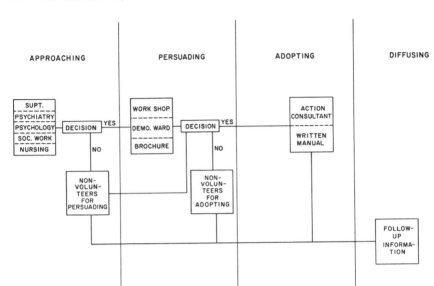

Fig. 2.2 Longitudinal stages of the research process showing the action occurring in approaching, persuading, adopting, and diffusing.

Table 2.3 Sequence of Events for each Experimental Phase.

I. Send letters to 50 Department of Mental Health Chiefs

II. Approaching phase

    A. Brochure condition

       1. Researcher calls hospital telephone information for chief and his name.

       2. Hospital contact is then called to obtain a decision about sending a *roster* of hospital personnel so that brochures can be mailed by name.

       3. A structured interview is conducted over the telephone with the contact pertaining to his: (a) attitudes toward mental illness, (b) a "yes" or "no" decision about entering the persuasion phase, (c) information about how the decision was made, and (d) who made the decision.

       4. If a decision cannot be obtained upon initial call, arrangements will be made for a second call.

       5. If the decision is *NO*, the hospital is placed in the non-volunteer group.

       6. If the decision is *YES*, the hospital is placed in the Brochure Condition of Persuasion phase.

    B. Workshop condition

       1. Researcher calls hospital telephone information for chief and his name.

       2. Hospital contact is then called to obtain a decision about holding a *workshop* at the hospital.

Table 2.3 *Continued*

3. A structured interview is conducted over the telephone with the contact pertaining to his: (a) attitudes toward mental illness, (b) a "yes" or "no" decision about entering the persuasion phase, (c) information about how the decision was made, and (d) who made the decision.
4. If a decision cannot be obtained upon initial call, arrangements will be made for a second call.
5. If the decision is *NO*, the hospital is placed in the non-volunteer group.
6. If the decision is *YES*, the hospital is placed in the Workshop Condition of Persuasion phase. Date when the workshop will be held is agreed upon.

C. Demonstration ward condition
1. Researcher calls hospital telephone information for chief and his name.
2. Hospital contact is then called to obtain decision to hold *demonstration* at the hospital.
3. A structured interview is conducted over the telephone with the contact pertaining to his: (a) attitudes toward mental illness, (b) a "yes" or "no" decision about entering the persuasion phase, (c) information about how the decision was made, and (d) who made the decision.
4. If a decision cannot be obtained upon initial call, arrangements will be made for a second call.
5. If the decision is *NO*, the hospital is placed in the non-volunteer group.
6. If the decision is *YES*, the hospital is placed in the Demonstration Ward Condition of Persuasion phase. Date when the demonstration ward will be established is agreed upon.

III. Persuading phase (volunteers)

A. Brochure condition
1. When rosters from hospitals are obtained, a letter is sent to professional staff about establishing the community treatment program.
2. Two days after the letter is sent, the brochure and postcard questionnaire about their interest in establishing the lodge program are sent to professional staff.
3. Follow-up postcard questionnaires are sent to staff who have not returned the first card.
4. After a response is received, a questionnaire about the effectiveness of the brochure is sent to hospital staff.
5. Each contact is then called for a decision about the community treatment program. At this time a structured interview is held on the telephone about: (a) what the hospital's decision is, (b) how the decision was made, and (c) who made the decision.
6. If a decision has not been reached at the time of the initial call, arrangements are made for a second call.
7. If the decision is *NO*, the hospital becomes a non-volunteer for activation.
8. If the decision is *YES*, the hospital enters the activation phase.

B. Workshop condition
1. When a date is set by us for holding the workshop, arrangements are confirmed by telephone with the hospital contact.

Table 2.3 *Continued*

---

2. After completion of the workshop, postcard questionnaires about interest in establishing a community treatment program are distributed to professional staff and a supply is left for those not able to attend workshop.
3. While at the hospital for the workshop, questionnaires about the effectiveness of the workshop will be completed. Those not attending will receive a different type of questionnaire later.
4. While at the hospital for the workshop presentation, a roster will be obtained so that follow-up postcard questionnaires can be sent to those not responding.
5. Each contact is then called for a decision about the community treatment program. At this time a structured interview is held on the telephone about: (a) what the hospital's decision is, (b) how the decision was made, and (c) who made the decision.
6. If a decision has not been reached at the time of the initial call, arrangements are made for a second call.
7. If the decision is *NO*, the hospital becomes a non-volunteer for activation.
8. If the decision is *YES*, the hospital enters the activation phase.

C. Demonstration ward condition
1. When a date is set for establishing the demonstration ward, arrangements are confirmed by telephone with our contact at the hospital.
2. While at the hospital for establishing the demonstration ward, a roster is obtained for postcard questionnaire follow-up to be initiated one month later.
3. Two months after completion of the demonstration ward, a postcard questionnaire about their interest in establishing a community treatment program is sent to the professional staff.
4. Different questionnaires about the effectiveness of the demonstration ward are sent to those who were involved in the demonstration and to those who were not.
5. Each contact is then called for a decision about the community treatment program. At this time a structured interview is held on the telephone about: (a) what the hospital's decision is, (b) how the decision was made, and (c) who made the decision.
6. If a decision has not been reached at the time of the initial call, arrangements are made for a second call.
7. If the decision is *NO*, the hospital becomes a non-volunteer for activation.
8. If the decision is *YES*, the hospital enters the activation phase.

IV. Adopting phase

A. These hospitals are matched in pairs for background experimental experiences and randomly assigned to one of two conditions—a condition where the hospital staff itself will attempt to activate the lodge through a written manual and a condition where activation will be attempted through a social action consultant's visits to the hospital.

V. Diffusing phase

A. All 255 hospitals in the sample are interviewed to ascertain if any dissemination of the lodge has occurred in the two years since the hospital had its last contact with the research team.

---

sample involved almost the entire mental hospital population in America—255 mental hospitals. Eight hospitals were eliminated because they were left as residual hospitals after the 255 hospitals were randomly assigned to the experimental conditions. Institutions that dealt mainly or solely with criminal populations, and those mainly concerned with medical problems that fell outside the realm of mental illness were deleted from the sample. Figure 2.1 shows the final design and the hospitals in each condition of the approach-persuasion phase of the project. The sample for the second phase of the experiment, which was concerned with the actual implementation of the lodge society, consisted of twenty-five hospitals that volunteered to establish the lodge in the persuasion phase. The twenty-five volunteer hospitals were matched in pairs so that each pair received the same treatment during the persuasion phase. Thus, for example, two hospitals that were both rural and had received the brochures were considered matched. One of each pair was then randomly assigned to either the written or action consultant condition for the implementation phase of the experiment. The one unmatched hospital was randomly assigned and fell in the action consultant condition. Twelve received the written manual and thirteen were seen by the action consultant during the implementation phase.

The final phase of the experiment involved a follow-up study of the diffusion of the lodge innovation. All 255 hospitals were included in the sample for this phase of the study and were contacted about the degree to which they had any knowledge of or had instituted any part of the lodge program themselves.

Assessment Devices

There were a large number of assessment devices used over the four years of this project in an attempt to measure the many aspects of social change. First of all, there was a telephone questionnaire completed at the time the interviewer first contacted a person in the hospital with whom he discussed the lodge possibility. This individual, of course, was randomly selected for social status (superintendent, psychiatrist, psychologist, social worker, or nurse). There was also concern about how effective the different conditions of persuasion were, that is, to what extent did the individuals who received the brochure, who participated in the workshop, or who established the demonstration model see this experience as satisfying and as influencing the hospital. These instruments were entitled the brochure effectiveness questionnaire, the workshop effectiveness questionnaire, and the demonstration model effectiveness questionnaire. Information was also obtained on another form about the effectiveness of the persuasive technique (brochure, workshop, demonstration ward) for those individuals who did not actively participate in the condition but were members of the same hospital staff.

Finally, in the persuasion condition there was a decision-making questionnaire that contained such items as who made the final decision, the degree to which the staff was involved in the decision, etc. A social status questionnaire was given to determine what the relationship was between hospitals that had very well-organized hierarchical social structures and those that did not upon the decision-making process.

There was, in addition, a voluminous amount of information obtained about the particular hospital itself. This concerned such information as the population density of the state and area where the hospital was located, the number of psychiatric beds in the hospital and in the state, the salaries and training of professional persons, etc.

After the persuasion phase was completed, those hospitals that had agreed to establish the lodge were divided into those that received extensive written instruction as to how a lodge could be established, and those that received the consultation of an expert in helping them actively pursue

Table 2.4   Assessment Devices.

Questionnaires:
   about the initial contact of the research staff with the hospitals
   workshop effectiveness
   brochure effectiveness
   demonstration ward effectiveness
   biographical information
   diffusion processes
   decision-making processes
   90-day follow-up of volunteers
   attitudes about social status
   attitudes about mental illness

Demographic Information:
   characteristics of the hospitals
   characteristics of the state in which hospital is located

Conference Discussions:
   interview about the persuading and activating processes
   recordings of social action consultant sessions

Research Journal:
   critical incidents and observations

---

their work on the lodge. The action consultants who visited the hospitals gathered descriptive information about the hospital itself, including such diverse items of information as its social climate, physical plant, and the staff's reaction to the consultant. In addition, other information about the implementation phase was collected every ninety days through follow-up telephone calls. In these calls to the twenty-five volunteer hospitals questions were asked about their progress in implementing the lodge. Finally, recordings were made of each session the hospital planning group had with the action consultant. This supplied an ongoing description of the internal workings of the small groups that had been designated by each hospital to help establish the lodge. From the outset, each experimenter had a research journal which he took on his trips. In it he made notes about critical incidents that occurred and other items of information. A list of the assessment devices is presented in Table 2.4.

From the outset of the study, arrangements were made for as many scores as possible to be recorded on computer sheets so that the scoring would be automatic and the data could be stored on computer cards and tapes.

Statistical Analyses

A chi-square technique was used to assess the various aspects of the experimental conditions in the approach-persuasion, activation, and diffusion phases of the experiment because of the non-parametric nature of the data. In addition, cluster analyses were performed to discover the relationships of the multitude of assessment devices to approach-persuasion, implementation, and finally to diffusion (Tyron and Bailey, 1970). The results of the analyses are presented in Chapters 5, 7, and 8.

Through its four phases (approaching, persuading, adopting, and diffusing) this study was designed to answer a series of questions about social change in mental health systems. The basis for these questions came from both daily experience and the social change literature presented in this chapter. Following are the major questions this study was designed to answer:

1. Are organizations more likely to change if persons contacted about the change hold high, middle, or low social status positions in the selected hospital?
2. Are hospitals with lengthy "chains of command"—such as federal hospitals—easier or harder to change than hospitals with shorter "chains of command"—such as state hospitals?

3. Are hospitals located in urban areas, where jobs are more clearly defined, more or less likely to change than hospitals that are rural and where, typically, job-definition rigidity does not exist?
4. Are active approaches, such as demonstration projects, used in persuading hospitals to change more likely to influence those organizations to adopt new practices than less active approaches, written material and verbal workshops?
5. Are change agents actually necessary? Is the effective role of the change agent simply to present new information or, to be effective, should it be a much more broadly defined role including some knowledge of group structure, leadership, and motivation?
6. Are organizations that are more bureaucratic and in which leaders make decisions without consulting their underlings more likely to change than more participative organizations?
7. Are hospitals that have better communication systems more likely to change than hospitals that do not?
8. Is there any relationship between the various phases leading to adoption: that is, are the methods of attempting to persuade hospitals actually related to what happens in the adoption phase?
9. Are hospitals more financially able to change more likely to do so? Are hospitals with more facilities more likely to change than those with few?
10. Are hospitals that have more well-educated staffs more likely to change than hospitals that do not?
11. Are demographic characteristics, such as the region in which the hospital is located, related to change?
12. Is there any evidence that even after adoption has occurred some hospitals will diffuse the new innovation while others will not?
13. If so, is diffusion related to a general innovativeness in hospitals or any other characteristic of those organizations?
14. Are there any characteristics of the superintendent that lead to social change? For example, is the cosmopoliteness of the leader, as mentioned by Rogers and Shoemaker (1971), related to change?

This study attempts to answer the aforementioned questions through an actual experiment which yielded observations, a series of measurements, and statistical tests varying from comparative to correlative techniques.

CHAPTER 3

The Process of Approach and Persuasion

PRELIMINARIES TO THE STUDY

As shown in the design of the study, one essential comparative dimension in the approach-persuasion phase involved an evaluation of the effectiveness of written, verbal, and active demonstration approaches in persuading organizations to change. In addition, randomly selected persons representing the different professions within the organizational hierarchy (superintendent, psychiatrist, psychologist, social worker, and nurse) were to be approached and offered the opportunity to serve as local advocates for the lodge within their hospital. This permitted an assessment of the effect that approaching persons in different social status positions within the hospitals had on effecting change. Finally, urban were to be contrasted with rural hospitals, and state with federal hospitals in their rate of adoption.

It was necessary to begin the process of making these evaluations by giving some information about the plans of the researchers to the mental health directors of each state. Therefore, the first step in initiating the research was the writing of a standard letter that was sent to all the directors of departments of mental health in all fifty states of the country. The purpose of this letter was to inform the chief mental health officer that a study was being carried out in the state system and that his support was being sought. Permission to contact the hospitals in the state was *not* requested; rather, the letter announced that the research team was planning to visit hospitals in that state. This approach was chosen because (1) we did not want to communicate with the various state hospitals without notifying the state director of our plans to enter the system, and (2) the mention of the National Institute of Mental Health as the sponsoring agency and our past NIMH researches would establish that the research team had some credibility in the mental health field. The letter to the directors illuminates these two purposes:

> John J. Jones, M.D., Director
> State Department of Health
> State Office Building
> Portland, Oregon
>
> Dear Dr. Jones:
>
> As the leader in mental health efforts in your state, interest in the constant improvement of your treatment programs must certainly be one of your paramount concerns. The National Institute of Mental Health is one of your major allies in this endeavor, financing numerous research projects each year which are directed toward extending knowledge about possible solutions to this major national problem. You may be aware that many of these studies have produced valid and valuable new treatment procedures, some possibly conducted under your own leadership, that have turned out to be extremely difficult to incorporate into current hospital practices.
>
> Those of us who have conducted some of these researches believe, however, that the quality of mental hospital treatment could be greatly improved if the knowledge gained from these researches could be more widely applied. This is particularly true nowadays because of the rapidity with which new knowledge is acquired, often resulting in a considerable gap between the best available knowledge in the field and everyday practice.
>
> As a consequence of the concern about facilitating the use of research results, a research project is being undertaken through an NIMH grant to explore how new research results can be used more adequately by mental hospital personnel. Accordingly, the research staff of this project plans to contact some of the mental hospital professional and administrative staffs in your state as an integral part of this study. We will be pleased to keep you informed of our progress, should you so desire.
>
> Sincerely,

Twenty-five state departments of mental health responded to the letter. All of the initial responses were positive; however, several different types of responses were received. The majority of the responses endorsed our efforts. Typically, such letters did not request that we do anything other than keep the director informed of our progress; they did not indicate any restrictions on our activities. A second type of response also contained an endorsement of the research effort, but, in addition, indicated that the state mental health division ostensibly was already engaged in a similar activity. Generally, this stated that some type of research diffusion or information-sharing was occurring within the state system.

The third type of response was in many ways a preview of things to come. It sanctioned the research effort, but asked specific questions about the research. An example is:

Dear _____:

We have had several communications from Directors of our State Hospitals concerning a demonstration project on the organization into problem-solving groups of chronic mental patients. Your inquiries were referred for 'our knowledge and consent,' and we are interested in the project, but would appreciate additional information concerning this proposal. (1) Further information about the mimeographed documents to be supplied to the staff and copies, if possible. (2) The commitment of the hospital to the project, in terms of time, space necessary, etc. (3) The follow-up, if any, on the part of the consultants who assist in establishing the program. (4) The kinds of ongoing evaluation, not only for staff, but of patients and the effectiveness of this program. Any other information you feel would be of value would be appreciated.

Yours very truly,

A fourth letter of reply incorporated some of the features of the previous letters, but went further by outlining in detail some of the roadblocks and hazards that the research group might encounter in this effort. An example is the following:

Dear _____:

Dr. Smith forwarded your letter to me which I found very interesting and with which I find I have considerable empathy. However, I do believe I have some reactions to your letter that I would like to share with you. My reactions, I am sure, will not be new to you, but perhaps it is just as well if I put myself on record. I also am impressed with the fact that there is a considerable lag between research discoveries and application; however, I would like to point out that there are several obstacles in the path of implementing new discoveries. One is to be sure the results obtained by research are really verifiable and that we not plunge into a new system of treatment without being very sure this new system would be applicable and that it has been adequately verified. Another consideration which I believe is important is that most institutions do have programs underway—some of which are relatively new—with the result that they are reluctant to uproot one program, substitute another, with the recognition that within six weeks or six months they may have to uproot that program and start over again. Needless to say, it takes time to initiate a program in a state hospital. Also, in my experience, one frequently has difficulty finding professionals whose attitudes are sufficiently progressive to enable one to move forward in these programs. And, finally, a consideration which should be dear to your heart as a psychologist, is that people are resistant to change; that when one suggests a new modus operandi it produces immediate resistance on the part of the hospital staff. I find not infrequently that when I ask people on the hospital staff how they would institute a program within the hospital, rather than facing the challenge of this intellectual exercise, they are more likely to begin telling me the reasons it can't be done. I believe the worthwhileness of your research is self-evident. I believe it is a very important piece of research. We would like to cooperate in any way we can to help you find the answers you are seeking. I shall notify the staffs at the State Hospital that you will be asking questions of them regarding this matter.

Sincerely,

Since the letters from the various mental health directors throughout the states suggested the research group would meet little resistance in contacting the various hospitals, the way was clear to proceed with implementing the research project itself. In order to clarify what we were offering the hospital in our initial contact with them, it is now important to review the manner in which the three persuasion conditions (brochure, workshop, and demonstration model) were developed and what was contained in each of them.

DEVELOPMENT OF MATERIALS

Brochure

The idea followed in developing the brochure involved creating a written document that would be visually attractive and also would summarize what the community lodge program was about. It was to be designed as a model of the kind of information often seen in the advertising material of the health professions—similar to pamphlets that pharmaceutical houses use to promote a new drug. In writing the brochure, the research staff attempted to condense into a relatively few pages approximately ten years of research leading up to the lodge program. The initial effort was a document nineteen pages long (double-spaced) including an introduction, a history of small group research with mental patients, a description of the lodge society, and the results of the community lodge research program. The researchers then met with a commercial artist who specialized in promotional advertising to review the draft of the brochure. The research project and its design were described to the artist so that he would understand exactly what we were attempting to communicate and could, therefore, make some judgment about how to best transmit the idea of the community lodge. He told us that the original brochure was too long and recommended that it be reduced in size, to hold reader interest. Several sessions were spent with the artist to give him a better feel for the information as well as a clearer understanding of the modality by which we were trying to communicate the information. Considerable effort was expended to reduce the original nineteen-page document and we eventually succeeded in reducing it to three pages. The decision was then made to develop an envelope-size brochure to be multicolored and thus eye-catching. The artist suggested that the cover design contain a drawing showing a symbolic summary of the purpose of the community lodge program, namely bringing patients out of the hospital into a living–working situation where they could become first-class citizens.

Workshop

After the brochure was developed, the research group turned its attention to creating the workshop presentation. The material for this was somewhat easier to develop than the presentation for the brochure. The speeches, other presentations, and research we had offered to various groups in the past served as the raw material for development of the workshop presentation. Unlike with the brochure, we were not too limited in the amount of information that could be presented in the workshop situation. Rather, we had a longer period of time in which to present the research that led us to the community lodge, and for this we prepared a speech that took approximately thirty minutes to give.

Since a twenty-five or thirty-minute speech might not hold the interest of many of the hospital personnel who were not research-oriented, we decided to enhance it with the addition of audio-visual materials, and so we developed a series of sixteen color slides to be shown on a screen. The first few slides showed graphs about the research results. Of the remaining slides, some showed pictures of the lodge grounds and residential facilities to give the audience some notion of where the lodge was located and how it appeared to the ex-patients who resided there. Other slides described the business aspect of the lodge. In these we attempted to depict the janitorial and yard work that the lodge members did as well as the business operations, such as bookkeeping, etc., with which they had become familiar. We showed slides of the accounting books and journals to demonstrate that the lodge members had become competent in operating a true business. The workshop presentation—the speech with slides—was first pilot-tested at a local mental health conference where preliminary feedback on its merit was possible. As the feedback was favorable, a question-and-answer period was added to the presentation. This open-ended question-and-answer period was not to last for more than thirty minutes, making the formal part of the workshop presentation approximately one hour long.

The second part of the workshop involved small group discussions around questions that were raised by the one-hour presentation. There were four such groups from the audience. Each group developed questions relating to topical areas that could be discussed by everyone. They met for about one hour during which time they also elected a leader and recorder (secretary). All the recorders later reviewed the discussions and the conclusions the groups had reached. The discussion following the small group meetings also lasted approximately one hour. Four areas of concern were commonly discussed: the procedural problems that arose in establishing a community treatment program; how living arrangements could be made; how work is conducted in an ex-patient run society; and what changes occurred in the roles for ex-patients and mental health personnel as a result of creating a lodge society.

This was the procedure that was followed for the hospitals placed in the experimental workshop condition. It involved a speech animated by pictures, followed by audience participation and small group discussions of the lodge society.

Demonstration Ward

The third persuasion condition was an active demonstration model, designed to enable hospital personnel to actually experience the decision-making processes of autonomous patient-led groups. In order to provide each hospital in the demonstration condition with an actual demonstration, the researchers decided that the only feasible avenue was to establish a patient-led small group ward in which the patients took over most of the functions of the professional staff. The prototype of this autonomous small group ward had been established in a previous experiment and had been replicated many times since then in several locations in and outside the United States. The program was described in an earlier publication in the following manner:

> . . . This system required that each patient remain in his assigned task group from the day he arrived until he left the ward. To complete successfully the program, the patient had to progress through four steps. The group was responsible, as a unit, for each of its individual member's progress through these steps. The first step level was personal care, punctuality on assignments, and orientation of new members. When in this step, the member received $10 and a one-day pass per week. Each patient ordinarily had some money in his personal funds to be used for expenditures, and the approved funds were taken from these accounts. Step 2 required adequate performance in step 1 as well as qualitatively acceptable work on the job assignment. After successful completion of step 1, patients were advanced to step 2. In step 2 the member received $15 per week and an overnight pass every other week. In step 3, members were responsible for steps

1 and 2 and, in addition, recommended their own money and passes commensurate with individual step level. Members were eligible for $20 per week and three overnight passes for the four weekends per month. In step 4 the patient had unlimited withdrawal of money and passes and was responsible for all preceding steps.

The task groups operated in the following manner: four out of every five days they met in their own room without staff members present. Here they evaluated each other and prepared recommendations for the staff when they met with them on the fifth day. During the autonomous task group meetings, the patients had recourse to request any staff member to appear before the group and to ask him for factual information which was needed to enable him to make a decision. The staff member could not recommend a course of action, but did reveal facts that were needed by the group to arrive at reasonable decisions.

On the fifth day, the staff met with the task group. The group presented specific recommendations about how their problems should be solved. This involved not only recommendations about more adequate group performance but also about how each member's money, privileges, job assignment, and problems should be handled. The staff then adjourned and made decisions regarding the merit of the task group recommendations . . .. (Fairweather, 1964, pp. 30–31)

One of the most impressive results of this early social experiment, and the reason it was chosen to demonstrate the feasibility of creating an autonomous lodge society, was the consistent response of surprise and excitement from the professional staff when they discovered that patients could actually be trained to administer and operate a social system.

Our attention now turns to an examination of how the demonstration ward was developed for those hospitals that fell by random assignment into that condition. The criteria for volunteering for the demonstration ward were: (1) the hospital had to be willing to meet with the action consultant for a period of three days; (2) the hospital had to agree to select a hospital ward team that could meet with the consultant for this period of time; and (3) a physical plant (usually an actual ward) where the demonstration project would take place needed to be designated. A final item of agreement guaranteed that the hospital would initiate the demonstration ward program and operate it for a period of not less than ninety days. When these criteria had been met, arrangements were made by the particular action consultant, who had been randomly assigned to that hospital, for a three-day visit.

The consultant's three-day visit was to be both an information giving and training period. On the first day he would present a discussion and review of the small group program and the community lodge program to give the ward staff necessary background in the steps that must be taken to establish a small group program. The objective of the discussion was to combine some theoretical notions about small groups and personal autonomy with a practical description of the operation of such a ward. A further goal of the first day's consultation was to help the staff take the demonstration ward materials presented to them from the prototype ward and adapt them to their particular hospital's situation. The second day's objectives continued the adjustment of fitting the small group program into the operations of the particular hospital with which the consultant was meeting. The major tasks for this day involved scheduling work assignments for patient groups, teaching the staff to give group assignments, arranging for meeting rooms for the patient-led groups, and establishing a reward system in preparation for the first day of the program.

To accomplish this, the action consultant brought with him several items of information. Among them were: a handout which described the five processes required to organize problem-solving small groups, a brief description of a functioning small group which met the five requirements, the modifications necessary in the traditional role of the ward staff so that autonomous groups could be created, several items of information about how to communicate with groups, and numerous practical hints about how the staff could improve small group performance. The third day of the three-day consultation visit was to be devoted to helping the staff evaluate a small group's performance and a discussion of the new staff and patient role behaviors required in this situation. To train the staff in making an evaluation of patient-led groups, materials were given to them which described an actual evaluation of a task group from the prototype ward. After the information and training sessions were completed, the action consultant would instruct the ward staff that they could call him collect for any further consultation desired. He also agreed to revisit the hospital if this was necessary. In addition he would inform the staff that he would be contacting them periodically for progress reports during the course of the small group demonstration model at their hospital.

After the small group demonstration model program had been completely planned as described above, it was tested on a large state hospital located near the research center. Generally, the plan worked out quite well, probably because it was actually based upon numerous past consultations about the small group program already completed by the experimental staff. Nonetheless, a few minor changes were made in the presentation and the demonstration aspects which enhanced the information and training procedures for the patient-led small group program.

CONTACTING THE HOSPITALS

Now the research group was ready to begin approaching eighty-five hospitals with the offer to send their professional staffs the attractive brochures, eighty-five other hospitals offering them the opportunity to have the workshop presented, and another eighty-five hospitals offering them the opportunity to establish a small group demonstration program. The appropriate contact in each hospital, as designated by random draw (either superintendent, psychiatrist, psychologist, social worker, or nurse), was telephoned and given an initial description of the research project. This was followed by a series of questions about the hospital, its management, and whether or not the hospital itself was willing to participate in receiving brochures, presenting a workshop, or establishing a demonstration program, depending upon the persuasion technique which had been experimentally assigned to that hospital.

In order to be designated as a participant in the *brochure* condition, the selected hospital had to send to the experimental staff a roster of professional persons in the hospital to whom the brochure could be sent. Those hospitals who did so had successfully completed the *approach* phase of the study. Those who refused to send lists were considered failures. Different hospitals responded to the request in different ways. Some sent telephone directories listing in detail the professional persons in the hospitals; others sent a typewritten list of their staffs; and still others sent lists of the personnel from hospital records. After the list had been received, the brochures were sent to each person on the hospital roster. In addition, questionnaires that were designed to assess the brochure's effectiveness were sent. When personnel did not respond to the questionnaire a follow-up letter was sent enclosing another questionnaire and asking the respondent's cooperation.

In approaching hospitals that fell in the *workshop* condition, the introductory telephone call followed the same path as that for the brochure. After the initial introduction to the lodge project was made to the randomly selected contact (superintendent, psychiatrist, psychologist, social worker, or nurse), arrangements were made for the hospital to decide whether a workshop could be held there. If the response was "yes," travel plans and arrangements to conduct the workshop were made with the person who was the hospital contact. If the answer was "no," the hospital was not recontacted until the diffusion follow-up phase that occurred after all workshops had been completed. Those hospitals that agreed to conduct a workshop had successfully completed the *approach* phase of the study. Those that did not were considered failures. In a manner similar to the brochure condition, questionnaires assessing workshop effectiveness were distributed to those attending the workshop and were mailed out later to those that did not.

In the *demonstration ward* condition, the introductory telephone call was the same as in the brochure and workshop conditions, except that the hospital was asked to establish a small group program for a ward and to provide the staff required for its operation. Here again the hospital could agree to participate or not to do so. As with the other two conditions, if the hospital volunteered to establish the demonstration project, arrangements were made with the hospital contact for an action consultation visit during which the consultant would aid the selected demonstration group in establishing a functioning model. If the answer was "no," the hospital was not contacted again until the persuasion phase had been completed. At, and after, the demonstration ward consultation visit, effectiveness questionnaires were distributed to hospital staff.

To briefly review, the outcome of the *approach* phase was a yes–no decision about whether the hospital was willing to expose itself to a persuasion attempt. Operationally, and by condition, a "yes" meant that: (1) the hospital submitted a list of personnel to whom the *brochure* could be sent, (2) the hospital agreed to host a *workshop* and did so, (3) the hospital agreed to establish a *demonstration ward* program and run it for ninety days and did so. The actual persuasion modalities—brochure, workshop, demonstration ward—were described in the previous section, and will be elaborated in subsequent sections. What followed the persuasion attempt was the actual decision about lodge implementation.

LODGE IMPLEMENTATION DECISION

The manner in which the hospital's decision was obtained about subsequent lodge adoption was straightforward. After a predetermined period following the completion of the persuasion attempt, a letter was sent to the contact person at each hospital requesting a decision about whether or not the hospital wanted to establish a community lodge. Also sent were open-ended and structured decision-process questionnaires about how the decision was reached, and what factors were relevant.

If no response was received within two weeks, another decision-making letter and packet of questionnaires were sent. If necessary, this was followed by a third mailed request two weeks later and, if all this failed, the decision was finally obtained by telephone. When a decision was reached, decision-process questionnaires were sent to other hospital staff. In addition to the hospitals who received the persuasion attempt, the hospitals which *refused* participation earlier in the approach phase were recontacted and asked for a decision about implementation.

The combination of this yes–no decision about implementation, and the previously discussed yes–no decision yielded three basic response patterns: the no–no hospitals which refused both the persuasion attempt and implementation; the yes–no hospitals which allowed the persuasion attempt, but refused implementation; the yes–yes hospitals which permitted the persuasion attempt, and were persuaded to try implementation.*

In the following section we provide illustrative examples of these response patterns.

Turned-Down-Cold

These hospitals constituted a group of organizations that refused to permit any entry. They would not permit brochures to be sent, workshops to be held, or demonstration projects to be started. From the outset, their response was that of a closed organization that would not permit communication input. Following are examples of the experimenters' relationships with the hospital leading to a rejection. An example from each persuasion condition is presented. The information was taken from the research journal.

Brochure: Carline State Hospital   The contact in this situation was the hospital superintendent and he was easily obtained on the telephone. He was barely able to control his hostility while the research and community lodge treatment program was described to him. He said the hospital already had such programs and that they had had them for twenty years, that he would not send a roster to us, so the brochures could not be sent to the staff but should be sent directly to him. He wanted to know why the researcher was asking all of "those" questions. He was irate "as a taxpayer" that the research team was calling long distance instead of writing. "Next time," he said, "send me a letter and use a six-cent stamp." He further said he was ashamed that people like us wasted tax money like this. "Save our money," he said in parting. Carline State Hospital was obviously a flat "NO."

At a later date when the superintendent was re-contacted for a decision

---

*A fourth, relatively rare, no–yes category was represented by two hospitals. These two refused initial persuasion attempts, but opted for implementation later on.

about implementation, a similar experience occurred. Several letters and calls were necessary to locate him, and he finally rejected implementation by telephone with considerable ill temper.

Workshop: Goodbody Mental Health Institute   The hospital contact here was the chief psychologist. On reaching him by telephone he said that he had a patient coming to see him and would call back in a few hours. He did indeed return the call and during the conversation indicated that their mental health institute was atypical in that it was a small teaching hospital with 200 beds handling mostly acute cases. However, he referred the researcher to the man who makes such decisions, namely the hospital director. The hospital director was not available. He was contacted in two days but was very busy and asked that the researcher call at a specific date and time, approximately five days later. When finally reached, the hospital director stated that the mental health institute was a part of a university and did not need this kind of program as they handled acute psychiatric cases and sent their chronic cases to a state hospital.

When Goodbody was re-contacted later for a decision regarding the lodge itself, the written reply was simply "no" with no illuminating reasons given.

Demonstration Program: Pavlov Psychiatric Hospital   The chief psychiatrist was the contact in this case. After being presented with the offer of a demonstration ward and a description of its relationship to the lodge community treatment program, the contact said that he already had such programs operating at the hospital and that, in any case, he would have to talk to the central office about any new programs. He further stated that he was an expert on Bulgarian psychiatry and was chairing a panel at a meeting to be held soon. He was mildly offended by our offer since he felt he was an expert in this field—he indicated that the Bulgarians did a lot of it and as a consequence had a low hospital population. He finally said he was a definite "no." Subsequent re-contact for an implementation decision resulted in the same response.

"Foot-in-the-Door But No More"

A number of hospitals permitted the persuasion (received the brochures, held the workshops, or established the demonstration program) but then decided they did not want to establish the lodge program. Following is an example of three hospitals representing the three experimental persuasion conditions as taken from the experimenter's notes.

Brochure: Rosebud State Hospital   The superintendent was randomly selected to be the contact and was reached by telephone. At the outset he was positive and responsive to the idea of establishing a community treatment program such as the lodge and volunteered to send a hospital staff roster in order to receive the brochures mentioned to him in the telephone conversation.

The next day the superintendent followed up this telephone conversation with a letter:

Dear ————————:

Pursuant to our telephone conversation yesterday morning, enclosed is the list of the hospital personnel directly involved in patient care, whose names I would like included in your mailing list.

Please allow me to express by appreciation to you for sharing your project study report with us. I am confident that we will find it very beneficial.

Thank you very much.

Sincerely,

In response to the mailing of the brochure and the appropriate questionnaires a positive letter was received from the director of the hospital:

Dear ————————:

We believe that our own community coordinated program has been helpful, but are aware that measures other than this may be in order. A community dormitory as described by you may be an excellent addition to the hospital's community program. Community dormitories may be suitable for several areas in the state.

Many questions about the operation of such dormitories and how they might be financed (especially initially) remain to be answered. More information about such projects would be very helpful. Project evaluation material, operational procedures, information on what help NIMH might provide, sources of consultative assistance, etc., would be useful in any developmental effort.

Thank you for your interest in our mental health program. I look forward to hearing from you.

Sincerely,

Follow-up on the questionnaires in the brochure condition went fairly smoothly and no further contact was initiated by the research staff nor received from the hospital other than the above mentioned letters until the research staff contacted the hospital regarding their willingness to volunteer for the community lodge treatment program. That letter follows:

> Dear _____:
>
> You will recall that a brochure entitled, 'A New Community Treatment Program for Mental Patients: An Alternative to Hospitalization' was distributed to the professional staff at your hospital after you had sent the roster requested by Dr. Watson. This information was designed to facilitate a decision by your hospital about whether or not it would be interested in actually establishing a community treatment program like that described in the brochure.
>
> It is now necessary for our research group to ascertain your hospital's decision. Of course, if your hospital should decide to implement the program our research staff would provide either written or active consultation depending upon its time commitments. I realize that such a decision may take time and involve more than one person. Although it may take time to discover how much interest your hospital has in this type of community treatment program, an answer from you is vital to us. The enclosed questionnaires request such a decision and some information about the factors surrounding it. Could we, therefore, enlist your support in completing and returning them at your earliest convenience?
>
> Sincerely,

The response received ten days later indicated that the hospital was not willing to establish a community treatment program such as that described in the brochure. The decision given thusly came from the hospital director:

> "This might be considered in the future. At present, the funds, or facilities, are not available."

The hospital is a "no" for implementation of the lodge.

Workshop: Magnolia V.A. Hospital   A telephone call was made by Dr. Edgar to the hospital contact who was the director of nursing. Initially, the hospital contact was surprised to hear from a Dr. Edgar in Omaha, which in return apparently surprised Dr. Edgar. The confusion was over a Dr. Edgar who was a psychologist and specialist in behavior modification at a local university. This aside, after listening to the information concerning the community treatment program and the offer to present a workshop at the hospital, the hospital contact reacted quite positively to the offer.

Approximately one week later a letter of confirmation was received from the hospital contact:

> Dear_____:
>
> This is in reference to your earlier call to me. Our vocational rehabilitation department is very much interested, as are the rest of us here at the hospital, in hearing you or one

of your co-workers on the subject of moving chronic patients out of the hospital for employment and living in the community.

I am picking, at random, a date in May, for you to spend the day with us, telling us about your project. If this is entirely unsuitable for you, please let me know and we will choose another date.

Also, let me know if there is anything special that you require for this speaking engagement; whether you want to limit the number of participants to a certain number.

Sincerely,

In response, the research team sent the following confirmatory letter:

Dear _____:

I am writing to confirm the date in May for the presentation of the workshop entitled, 'The Effect of Group Membership on Community Adjustment: Maintaining Productive Groups in the Community.'

The workshop will be conducted by Dr. Watson, a research associate with the Institute. He will arrive at the hospital at approximately 8:00 a.m. on May 20 to meet with you.

As previously mentioned, we will require the use of a 35 mm slide projector and screen for the presentation. Although the workshop is primarily directed at the hospital professional staff, you are certainly welcome to invite other staff members as well as local community and county mental health workers and people from local industry and business. We are requesting that you do not invite personnel from other state and V.A. hospitals in your locale as independent contacts with them have already been completed.

Dr. Watson and I hope that the workshop is informative and successful. He is looking forward to meeting with you and your hospital staff.

Sincerely,

A report of the research consultant's trip to the hospital read:

Upon arrival at the contact's office (director of nursing) there was no one to meet me other than the secretary who seemed vaguely aware that I was supposed to be there. After about one-half hour, the director of nursing appeared, excusing herself by stating that she had had to attend a general staff meeting. After formal introductions, she took me next door to the nursing education office where she essentially 'dragged me' into the hands of three nursing education supervisors who immediately started catering to my needs. They were all obviously well aware of my arrival and what I was going to be doing at the hospital. Preparations had been made to hold the workshop in a very old auditorium in which the lighting and ventilation were poor and where no one could smoke. Nevertheless, a lectern was provided, a carousel 35 mm projector and screen were provided as well. No sound system was needed as the acoustics were surprisingly good and the audience turned out to be painfully small. The workshop was attended by about twenty people, mostly nurses, social workers, and vocational rehabilitation personnel. No M.D.'s or Ph.D.'s attended nor did I meet one while I was at the hospital. In fact, I was not even introduced to the hospital director or the assistant hospital director during my stay. Nevertheless, the workshop went well although we did not break down into the four small groups as usual after the workshop because of the size or rather lack of size of the audience. I conducted it as one small group with me acting as the leader and the group discussing all parts of all four of the usual small group topics and questions. The response was surprisingly good considering the smallness of the group. The group was not overly enthusiastic but neither were they lethargic. The lodge proposal seemed a bit sophisticated for them but they grasped it as they did have some experience with halfway houses and foster home care, etc. Only one person was in attendance from the community.

The hospital and grounds were moderately run down. The grass was not well manicured, and the buildings were quite old. The interiors were poorly lighted and quite dingy although some attempts had been made to improve conditions by the hanging of new fluorescent fixtures. Although dingy and old, the interiors were fairly well kept and clean. Some patients were roaming around in typical hospital garb. The hospital was located in a rural part of the town, more accurately the country, which did not even appear to be part of the city. Although the majority of buildings were old, there were a group of buildings near the entrance to the hospital (one-half mile from the main section) that were new and modern. They were used for vocational rehabilitation and the criminally insane. They also housed a very handsome cafeteria–dining room for the staff. The director of nursing did say that one of the reasons for the poor attendance at the workshop was that a conference was being held at the hospital with the new personnel director for the state. This situation, according to her, developed after the workshop was first established.

Shortly after the presentation of the workshop, a letter was received from the hospital superintendent stating that he would like to have a copy of the speech given at the workshop. In response to his request a letter was sent on May 31:

Dear _____:

I would like to thank you for the cooperation I received at Magnolia V.A. Hospital from your staff in conducting a recent workshop.

Pursuant to your request, I am enclosing a speech that I made regarding the community treatment program. I am sending a copy of this presentation in lieu of the workshop presentation as we have no copy of it available at this time.

The superintendent's reply was prompt—on June 4:

Dear _____:

Thank you for sending me the paper on the community treatment program. I enjoyed reading this paper and will circulate it to other interested personnel.

Subsequent to the presentation of the workshop and the previously mentioned letter, no further contact was made with the hospital other than to attempt to obtain the usual follow-up on the questionnaires. On December 6 a letter was sent to the hospital concerning their decision about volunteering for the implementation of the lodge itself. There was no response to this initial decision-making letter, so two weeks later a duplicate follow-up letter was sent.

The second letter received no response so a similar third letter was sent on January 3. The hospital contact responded by letter on January 24:

> Dear ———————:
>
> In reply to your letters of December 6 and January 3, I would like to make my position perfectly clear.
>
> In the first place, I urged all R.N.'s and staff members to send in the questionnaires they received from you. Secondly, I could not reply concerning a decision on the project for no decision was truly made. Our hospital this past year was in a financial bind due to a political change and we were unable to push through any new programs. The administration and nursing staff were enthusiastic about the project but I was told that it would be up to vocational rehabilitation to put it into effect here, as the hospital had no funds to take over the expense of housing patients in a building in town.
>
> Miss Joan Smith, R.N., is the new director of nursing since October and I talked to her about your visit. She is interested, as we all are, in moving chronic patients out of the hospital, using janitorial skills to keep themselves in the community. She thinks we can surmount the problem of housing and we would be obliged if you would send her any information you have available regarding the community treatment program. A more definitive decision on this matter would come from her.
>
> Sincerely,

As a result of this letter a slightly modified decision-making letter and the related questionnaires were sent to Miss Smith, the new contact, on February 14. As no response was received to this, a follow-up was sent on February 28, and an additional follow-up letter was sent on March 19.

The second follow-up letter and a telephone call to stimulate an answer finally brought a response on April 23. The decision concerning the establishment of a community treatment program such as that described in the workshop was "no." The reasons given were that they had other programs ongoing and that staff time was not available. Furthermore, they wanted the women's service group to underwrite the new program but they needed financial information and could not present this plan to the hospital without it. They were willing to seek information so that they could present it to an outside organization for financial support. Only if they could obtain outside support were they interested in this as a possible project.

Demonstration Ward: Hardhat State Hospital   Dr. Sykes initially telephoned the hospital whose contact for the research was the chief social worker. The contact said that he would be willing to assist the research group but he had to obtain approval from the superintendent and would like a letter outlining the research and exact plans. He stated that he worked as a therapist and saw himself primarily as a clinician but that he had some administrative duties. In response to his request the following letter was sent to the director of social services at the hospital:

Dear _____:

I am writing to you pursuant to your recent conversation with Dr. Sykes regarding the establishment of a small group demonstration ward at your hospital. Dr. Sykes indicated to me that you would desire some information concerning our ward and the purpose of this demonstration ward. I believe that Dr. Sykes indicated to you that our research team at the Institute has entered into an agreement with the National Institute of Mental Health to inform the mental hospitals in the nation of a new program for treating mental patients.

About five years ago, we established a business and living organization in the community for the treatment of chronic mental patients with many years of previous hospitalization. The patients lived in a dormitory and operated the business. We have been able to demonstrate that most chronic patients can live in such a community situation. Furthermore, it greatly reduces costs compared with hospitals and demonstrates that current hospital personnel can be trained to operate such organizations. In addition, these chronic patients who have gone to live and work in such community situations are much improved. Chronic hospitalization and recidivism can be greatly reduced by this means.

We would appreciate the opportunity to send a consultant to your hospital, at our expense, for three days. The purpose of this consultation would be to assist you in establishing on one small ward in your hospital a demonstration program, to last about two months, which would show you and other staff members the increase in responsible behavior that is possible when chronic mental patients are organized into problem-solving small groups.

During the three-day consultation, we would hope to accomplish several objectives. The first day would be devoted to a discussion and review of the small group ward program and the necessary steps for establishing such a ward. The discussion would be combined with a practical description of the procedure for implementation. The entire staff will be provided with several mimeographed documents which should assist greatly in the practical matter of actually establishing the ward.

The second day would be devoted to the major portion of the tooling-up procedures for implementation. This refers to the procedures relating to scheduling, work assignments, group assignments, meeting rooms, etc. We would also hope to accomplish some preparation for the first day of the program.

The third day would be utilized for a demonstration of the staff evaluation procedure, which is crucial to the operation of the program. Additionally, we would hope to discuss the various roles of staff members in this situation and in the program. Finally, we would devote the remaining time to the completion of any tooling-up procedures that might be necessary.

Hopefully, the consultation will serve to inform you and the members of your hospital staff more fully about how such programs might be developed as a part of your particular hospital treatment program.

Sincerely,

The initial call by Dr. Sykes was made on April 9 and the above letter was sent out on the same date.

On April 15, a letter was received from Dr. N. H. Smaltz, the clinical director to whom the chief social worker had obviously forwarded our letter for a decision. His letter stated:

Dear _____:

Your letter of April 9 addressed to Mr. Gunn has been brought to my attention.

We are indeed interested in this program as we are in the process of initiating a program of this type at our hospital. We have made application for a NIMH grant for this in-service training plan and I am presently awaiting approval of this, but in the meantime we are proceeding with a self-help project involving one ward of chronic patients. We have also a hospital improvement program which is in its last year and we are considering applying for a renewal H.I.P. grant relating to chronic patients.

The hospital personnel selected to work in the project are enthusiastic and will welcome any help you could offer to us in revising or continuing our present program.

We shall be happy to meet with you and make any necessary arrangements.

Sincerely,

The following letter was sent in reply:

Dear Dr. Smaltz:

I am writing to acknowledge your acceptance of a three-day consultation, which will take place on July 16, 17, and 18 to establish the demonstration ward at your hospital. It is our understanding that you have agreed to commit, for a two-month period of time, a ward staff, typical for your hospital; a group of patients ranging in size from twenty-five to one hundred; and a ward for the purpose of this demonstration.

The consultation will be conducted by Dr. Watson, a research associate with the Institute. We hope that the three-day consultation and subsequent demonstration ward will be informative as well as successful.

Sincerely,

A response to our letter was received on May 17:

Dear _____:

Thank you for your letter of May 9. I regret that a temporary absence delayed my reply.

The personnel and the ward have been selected. We are looking forward to your visit and are sure that we will benefit from the consultation and demonstration of your team members.

Sincerely,

The three-day consultation did take place on July 16, 17, and 18 and was quite successful. The demonstration ward consultation was followed by communication with the hospital every two weeks to lend telephone advice and to gather data on current progress.

The first follow-up call was made on August 9. It disclosed that the hospital had not yet started the full program, but had assigned patients to groups, and had established on paper a reward system as required by the small groups system. They had not arranged for specific group-work assignments, nor had they developed a daily ward schedule. The call also disclosed that they were having some difficulties in getting the program started because the superintendent and the clinical director had decided they should focus their efforts on securing the approval and funding of the current NIMH grant proposal. If and when it was approved, they planned to utilize selected aspects of the demonstration ward program. Dr. Grabotz, the current contact, appeared pessimistic about the situation, but felt that the demonstration ward program would be implemented. A second demonstration ward follow-up was made on August 26. The full development of the ward was on schedule. More of the concrete details had been worked out in terms of work assignments, daily schedule, group meeting format, etc. Some of the necessary forms needed to be developed.

On August 30, a letter was received from the clinical director of the hospital:

Dear _____:

I regret that my absence from the hospital delayed my writing to you until now, although I understand that Dr. Watson has spoken to Dr. Metzer on this matter.

Following your group's visit we had several discussions about the application of your program to our particular hospital, and it was felt that because of the physical layout, age and type of our patients and economic factors, a modified program could be applied.

We are, as I mentioned in earlier correspondence, committed to an in-service training program under a NIMH grant and the hospital administration feels that the two programs can be conducted at the same time since the ultimate goals are the same. We feel that your visit was most profitable to us in clarifying our aims and thinking in terms of care of the patients. We wish every success to you and your colleagues.

Sincerely,

The next follow-up, on September 10, indicated that the demonstration ward was in full operation. There had been some problems with staff assignments, and the staff was under continuous pressure to integrate the program into the H.I.P. project, but generally everybody was satisfied. The subsequent demonstration ward follow-ups indicated much the same situation throughout the compulsory demonstration ward ninety-day follow-up period. The hospital continued the ward in excess of the ninety-day period and was considered a "yes" for the persuasion phase.

Nothing further was attempted with this hospital until some weeks later. On January 10, a decision-making letter was sent to the hospital attempting to obtain a response and decision concerning their willingness to volunteer for the lodge program.

Two weeks passed. No response had been received; therefore, a follow-up letter was sent:

Dear _____:

Approximately two weeks ago you received a letter requesting cooperation in securing a decision about your hospital's interest in establishing a new community treatment program with some help from our research staff. Since I have not heard from you, I am wondering what progress you have made. In case you have misplaced the questionnaires, I have included them. I would be deeply appreciative if you would complete the enclosed forms and return them to me at your earliest convenience. Thank you for your help in this matter.

Sincerely,

On February 26 the following letter and the responses to the questionnaires were received:

Dear _____:

Your letter of February 12 is acknowledged. It is regretted that reply was delayed because of my absence from the hospital. We appreciate your interest in helping us develop a community treatment program; however, we are commited to a NIMH grant for hospital staff development, and this precludes, at least at this time, development of a subsidiary program.

Sincerely,

The hospital also answered "no" to a questionnaire item about whether they wished to establish a lodge program.

"All the Way with the Lodge"

Twenty-five hospitals finally volunteered to establish the lodge society. These twenty-five hospitals were later to be subjected to another experiment concerning the implementation process (Chapters 6 and 7), but for the moment let us review the long and tedious process leading to the act of volunteering itself. A description of what happened to three hospitals, each representing one of the three persuasion techniques, follows.

Brochure: Arrowhead Acres State Hospital   This hospital randomly fell into the brochure persuasion condition, and the superintendent was randomly chosen as the hospital contact. On initial telephone contact with the superintendent, a positive reply was received regarding his willingness to have the hospital staff receive information via the brochure concerning the new community lodge treatment program.

Within a few days after receiving the initial telephone contact, the superintendent sent a list of hospital staff, as requested, with the following letter:

> Dear ————————:
>
> Attached is the list of the professional and administrative staff of this hospital which was requested in the telephone conversation this morning. The attached list is a copy of the mailing list for the hospital newsletter and includes administrative personnel as well as professional and ancillary personnel at the hospital.
>
> Sincerely,

Approximately three weeks later a spontaneous letter was received from the superintendent after his receipt of the brochure from the research group. This letter of May 22 read:

> Dear ————————:
>
> I enjoyed our recent conversation regarding a hospital community treatment program, and thought the information you sent me extremely interesting. You may also be interested in knowing there have been many favorable comments and a great deal of interest expressed from other staff members who received your information pamphlet.
>
> In view of this, I should like to suggest again that perhaps you and other members of your staff might enjoy visiting our hospital to discuss this project further.
>
> Sincerely,

Apparently there had been no problems in either sending or receiving the brochure. No further contact other than the usual research follow-up regarding this condition was necessary during the next several months. The next contact was made approximately nine months later in February when the decision-making letter to the hospital superintendent was sent.

A response to this was not immediately forthcoming and a follow-up letter was sent two weeks later:

Dear ――――――――――――――:

Approximately two weeks ago you received a letter requesting cooperation in securing a decision about your hospital's interest in establishing a new community treatment program with some help from our research staff. Since I have not heard from you, I am wondering what progress you have made. In case you have misplaced the questionnaires, I have included them. I would be deeply appreciative if you would complete the enclosed forms and return them to me at your earliest convenience. Thank you for your cooperation in this matter.

Sincerely,

An immediate reply, dated March 2, indicated that Arrowhead Acres State Hospital was willing to establish a community treatment program such as that described in the brochure previously sent to the hospital staff. The superintendent who responded concerning this decision wrote that the hospital was interested in new programs, that the lodge fitted in with what they wanted to do, and, thus, it would be rather easy to add this new program to their ongoing program. As a consequence of the early reply, a letter was sent from the research staff to the hospital on March 6:

Dear ――――――――――――――:

This will confirm receipt of your letter stating that your hospital is willing to establish a new community treatment program. I will be contacting you in the near future about the kind of assistance our research staff will provide you in helping to establish this program. Consequently, one of our research staff will be looking forward to working closely with you within the next few months.

Sincerely,

As a result of the hospital's decision to install a community treatment program and our follow-up letter of March 6, several telephone calls as well as written communications in late May fixed dates for the first consultation visit to Arrowhead Acres State Hospital to establish a community lodge program.

Workshop: Lemongrove V.A. Hospital   Dr. Sykes initiated the telephone approach and his first contact was the chief social worker at the hospital. Dr. Sykes presented himself and the research program by outlining the project, reviewing the previous research efforts, and attempting to enlist the contact's support in sponsoring a workshop at the hospital.

Mr. Grubb, the contact, appeared to react quite positively and Dr. Sykes requested information on our personal data inventory. However, Mr. Grubb was not entirely sure that he was the responsible party to act in the matter and referred us to the assistant hospital director who arranged workshops such as the one being proposed. Mr. Grubb said that he would talk to the assistant hospital director and relay his response to us when appropriate. On the following day, the chief social worker called back to make his appointment for a workshop. He had apparently discussed matters with members of all the professional staffs and then took the proposition to the professional staff meeting with the hospital director present. He said that he had spoken first to the chief of staff of the hospital and to another physician in the department of physical medicine who apparently had some responsibility in the matter. All of the professionals to whom he spoke thought it was a good idea and, in addition, the hospital director also approved of the plan. However, in discussing the content of the workshop, the chief social worker said that he wanted some information on the lodge for help in making up the invitations to the workshop. An informational letter was sent to our contact to assist him in establishing the workshop.

A response to that letter was received from the chief social worker confirming the fact that they would be willing to have the workshop conducted at their hospital and giving the date on which the workshop would be held. After appropriate travel and accommodation arrangements were made, a letter was sent to Lemongrove V.A. Hospital confirming the workshop.

Following is the research team member's notes about his visit for the workshop:

> Arrangements were made by the chief social worker to pick me up at my motel and take me to the hospital. In talking to him it was obvious that he had prepared well for the workshop and that he was well motivated to have the workshop. Upon entering the hospital grounds, one was presented with a more or less typical V.A.-NP hospital, It was clean, well manicured, generally in good repair with moderately old buildings showing their wear fairly well but quite presentable. I did not observe any new buildings on the grounds. The workshop was held in a chapel building, used for religious services, lectures, etc. Mr. Grubb, the chief social worker, had arranged for the music therapist to

have available a carousel 35 mm projector, screen, lectern, and sound system. The auditorium could probably seat about 300 to 400 people but they had roped off about two-thirds to three-quarters of its as they expected about 100 people from the hospital and community. As it turned out, no one arrived from the community and about eighty were in attendance from the hospital. The attrition increased after about two breaks but was minimal, running about ten to fifteen percent. The workshop went off without a hitch and the participants reacted and responded quite well, even enthusiastically in the small groups and the discussion. In general, they seemed well motivated to have such a community treatment program, particularly the S.S. (Social Service) department. The chief social worker stayed on after the workshop with a small party of about five to six people asking questions of a more personal nature and they all reiterated their desire for us to keep in contact with them and to attempt to establish a lodge. This theme continued when the chief social worker returned me to the office of the assistant hospital director and during our drive back to the motel.

At the termination of the workshop, a questionnaire was handed out to all the participants and they were asked to complete it prior to leaving. The final act for the workshop was the task of obtaining from the chief social worker a complete list of his professional staff including psychiatrists, psychologists, social workers, and psychiatric nurses, so that follow-up information could be obtained from them.

The apparent success of the workshop of May 8 resulted in the hospital volunteering to establish a community lodge on December 20. In volunteering for the lodge, the contact mentioned that one unit at the hospital was developing a plan and that a physician and a social worker from this particular unit had visited the original lodge project. Furthermore, the chief of psychiatry at the hospital planned to discuss this matter with all unit chiefs of psychiatry about a month later. In response to why the decision to volunteer was made, the contact stated:

This hospital has been organized on the unit system since June, 1965. It has been made up of four male psychiatric units, (one of which includes a female psychiatric building) and a medical unit composed of an acute medical ward and a physical ward. Top management expressed interest in the idea and the personnel of one of the male psychiatric units established a committee to explore the possibility of establishing a unit. The decision was made because the personnel of this unit were interested in developing this kind of resource for patients.

Demonstration Ward: Kesey State Hospital   Kesey State Hospital was initially contacted on April 9 by Dr. Watson whose randomly assigned contact at the hospital was the chief social worker. Initially, the social worker was quite responsive to the idea of establishing a demonstration ward at Kesey and stated that he would help in any way he could. However, he further indicated that he would probably need the approval and support of the superintendent and the director of nursing at the hospital. To accomplish this, he requested that we forward a letter to him which would outline and structure exactly what we were proposing. A letter was sent to the chief social worker that day.

Within two weeks a letter was received from the contact at Kesey State Hospital stating that our letter had been referred to their unit for planning and coordination and that a committee had been established for its consideration. The letter further stated that the committee had agreed to undertake this project and that they would contact us for additional information about the project itself and what steps were needed to undertake the project in order to be prepared to carry it through. He concluded the letter by stating that the hospital staff

> appreciate the opportunity to participate in this type of project and look forward to working with your research group.

This was quickly followed by a second letter from Kesey State Hospital as follows:

> Dear _____:
>
> Your letter of April 9 regarding the research team and consultation provided by your Institute was quite interesting. As I indicated to Dr. Watson when he called me, I first discussed your letter with our superintendent and chief psychologist.
>
> Our hospital evolved into the unit system in January of this year and the staff has, for some period of time, exhibited considerable enthusiasm in developing a more efficient milieu. In keeping with these efforts your letter was referred to the unit chief. This unit's planning and coordinating team can properly position specialized projects into the unit's overall treatment program.
>
> It will be most helpful if you can provide us with more information during your visit regarding the demonstration program. Such would be especially helpful in the utilization of personnel in carrying out existing programs and implementing new ones. The population of the ward to be used, and the staff requirements in this program will be helpful.
>
> The hospital is limited in carrying over programs into the community; however, we are interested in carrying forward so far as our limitations permit.
>
> Sincerely,

The response to the contact at Kesey on May 14 was:

> Dear _____:
>
> I am writing to acknowledge your acceptance of a three-day consultation to establish a demonstration ward at your hospital. It is our understanding that you have agreed to commit, for a two-month period of time, a ward staff typical for your hospital; a group

of patients ranging in size from twenty-five to one hundred; and a ward for the purpose of this demonstration.

We are proposing the dates of August 13, 14, and 15 for the consultation. If you do not find these dates acceptable, we would appreciate an early response proposing an alternative time. As soon as the three-day period is mutually agreed upon, we will inform you of the research member who will conduct the consultation.

We hope that the three-day consultation and subsequent demonstration ward will be informative as well as successful.

Sincerely,

The hospital contact responded approximately one month later on June 10:

Dear _____:

The unit chief of unit four and the planning and coordination committee have agreed on the proposed dates of August 13, 14, and 15 for the consultation.

The hospital's demonstration ward will be housed on unit seven and will consist of approximately forty to ninety patients. Our wards are divided into two sections with a large day room for use of both wards. Male patients are housed in one section with females in the other. We may decide to involve both in the project. Any comments or opinions on these arrangements prior to the consultation will be appreciated.

It is our understanding that the extent of our obligation will be limited to the consultation, demonstration ward, and staff that would be currently used by a ward with this patient load. We also understand that we will be under no financial obligation in carrying out this project, nor will it conflict with our present roles of operation and existing state law.

The above are specific questions that we need an answer to prior to entering into the consultation. Other questions center around involvement of the other departments such as, psychology, vocational rehabilitation, social service, etc., and extent of involvement.

Should there be questions directly involved with the rules of operating procedure then please direct your request to the superintendent, Kesey State Hospital. Involvement of this project with our psychology department should be cleared through the chief, psychology department, Kesey State Hospital.

The unit chief and the committee will await your confirmation of the above dates and assignment of the consultant.

Sincerely,

A response to the letter was sent two weeks later on June 25:

Dear _____:

I am writing to confirm the dates of August 13, 14, and 15 for the three-day consultation to establish a demonstration small group ward at your hospital.

The consultation will be conducted by Dr. Rosen, a research associate with the Institute and a clinical psychologist. He will arrive at the hospital at approximately 8:00 a.m. on August 13 to meet with you and the ward staff that has been selected.

The number of patients that you are planning to utilize for the ward is quite acceptable and we see no reason why you cannot involve both male and female patients.

The extent of your obligation, both financial and otherwise as outlined in your recent letter, is approximately correct. There is no reason to believe that this obligation will be in conflict with your present rules of operation or state law. We have had no conflicts in any of these areas while establishing such wards in other states. I hope that the above satisfactorily answers your questions.

As to the involvement of other departments such as psychology, vocational rehabilitation, social service, etc., this will be entirely within our purview. If the personnel from these departments are normally considered to be part of the typical ward staff for the hospital, then certainly they are welcome to participate in the project.

We would appreciate your recommending a good motel in your locale that is relatively close to the hospital. It would be of great assistance if you could forward to us the name of the motel, its location, and the telephone number so that we might attempt to make reservations.

Dr. Rosen is looking forward to meeting with you and the ward staff. Hopefully the visit will be of benefit to all.

Sincerely,

A rather brief response was received from the hospital on July 12 stating that they had received our letter and were looking forward to our consultant's visit on August 13. They recommended a local motel and gave its location and telephone number. The letter concluded with the contact asking if he might be of any additional help to us.

The consultation visit was held on August 13, 14, and 15 with no major problems. Although there was some initial lack of understanding of the lodge concept, the staff was generally enthusiastic and willing to learn. Participation at the meetings was active, and included some staff from other units in the hospital, but there was little higher administration representation at the meetings.

The first demonstration ward follow-up was made two weeks later on August 30, with the sending of the usual behavioral checklist to determine the progress in developing the ward. By this time the appropriate preparations for the program had been initiated; patients had been assigned to small groups; a reward system had been established; group work assignments had been arranged for; and a daily ward schedule had been developed. In addition, the unit had completed preparation of all the necessary forms for the program and was having no difficulty in getting the program underway. In fact, they had obtained the services of a psychiatric technician to be permanently assigned to the ward.

The full program was initiated on September 3 at Kesey State Hospital and a second contact was made ten days later on September 13. At this point, the unit staff stated that they were amazed and elated that the four groups (two male and two female) that had been formed were actually functioning effectively. Apparently, in this brief time the groups had organized themselves sufficiently well to handle their problems, and the staff for the most part was learning to permit the groups to function autonomously by refraining from interfering with them. The reward system seemed to be working satisfactorily. Staff members were participating in evaluating the groups and they seemed to be accepting their new role as evaluators rather than helpers.

The third contact was made on September 27 at which time the program had been in operation for three and one-half weeks. Although the groups had organized themselves well and the staff was still moving toward permitting the groups to function with increasing autonomy, the unit staff was beginning to make some modifications in the reward system as well as in some general procedures to make the program more appropriate for their population. The job assignments for the groups worked out well despite some friction among a few of the staff members who believed the work assignments were not essential to the group's progress. In addition, some resistance was developing from the hospital's clinical director who had refused to sign town passes for the patients. This was the first administrative block to the program, but the hospital contact stated that some compromise was made so that town passes could be utilized if the patients went to town in groups of three rather than individually.

The fourth contact was made on October 11 at which time the ward program was progressing well although there were some minor problems. Some revisions in the program had been made and the groups were working as effective units despite some interference. The staff was becoming a much more cohesive unit, as evidenced by the support it gave its own members. In this recent contact, it was observed that the unit staff was having nurses, nursing supervisors, and graduate students attend their lodge group community meetings, and they planned to invite affiliate nurses to observe the ward during the day. To highlight the cohesiveness of the work groups, the contact stated that the groups had received $20 for a month's laundry work and had divided it among eighty members of the ward with each patient receiving approximately 64¢. The final contact was made on October 25 and there still appeared to be no major problems.

The unit staff seemed to be functioning as disseminators of the program throughout the hospital, demonstrating the program to the various unit chiefs and inviting many people, both on the staff and others, to visit the ward program.

Approximately two months later, on December 16, the following spontaneous letter was received from the contact at Kesey State Hospital:

> Dear ———————:
>
> We thought we'd include a note regarding the program with our Christmas greeting.
>
> You will recall our demonstration period ended on November 3 and all seemed too good to be true during that time. Well, by the end of the first week following, we did have some complaints from a work area. The staff on ward Q-16 decided they would like just four of the group, the best workers, to come; that the other sixteen were more nuisance than help; they used up the limited sitting area; they asked for various doors to be opened and closed; and they smoked in the visitors' area. To make a long story short, the staff was given a choice of keeping the group intact or having none; they chose to have none, so we found another work area, this time within our own unit, so that we could deal with staff attitudes. The new area has welcomed the work group and found it most helpful, so we can conclude it was a matter of work area staff feelings.
>
> Around the middle of November some of the residents on ward 803 decided they would like to prepare a Thanksgiving dinner. Of the residents, thirty chose to take part; planning, shopping, cooking, inviting, serving, etc., was managed.
>
> Twelve guests, including the superintendent and his wife, were present on the Saturday evening preceding Thanksgiving day. It was impressive.
>
> Our Kesey State Hospital Newsbulletin of December 1 carried the following ad: 'GET READY FOR CHRISTMAS. TRY OUR SERVICES FOR HIRE: WE GO IN A GROUP OF INDIVIDUALS ON SATURDAY AND/OR SUNDAY. IRONING, HOUSEWORK, YARDWORK, AND GENERAL HELP. LEAVE YOUR REQUEST AT PHONE NUMBER 27 or 29. THE RESIDENTS ON WARD 803 TRAINED IN THE GROUP PROGRAM.' Four requests were received.
>
> Since the above was done in free time, there was no problem. However, a couple of people have had offers to work during the week as a more reality type testing of their ability to perform outside the hospital. It would be a couple of weeks trial for those who have been institutionalized many years. The question arises whether this adjustment period could be an important in-between step—or is it a protective delaying tactic?
>
> We also have private individuals who remain as part of the program, but who are getting individual work assignments in training areas in a cooperative effort for vocational rehabilitation, who can offer a living allowance for a few weeks following release, and a referral to a vocational rehabilitation field worker.
>
> We wonder if these things are modifications or disintegrations.
>
> We have added another part to step four; that is including letter by patient to family advising them of the plans, getting their approval, or at least keeping them aware of

their progress. The social workers feel that unless the family is aware, firm, stable arrangements for work and release are not possible.

The last Group G evaluation meeting I attended was again with Mr. C., the leader, and my quote from this time is 'This is a begrudgin' place—I need cooperation or else I get the blame.'

We had a full discussion regarding each group member's responsibility to contribute and not to be dependent on the leader only.

Another quote, 'I think I am doing better—I know I am!'

Staff has decided to have group evaluations every two weeks instead of every week! I can hear you exclaim, 'staff decided!'

We are planning to replay the tapes of the workshop. From some of the above developments, you can see we need to.

Please give us a boost for the New Year with some comments about our progress and answers to some of our questions. At the very least we are still rolling.

Sincerely,

This spontaneous letter was answered on January 7:

Dear _____:

You will have to pardon me for the delay in answering your interesting letter of December 16. A number of work problems, in addition to a crippling winter storm in this area, have meant that things are somewhat behind schedule.

I want to thank you for the information you sent about the workings of the program. I think that the way in which the staff is handling the work area problems is entirely appropriate. The Thanksgiving dinner story and the ad in the hospital newspaper are both indications of the kinds of side effects which can be expected once a program like this gets going. They are very encouraging signs indeed.

On the second page of your letter you mentioned two kinds of problems which you seem to feel might be either dangerous or beneficial to the overall program—but you did not seem to know which. With respect to the problem of program participants working outside the hospital during the week, all you need to remember is that to the extent that those members are outside the control of their patient small grouping, they consequently escape supervision and guidance. So long as the group maintains the prime control over the member when he is on the hospital grounds, the effect of working off the grounds ought to be minimal. If the staff, however, takes control away from the group of which the person is a member, the damage to program should be obvious.

With respect to the five persons who may be able to get individual work assignments, the effect on the program need not be detrimental. As a matter of fact, when the program was first begun as a service program, only individual work assignments were used. Later on the work assignments were changed into group work assignments because of the increased cohesion and morale to be expected from such new roles. If you decide to set these people up in individual work assignments (and perhaps you have already done so), it will be interesting to see what happens since we never operated a small group ward program with both individual and group work assignments simultaneously available. The important thing to remember is that evaluation should be sought from the patient's individual work supervisor and incorporated in a note to the group of which the patient is a member. The procedure is thus the same as when evaluations are sought for group work assignments. If this supervisor's evaluation does not work out, of course, you can always go to the work area where the individual assignment is located and get, or make, the evaluation yourself. If these patients also perform work as a member of the group or on the group work assignment, in addition, an evaluation of their contribution in this area should also be made a part of the information provided for the group through the note system. In other words, except for the fact of the individual work assignment, the patient ought to be treated like any other group member of the program.

As you can see, modifications from the basic small group program are always possible as long as you keep in mind the treatment goals for which the group-oriented program was devised in the first place. I hope the information in this letter will help you. Best wishes for the continued success of the program at Kesey. Keep us in touch, as you have, if anything new should develop. Thank you again and best wishes to all for a fine New Year.

Sincerely,

No further contact was made until May 19 when a letter was sent to the hospital contact reminding him of our consultation and the small group demonstration ward program and requesting that we ascertain his hospital's decision concerning implementation of the community treatment program. As no responses were received to the initial letter two follow-up letters to this request were sent on June 3 and June 18.

A response to our questionnaire concerning the decision to implement the small group community treatment program was finally received on July 1. The hospital indicated a willingness to do so with the understanding that the hospital would not be financially obligated in any way. Attached to the response was a letter from the contact as follows:

Dear _____:

We are pleased to report that our 'Community-Ward 803 Project' has been very successful and going stronger each day. We have recently completed a two-week companion project involving some thirty-five patients from ward Z. During these two weeks they assume the responsibility of taking care of their own personal needs in addition to program planning and activities.

We are, however, all acutely aware of the fact that our weakness now lies in the absence of a community lodge. We have the staff's willingness to proceed toward the establishment of this type of facility but the financing part seems to be our major problem.

We would like to make arrangements with you for securing your staff's assistance in establishing a community lodge, if possible, and with the understanding that the hospital would not be obligated financially in any way.

In this chapter we have attempted to impart some of the "flavor" of the approach-persuasion phase of the project. We have also tried to present examples of the different types of responses received from hospitals during our initial intervention efforts. For a more generic clarification of the dynamics of approaching and persuading institutions to adopt an innovation, a hard look at the data itself is necessary. This is the burden of the next chapter.

CHAPTER 4

Factors Affecting the Decision to Adopt

The experience of the lodge advocates in the various hospitals across the nation, examples of which were presented in Chapter 3, should have given the reader a "feel" for the workaday processes that occurred in approaching and persuading organizations to adopt the lodge treatment program. This chapter views the same processes from a quantitative perspective. It summarizes the experiences of the researchers by addressing itself to the specific questions this study was designed to answer. While the preceding chapter described the change processes in selected and illustrative hospitals, the analyses in this chapter are based upon all 255 hospitals in the study.

It will be recalled that the design of the study set forth four experimental conditions to be evaluated in the approaching-persuading period of the experiment. They were: mode of persuasion, status of the initial contact, geographic locale, and governmental affiliation. The basic outcome criterion was a social change score varying from one to three. It was based upon the two yes–no decisions made by the hospital during the approaching-persuading process. These two decisions were reflected in answers to the following two questions: (1) whether the hospital agree to expose itself to a persuasion attempt, and (2) whether it expressed a commitment to attempt lodge implementation. A hospital which would neither expose itself to a persuasion attempt (answer of no), nor agree to establish a lodge (also an answer of no) received a score of one. A hospital which agreed to receive a brochure (or hold a workshop, or set up a demonstration ward) (answer of yes), but would not agree to establish a lodge (answer of no) received a score of two. A hospital willing to receive a persuasion attempt (answer of yes) and ultimately to establish a lodge (also an answer of yes) received a score of three.

Table 4.1 presents a chi-square comparison of the effectiveness of the brochure, workshop, and demonstration ward on the social change score described above. Cell entries indicate the number and percentage of hospitals in each condition that received a particular change score.

Table 4.1 Comparison of Passive–Active Modes of Presentation.

| | Mode of Presentation | | | | | |
| | Brochure | | Workshop | | Demonstration Ward | |
Change Score	(N)	(%)	(N)	(%)	(N)	(%)
1. No Change	26	30	17	20	64	75
2. Permitted Persuasion Attempt	55	65	58	68	12	14
3. Persuaded to Change	4	5	10	12	9	11

$$\chi^2 = 69.39* \; (4 \, df)$$

*Significant at 0.001 level.

From these results it is apparent that the modes of presentation had significantly different effects both on the approaching decision and when a decision about lodge implementation was finally made. Thus, initial entry into the hospital was considerably easier in the brochure and workshop conditions (69.4 percent and 80 percent respectively permitting the persuasion attempt), than in the demonstration ward condition (only 22.4 percent of the hospitals permitting the demonstration project). However, of those hospitals that received the treatments, it is clear that the more active the persuasion intervention the greater the likelihood that a positive decision about the lodge would be reached (6.8 percent for the brochure condition, 14.7 percent for the workshop condition, and 47.4 percent for the demonstration ward condition). Using an anthropomorphic view of institutions, it could be said that a hospital avoids external interventions which it believes will cause it to change. It does appear that a two-step process is involved: interventions which might make an impact on an organization are screened out while interventions which will probably not be effective in creating change are permitted. The implications for approaching and persuading hospitals seem clear. Combining modes of intervention to create a sequential use of more active approaches

Table 4.2 Comparison of the Social Status of the Hospital Contact.

| | Initial Contact | | | | | | | | | |
| | Superintendent | | Psychiatry | | Psychology | | Social Work | | Nursing | |
Change Score	(N)	(%)	(N)	(%)	(N)	(%)	(N)	(%)	(N)	(%)
1. No Change	19	37	28	55	19	37	21	41	20	39
2. Permitted Persuasion Attempt	28	55	19	37	28	55	23	45	27	53
3. Persuaded To Change	4	8	4	8	4	8	7	14	4	8

$\chi^2 = 6.718$ (8 df)

(sometimes called getting a foot-in-the-door technique) would probably be the most productive technique.

Table 4.2 presents the effectiveness upon persuading a hospital to change that approaching persons of different social status will have. The results show that the social status of the person contacted within the hospital is not a significant factor in persuading organizations to change. These findings are extremely interesting in themselves. They strongly argue against a simple bureaucratic structural model of hospital functioning and change. The fact that initial intervention at higher levels in the administrative and status hierarchy did *not* result in greater change argues against a simple relationship between hierarchy and *de facto* influence. From these data (and other data to be presented later) it is apparent that a more diffuse pattern of influence and power exists relative to responding to an external intervention. While the mental hospital cannot be considered as an exact model of a Weberian bureaucracy, these data also do not support a view of the mental hospital as a totally democratic and participatory organization. While *de facto* authority and power do not automatically come from the top of the organization, neither do they emanate exclusively from the bottom. Some mix of higher administrative and lower staff involvement in decision making is suggested by these data (and more firmly supported in data to be reported later).

As described earlier, the rationale for including the urban–rural location of the hospital as an experimental condition involved an attempt to determine if this dimension—presumably related to cosmopoliteness, socioeconomic milieu, norms concerning change, and the like—would have an effect on lodge adoption. From the data presented in Table 4.3, it

Table 4.3   Comparison of Geographic Locale.

	Geographic Locale			
	Urban		Rural	
Change Score	(N)	(%)	(N)	(%)
1. No Change	54	44	53	40
2. Permitted Persuasion Attempt	59	48	66	50
3. Persuaded To Change	9	8	14	10
$\chi^2 = 1.016$ (2 df)				

is obvious that the urban or rural location of the hospital does not influence the change process to any significant degree. At least two possible explanations for these findings come quickly to mind. One is that the mental hospital is such a total institution, described elsewhere by Goffman (1962) and Stanton and Schwartz (1954), that it is relatively immune to the surrounding cultural milieu and is therefore uninfluenced by it. Another possible interpretation is that the cultural milieu is important but that it is not reflected in the urban–rural dimension. Subsequent data analyses will shed some light on this question.

Table 4.4 presents the final comparative result that concerns the effect of governmental affilitation (basically a comparison between Veterans Administration and state mental hospitals) on a hospital's decision to adopt new practices. As the reader will recall, the guiding assumption in

Table 4.4   Comparison of State and Federal Hospitals.

| | Government Affiliation | | | |
| | State | | Veterans Administration | |
Change Score	(N)	(%)	(N)	(%)
1. No Change	97	43	10	33
2. Permitted Persuasion Attempt	109	48	16	54
3. Persuaded To Change	19	8	4	13
	$\chi^2 = 1.434$ (2 df)			

using this variable in the experiment was the notion that federal hospitals would have less local decision-making autonomy, and as a result would be less likely to be receptive to a change intervention. Table 4.4 shows that there is no evidence to support this notion, or to support any differences on adoption practices between state and federal hospitals.

CLUSTER ANALYSES OF APPROACH-PERSUASION PHASE

As an essential supplement to the comparative results just reported, additional analyses were used to determine if there are any significant associative relationships between social change and other variables measured in the study. As previously described, data were gathered on a number of variables including the hospitals' internal social processes, demographic characteristics, staffs' opinions about the decision process, etc. To find the dimensionality of these variables, Tryon and Bailey's (1970) cluster analysis was used.

A V-analysis (cluster analysis of variables) was done independently for each of the three persuasion conditions (brochure, workshop, demonstration ward). The use of three separate analyses was considered necessary because of the significant differences that obtained among them, as shown in Table 4.1. In turn, it was decided to use the other experimental conditions (contact status, urban–rural, governmental affiliation) as variables because no significant comparative differences could be attributed to them as shown in Tables 4.2, 4.3, and 4.4. In order to determine the relationship of all variables to social change, the social change score was selected as the key variable in the first derived cluster. The other clusters were permitted to form empirically from the residual matrix. Thus, the cluster analysis for each persuasion condition includes: (1) a social change cluster, (2) a number of residual clusters, and (3) the relationships among the clusters.

The Brochure Clusters

The clusters obtained from the hospitals that participated in the brochure condition are presented in Table 4.5. The variables in each cluster are listed with their oblique factor coefficients. Within each of the clusters the variables are grouped by conceptual categories for ease of interpretation.

Table 4.5   The Brochure Clusters.

Cluster		Loading
Cluster 1 Social Change	A. Social Change 1. High social change score.	0.74

	B. Efficiency and Promptness of Hospital Response
	  1. Greater likelihood that decision about
	  receiving brochures was made during the
	  initial telephone call.
		0.74

	2. Decision about implementation was made in less time after initial contact.	0.70
	3. Decision about implementation was made promptly, with less need of follow-up letters.	0.67

Table 4.5 *Continued.*

Cluster		Loading
	4. Greater likelihood that decision about receiving brochures was made by contacting fewer persons, fewer times.	0.58
	C. Staff Status Hierarchy	
	1. Psychologist is perceived by staff as having relatively high status.	0.61
	2. Attendant is perceived by staff as having relatively high status.	0.54
	D. Superintendent–Staff Interaction and Decision Making*	
	1. Greater likelihood that superintendent discussed the decision about implementation with other professional staffs.	0.61
	2. Persons responding to questionnaire about the decision-making process were likely to be lower status staff.	0.58
	3. Greater likelihood that superintendent saw the entire professional staff involved in the decision about implementation.	0.53
	4. Greater likelihood that superintendent saw other members of his professional staff being satisfied with the decision about implementation.	0.49
	5. Greater likelihood that superintendent discussed the decision about implementation with members of his own professional staff.	0.43
	E. Attitudes Toward Patients	
	1. Staff tends to see ex-patients as *not* more dangerous than average citizen.	0.40
	2. Staff tends to disagree with idea that anyone who tries hard to better himself deserves the respect of others.	0.38
	3. Superintendent tends to see ex-patients as *not* more dangerous than average citizen.	0.37
Cluster 2 Urban Mental Health Facilities	A. Large Health—Mental Health Program in State	
	1. Greater total mental health institutions expenses in state.	0.99
	2. Greater state hospital expenses.	0.99
	3. Greater state health expenses.	0.99
	4. Greater number of beds in state mental hospitals.	0.99

Table 4.5 *Continued.*

Cluster	Loading

	5. Greater number of state hospital psychiatric beds.	0.99
	6. Greater number of VA hospitals.	0.75
	7. Greater number of state hospitals.	0.73
	B. Urbanism	
	1. Greater number of employees in manufacturing in state.	0.89
	2. Larger state population.	0.87
	3. Greater manufacturing payroll in state.	0.87
	4. Less native white population in state.	0.55
	5. Less owner-occupied housing in state.	0.55
	6. Less white Anglo-Saxon protestant in state.	0.49
	7. Greater number of unionized labor.	0.49
Cluster 3 Family Structure— Women's Role	A. Women's Employment	
	1. Greater number of working women in state.	0.99
	2. Greater number of females working in the hospitals responding to questionnaires.	0.99
	3. Lower state per capita income.	0.51
	4. Less percentage skilled males employed in state.	0.41
	B. Family and Marital Patterns	
	1. Greater percentage of young children in state population.	0.99
	2. Greater percentage of large families in state.	0.94
	3. Less percentage married females with a spouse.	0.64
Cluster 4 Hospital Financial Priorities	A. Superintendent's Financial Priorities	
	1. Superintendent saw hospital as less willing to reduce support of current programs to start a community treatment program.	0.78
	2. Superintendent saw hospital's decision to accept–reject lodge as not affected by availability of funds.	0.50
	3. Superintendent did not expect support from outside funds to establish a community program.	0.42
	B. Staff Financial Priorities	
	1. Hospital staff did not expect support from outside funds to establish a community program.	0.65

Table 4.5 *Continued.*

Cluster		Loading
	2. Hospital staff saw hospital as less willing to reduce support of current programs to start a community treatment program.	0.58
Cluster 5 Hospital Decision Process	A. Decision Process as Perceived by Staff	
	1. Greater likelihood that staff discussed decision about lodge with members of their own professional staff.	0.88
	2. Greater likelihood that staff members discussed decision about lodge with members of other professional staffs.	0.86
	3. Staff saw decision to accept–reject lodge as involving entire hospital professional staff.	0.82
	4. Greater likelihood that staff saw decision to accept–reject lodge as being made by consensual agreement of administrative and professional staffs.	0.43
	B. Decision Process as Seen by Significant Others	
	1. Superintendent likely saw decision to accept–reject lodge as being made by consensual agreement of administrative and professional staffs.	0.61
	2. Contact likely saw decision to accept–reject lodge as being made by consensual agreement of administrative and professional staffs.	0.63
Cluster 6 Hospital Size	A. Hospital Size	
	1. Number of personnel.	0.99
	2. Hospital budget.	0.88
	3. Hospital census.	0.85

The cluster analysis of those hospitals participating in the brochure condition yielded six clusters. The six clusters in the analysis have been given the following titles: (1) social change, (2) urban mental health facilities, (3) family structure—women's role, (4) hospital financial priorities, (5) hospital decision processes, and (6) hospital size.

1. *Social Change* The social change cluster, in addition to the social change score, is essentially comprised of four conceptual units. The first—which is labeled "efficiency and promptness of hospital

response"—contains a number of indicators that show a delayed response was likely to be a negative one and a quick response was likely to be a positive one. Although some of these variables appear in the workshop and demonstration clusters, presented in the next two sections, they are not as apparent as in the brochure cluster. A second component that appears—"staff status hierarchy"— is one indicating a relatively more flattened prestige hierarchy in those hospitals that were changers. This is congruent with the third component of the social change cluster—which we have labeled "superintendent–staff interaction and decision making." This group of variables encompasses a consistent theme: participative and broad-based decision making. In those hospitals that were change-oriented there was a significant degree of upward, downward, and lateral discussion about the decision to implement. Finally, a group of variables appears in the social change cluster which might be construed as a supportive ideology for the lodge and small group concept. These "attitudes toward patients" view the ex-patient as a relatively benign person. In turn, there is a hint that the hospital staff are a bit "hard-nosed" about the patient and/or ex-patient in that they disagree with the notion that "trying to better oneself" deserves respect.

Taken together, the variables within the social change cluster clearly point out the importance of the intra-hospital processes in creating social change. This is even more apparent when we consider the relationship between this cluster and other cluster domains as shown in Table 4.6. The intercorrelations are negligible with the exception of that between social change and hospital decision processes (0.39). This is congruent with the other information contained in this cluster because it represents another group of variables that focus on participative and broad-based decision making. Prominent by their absence are any relations between organizational change and attitudes about being persuaded. It is informative to note the absence of any relationship between positive attitudes and tangible change decisions. Also interesting is the limited relationship between hospital financial priorities, hospital size, and organizational change. These correlations are negative, but very limited in size. Since these are the variables that are most directly affected by legislative and administrative action it appears that such routes to effecting specific innovation are of limited usefulness.

2. *Urban Mental Health Facilities*   This cluster is essentially a group of state demographic variables that are descriptive of large urban and industrialized states. It includes the obvious indicators of the amount of

Table 4.6 Correlations Between Oblique Cluster Domains for the Brochure Condition.

Clusters	1	2	3	4	5	6
1. Social Change		−0.04	0.07	−0.15	0.39	−0.12
2. Urban Mental Health Facilities	−0.04		−0.13	0.02	−0.08	0.48
3. Family Structure– Women's Role	0.07	−0.13		−0.22	−0.07	0.00
4. Hospital Financial Priorities	−0.15	0.02	−0.22		−0.46	−0.56
5. Hospital Decision Processes	0.39	−0.08	−0.07	−0.46		−0.01
6. Hospital Size	−0.12	0.48	0.00	−0.56	−0.01	

manufacturing, ethnic composition, as well as others that are associated with a large state mental health apparatus. It is only marginally related to any of the other clusters, as shown in Table 4.6 and, most important, is unrelated to social change. It is clear that the often mentioned urbanism-cosmopoliteness-social change relationship is unsupported by these data.

3. *Family Structure—Women's Role* This cluster is basically a group of state demographic variables showing a greater participation of women in the state work force, coupled with a constellation of variables pointing toward larger families. Its relationships with the other clusters are negligible (Table 4.6).

4. *Hospital Financial Priorities* The group of variables essentially focuses on the hospital's unwillingness to reallocate money for new programs, and its pessimism about receiving outside funds to support new programs. This cluster is minimally negatively related to social change (−0.15), negatively related to hospital decision processes (−0.46), and negatively related to hospital size (−0.56) (Table 4.6).

5. *Hospital Decision Processes* This cluster is basically an extension of the decision-making variables found directly in the social change cluster. All of the variables focus on the implementation decision process as being a consensual one, involving many staffs, and a great deal of intraor-

ganizational communication. Not surprisingly, this cluster is related to social change at a relatively high level (0.39) (Table 4.6).

6. *Hospital Size*   This small cluster is concerned exclusively with the size of the hospital in terms of staff, beds, budget, etc. Its relationship to urbanism and financial considerations has been pointed out above.

The Workshop Clusters

The clusters obtained from the hospitals in the workshop condition are presented in Table 4.7. The variables in each cluster are listed with their oblique factor coefficients. Within each of the clusters the variables are grouped by conceptual categories for ease of interpretation.

Table 4.7   The Workshop Clusters.

Cluster		Loading
Cluster 1	A. Social Change	
Social Change	1. Social change score.	0.88
	B. Efficiency and Promptness of Hospital Response	
	1. Greater likelihood that decision about having a workshop was made by contacting fewer persons, fewer times.	0.41
	C. Pre-Persuasion Participative Decision Making	
	1. Decision about having a workshop was made by relatively *low* status persons.	0.81
	2. Decision about having a workshop involved a *number* of different professions.	0.78
	D. Superintendent–Staff Interaction and Participative Decision Making	
	1. Persons responding to questionnaire about the decision-making process were likely to be lower status staff.	0.70
	2. Greater likelihood that superintendent saw the entire professional staff involved in the decision about implementation.	0.55

Table 4.7 *Continued.*

Cluster	Loading
3. Greater likelihood that contact discussed decision about the implementation with members of his own professional staff.	0.54
4. Staff was generally satisfied with decision concerning implementation.	0.54
5. Greater likelihood that superintendent discussed the decision about implementation with members of his own professional staff.	0.52
6. Greater likelihood that staff had heard about the decision to accept–reject lodge implementation.	0.47
7. Greater likelihood that contact person had discussed decision about lodge implementation with members of other professional staffs.	0.47
8. Greater likelihood that superintendent had discussed decision about lodge implementation with members of other professional staffs.	0.47
E. Hospital Communication with Research Team	
1. Letter, and correspondence, to team regarding lodge implementation was likely to be very positive.	0.65
2. Greater number of spontaneous calls and letters to research team from hospital staff members.	0.41
F. Financial Considerations	
1. If implementation was refused greater likelihood that lack of money was given as a reason.	0.44
2. Greater likelihood that hospital staff expected financial support from outside funds.	0.41
3. Superintendent felt that decision about implementation was affected a great deal by the availability of funds.	0.39

Table 4.7 *Continued.*

Cluster	Loading
Cluster 2 Urban Mental Health Facilities	A. Large Health—Mental Health Program in State	
	1. Greater total mental health institutions expenses in state.	0.99
	2. Greater state hospital expenses.	0.99
	3. Greater state health expenses.	0.99
	4. Greater mental hospital expenses.	0.99
	5. Greater average daily census in state psychiatric facilities.	0.99
	6. Greater number of V.A. hospitals.	0.71
	7. Higher salaries for rehabilitation counselors in state.	0.70
	8. Higher salaries for psychiatrists in state.	0.60
	9. Greater likelihood of having centralized administration of state mental health system.	0.42
	B. Urbanism	
	1. Greater number of employees in manufacturing in state.	0.86
	2. Less percentage owner-occupied dwellings in state.	0.64
	3. Greater number of live-in servants in state.	0.63
	4. Greater per capita income in state.	0.59
	5. Lower percentage of young children in state.	0.55
	6. Lower percentage of large families in state.	0.55
	7. Lower percentage of native-white population in state.	0.52
	8. Lower percentage of WASP in state.	0.52
	9. Greater number of unionized labor.	0.50
	10. Greater percentage of management-professionals in state labor force.	0.45
Cluster 3 Hospital Size	A. Hospital Size.	
	1. Number of personnel.	1.00
	2. Hospital census.	0.96
	3. Number of beds.	0.95
	4. Total hospital payroll.	0.85

Table 4.7 *Continued.*

Cluster		Loading
Cluster 4 Response to Workshop by Those Attending	A. Agreement with Content 1. Staff agreed that the lodge program as described affected them positively.	0.86
	2. Staff agreed with the information presented in the workshop.	0.85
	3. Staff was satisfied with the information presented in the workshop.	0.67
	B. Assessment of Workshop as a Way of Presenting Information 1. Staff agreed that the workshop effectively conveyed fact that chronic patients can live useful lives in the community.	0.84
	2. Staff would recommend the workshop presentation to others.	0.82
	3. Staff thought workshop was an effective way of presenting information.	0.54
	4. Staff believed that the workshop information described a new program of treatment.	0.54
	5. Staff liked the format of the workshop.	0.46
Cluster 5 Response to Workshop by Those Not Attending	A. Heard About and Interested in Workshop 1. Non-attending staff would be interested in attending another workshop if held.	0.57
	2. Non-attending staff had heard about the workshop.	0.51
	B. Agreement with Content 1. Non-attending staff agreed with the information presented in the workshop.	0.89
	C. Assessment of Workshop as a Way of Presenting Information 1. Non-attending staff agreed that workshop effectively conveyed fact that chronic patients can live useful lives in the community.	0.83

Table 4.7 *Continued.*

Cluster		Loading
	2. Non-attending staff believed that the workshop information described a *new* program of treatment.	0.74
	3. Non-attending staff thought the workshop was an effective way of presenting information about the community program.	0.67
Cluster 6 Differential Involvement In, and Perception of, the Decision-Making Process	A. High Status Control of Decision Making	
	1. Superintendent felt very personally involved in the decision about lodge implementation.	0.76
	2. Superintendent of hospital tended to be high status.	0.69
	3. Superintendent was personally satisfied with decision about implementation.	0.62
	4. Initial contacts tended to be high status persons.	0.45
	B. Perception of Decision by Superintendent and Contact	
	1. Superintendent did not expect support from outside sources for implementation.	0.76
	2. Contact felt other members of his own professional staff were satisfied with decision about implementation.	0.57
	3. Superintendent felt that decision about lodge implementation was a consensual one.	0.47
	C. Reaction to, and Involvment with, Decision about Implementation by General Staff	
	1. Staff felt few groups were involved with decision about implementation.	0.67
	2. Staff less likely to respond at all to questionnaires about implementation decision.	0.40

Six clusters were found to account for all but negligible variance in the cluster analysis of hospitals that participated in the workshop condition. They are: (1) social change, (2) urban mental health facilities, (3) hospital size, (4) response to workshop by those attending, (5) response to workshop by those not attending, and (6) differential involvement in, and perception of, the decision-making process.

1. *Social Change*   The workshop social change cluster has numerous similarities to that obtained in the brochure condition. There is some (but less) indication that promptness in reply to the initial contact is related to change. The internal communication and decision-making variables emerge, but in comparison with the brochure change cluster they emerge early in the approach-persuasion process. Thus, the involvement of lower status persons and different professional groups in the initial decision about whether to have a workshop is part of the change cluster. Also, the later decision concerning implementation of the lodge is clearly a broad-based one involving upward, downward, lateral, and cross-disciplinary discussion and decision making. In addition to this intra-hospital communication, the change hospitals tended to have greater and more positive communication with the research team. A final group of variables that enter into the social change cluster seems to reflect a cautious optimism about being able to secure funds for new community programs.

Table 4.8 shows that the relationships between the change cluster and the other clusters are minimal. The relationship to urban mental health facilities is negligible as is the relationship to hospital size (0.12). An even clearer picture emerges about the relationship between attitudinal "persuasion" and the behaviorally based social change indicator. Two of the workshop clusters (4 and 5) are based upon questionnaire responses by the staff regarding attitudes to and about the workshop. Table 4.8 shows these two clusters are essentially unrelated to social change (both 0.09). The only cluster that is moderately negatively related to social change (−0.21) is one that encompasses a group of variables that depict a relatively authoritarian, non-participatory form of decision making.

2. *Urban Mental Health Facilities*   The cluster is comprised of a group of state demographic variables that are related to large industrialized and urban states, quite similar to Cluster 2 in the brochure analysis (Table 4.5). It includes obvious indicators of urbanism such as ethnic composition, manufacturing payroll, and a number of variables related to a large, fairly cumbersome state mental health apparatus. Table 4.8 shows that the cluster is essentially unrelated to the other clusters with the

Table 4.8 Correlations Between Oblique Cluster Domains (Workshop).

Clusters	1	2	3	4	5	6
1. Social Change		−0.01	0.12	0.09	0.09	−0.21
2. Urbanism and Mental Health Problems	−0.01		0.25	−0.17	0.01	0.08
3. Hospital Size	0.12	0.25		−0.23	0.07	−0.05
4. Response to Workshop by Those Attending	0.09	−0.17	−0.23		0.27	−0.03
5. Response to Workshop by Those Not Attending	0.09	0.01	0.07	0.27		0.22
6. Differential Involvement and Perception of Decision Making	−0.21	0.08	−0.05	−0.03	0.22	

exception of hospital size (0.25), and has an unusual negative relationship to the "response to workshop by those attending" cluster (−0.17). If any trend obtains, it is the indication that in urbanized states there is a greater likelihood that the workshop and its contents would be poorly received.

3. *Hospital Size*   This small cluster of variables includes number of personnel, census, number of beds, and total payroll. Table 4.8 shows it is slightly positively correlated with the social change cluster (0.12), related to the urbanism of the state (0.25), and also to a negative response to the workshop (−0.23).

4. *Response to Workshop by Those Attending*   This group of variables basically constitutes a positive response to the content and format of the workshop by those who attended. The workshop participants were affected positively, agreed with the information presented, saw it as an effective way of conveying program information, etc. As indicated in Table 4.8, this cluster is negatively related to urbanism and hospital size, and, of most importance, is essentially unrelated to the social change cluster (0.09).

5. *Response to Workshop by Those Not Attending*   This cluster probably represents the "overflow" from the workshop participants.

Thus, even though the variables in this cluster are primarily attitudinal questionnaire items from staff members who did not attend the workshop, the thrust of the cluster domain is a positive evaluation of the workshop content and format. The non-participants had heard about the workshop, were interested in attending if another one was held, agreed with the information presented, and with the effectiveness of the workshop as a training vehicle. As with the previous cluster, this too is essentially unrelated to change (0.09), as shown in Table 4.8.

6. *Differential Involvement In, and Perception Of, the Decision-Making Process*   This cluster likely involves a high status, low participation, decision-making process. The superintendent—who was likely to be a fully qualified psychiatrist—felt quite personally involved in, and satisfied with, the implementation decision. The initial contact persons were likely to be high status persons, and the contact at the time of the implementation decision felt that other staff members were satisfied with the decision reached. Feeling that outside funds for additional programming was unlikely, the superintendent further felt that the implementation decision reached was essentially a consensual one. Juxtaposed against this is the general staff's feeling that few groups were involved in the implementation decision, and indicating this behaviorally by not responding to questionnaires about the decision.

Not surprisingly, this cluster of essentially hierarchical decision making was negatively related to change (-0.21), as shown in Table 4.8. Also, for somewhat undetermined reasons, it was positively related to the previous cluster (0.22) which involved a positive response to the workshop by non-attenders.

The Demonstration Ward Clusters

The clusters obtained from the hospitals in the demonstration ward condition are presented in Table 4.9. The variables in each cluster are listed with their oblique factor coefficients. Within each of the clusters variables have been grouped by conceptual categories for ease of interpretation.

Five clusters were generated by the hospitals that participated in the demonstration ward condition. They are: (1) social change; (2) observers' demonstration ward enthusiasm, and unilateral decision making; (3) quasi-participative decision making; (4) non-observers' demonstration ward enthusiasm, general interest, and the medical model; and (5) general hostility, hospital capability, and decision making.

Table 4.9   Cluster Analysis—Demonstration Ward Condition.

Cluster		Loading
Cluster 1 Social Change	A. Change 1. Social change score.	0.90
	B. Hospital Communication with Research Team 1. Staff more likely to respond to questionnaires about implementa- tion decision.	0.83
	2. Letters, and correspondence, to us regarding lodge implementation was likely to be very positive.	0.73
	3. Greater number of spontaneous calls and letters to us from hospital staff members.	0.63
	4. Greater number of contact persons during our interaction with the hospital.	0.38
	C. Success of Demonstration Ward Consultation 1. Consultant rated hospital, at time of consultation, as likely to implement a lodge.	0.51
	2. Consultant assessed reaction to demonstration ward consultation as more positive.	0.41
	D. Lower Status Staff Awareness of Decision Making 1. Greater likelihood that the staff had heard about the decision to accept– reject lodge implementation.	0.66
	2. Greater likelihood that those responding to questionnaire about lodge decision were lower status staff.	0.52
	4. Staff who observed demonstration ward were satisfied with it.	0.68
	5. Staff who observed demonstration ward saw it as an effective way of demonstrating a new form of treat- ment.	0.64
	6. Staff who observed demonstration ward were affected positively by it.	0.60

Table 4.9 *Continued.*

Cluster		Loading
	7. Staff who observed demonstration ward were convinced that patients would be maintained in community treatment with minimal supervision.	0.60
	B. Unilateral Decision Making	
	1. If primarily an individual made decision to have/not have a demonstration ward he was likely to have consulted few professional groups.	0.99
	2. People responding to questionnaire about hospital status structure were likely to be high status persons themselves.	0.49
	3. Superintendent felt quite personally involved in decision about lodge implementation.	0.47
	4. Superintendent did not see the entire professional staff involved in the decision about lodge implementation.	0.43
Cluster 3 Quasi-Participative Decision Making	A. Participative Initial Decision to Have/Not Have a Demonstration Ward	
	1. If initial decision was made by a group a greater number of professional staffs were represented in the group.	0.99
	2. If initial decision was made by an individual he was likely to be of lower status.	0.45
	B. Quasi-Participative Decision About Lodge Implementation	
	1. Contact saw implementation decision as involving a number of professional staffs.	0.97
	2. If implementation decision was seen as made by a particular staff it was likely to be a lower status staff.	0.88
	3. Staff as a whole saw implementation decision as involving few professional staffs.	0.60

Table 4.9   *Continued.*

Cluster		Loading
	4. Staff considered as a whole did not feel personally involved in lodge implementation decision.	0.55
	5. Greater likelihood that staff felt that decision about lodge implementation did not involve entire professional staff.	0.46
Cluster 4 Non-Observers' Demonstration Ward Enthusiasm, General interest, and the Medical Model	A. Non-Observers' Enthusiasm	
	1. Staff who did not observe demonstration ward felt positively affected by it.	0.99
	2. Staff who did not observe the demonstration ward expressed high interest in a community program one month after the consultation.	0.99
	3. Staff who did observe demonstration ward agreed with it as a method of treatment.	0.92
	4. Staff who did not observe demonstration ward believed it offers a new method of in-hospital treatment.	0.89
	5. Staff who did not observe demonstration ward were convinced that patients could be maintained as autonomous groups in the community.	0.67
	6. Staff who had not observed demonstration ward had heard a great deal about it.	0.67
	B. General Interest and Cooperation	
	1. Hospital staff willing to reduce financial support of current programs to start a community program.	0.99
	2. Staff who observed demonstration ward agreed that it enhances role of patient.	0.99
	3. Hospital was not seen by contact as hindering development of the demonstration ward at the time	0.97

Table 4.9   *Continued.*

Cluster		Loading
	of the second follow-up after consultation.	
	4. Demonstration ward was functioning well at time of third follow-up after consultation.	0.84
	5. Greater percentage of questionnaires returned that dealt with perceived effectiveness of demonstration ward.	0.52
	6. Greater percentage of hospital staff attended demonstration ward consultation.	0.49
	C. The Medical Model	
	1. Staff sees patients as in many ways like children.	0.81
	2. Hospital superintendent agrees that mental illness is illness like any other.	0.74
	3. Superintendent was satisfied with decision about lodge implementation.	0.66
	4. Contact agrees that mental illness is illness like any other.	0.55
	5. Contact was satisfied with decision about lodge implementation.	0.54
Cluster 5 General Hostility, Hospital Capability, and Decision Making	A. General Hostility	
	1. Staff who observed demonstration ward were disinterested in having a community treatment program.	0.75
	2. Staff who did not observe demonstration ward were not interested in participating in another demonstration ward as a staff member.	0.75
	B. Hospital Capability	
	1. Patient has relatively high status in the hospital.	0.61
	2. Hospital was well prepared for demonstration ward consultation.	0.49
	3. Hospital was likely to be in a state with a decentralized mental health system.	0.48

Table 4.9 *Continued.*

Cluster	Loading
4. Better staff–patient ratio in hospital.	0.39
C. Decision Making	
1. Initial decision to have demonstration ward involved considerable consultation with a single lower status professional group.	0.42
2. Implementation decision was reached rapidly with few deadline letters.	0.41
3. Greater likelihood that those responding to questionnaire about lodge decision were women.	0.50
E. Satisfaction with Lodge Implementation Decision	
1. Staff felt personally satisfied with decision about lodge implementation.	0.89
2. Staff saw others as being satisfied with decision about lodge implementation.	0.74
F. Establishment of Demonstration Ward	
1. Greater likelihood that hospital has made significant progress toward establishing a demonstration ward at the time of the second follow-up after consultation.	0.74
2. Greater likelihood that a demonstration ward had been established by the time of the third follow-up after consultation.	0.66
3. Greater likelihood that a demonstration ward had been established by the time of the fourth follow-up after consultation.	0.60
4. Greater likelihood that a demonstration ward had been established by the time of the second follow-up after consultation.	0.51

Table 4.9   *Continued.*

Cluster		Loading
Cluster 2 Observers' Demonstration Ward Enthusiasm, Unilateral Decision Making	A. Demonstration Ward Enthusiasm	
	1. Staff who observed demonstration ward felt that it demonstrated that chronic patients could function as autonomous groups.	0.99
	2. Demonstration ward was likely to be highly developed at time of second follow-up call after consultation.	0.85
	3. Staff who did not observe the demonstration felt that it had affected the hospital positively.	0.73

1. *Social Change*   The variables entering into this change cluster are *markedly different* from those related to change in the brochure and workshop conditions. Most apparent is the absence of variables related to a broad-based, participative process of internal decision making. Although there is indication that in the change-oriented hospitals there was among the staff a greater awareness of, and satisfaction with, the decision about implementation, there was apparently only a small group of people actually involved. There are a number of items related directly to demonstration ward consultation, and the establishment of the demonstration ward. It appears that if the hospitals reacted positively to the consultation (as perceived by the consultant), and rapidly proceeded to establish wards, there was a likelihood that they would continue in the change process. This is an example of action begetting further action. Perhaps, as a reflection of this activity, the change hospitals also tended to have greater communication with the research team and responded readily to requests for questionnaire information.

Table 4.10 shows that the change cluster is related to two of the other obtained cluster dimensions. It is related 0.33 to Cluster 3 which is essentially descriptive of a delimited mode of decision making and it is related 0.21 to Cluster 5 which involved features including isolation of the demonstration ward, better demonstration ward preparation, and a somewhat delimited pattern of decision making. Once again the change cluster was essentially unrelated to clusters that tapped general staff attitudinal acceptance of the demonstration ward. This independence of attitude and

Table 4.10   Correlations Between Oblique Cluster Domains for the Demonstration Ward Hospitals.

Clusters	1	2	3	4	5
1. Social Change		0.08	0.33	-0.10	0.21
2. Observers' Demonstration Ward Enthusiasm, Unilateral Decision Making	0.08		-0.32	-0.09	-0.01
3. Quasi-Participative Decision Making	0.33	-0.32		0.00	-0.15
4. Non-Observers' Demonstration Ward Enthusiasm, General Interest, and the Medical Model	-0.10	-0.09	0.00		-0.39
5. General Hostility, Hospital Capability, and Decision Making	0.21	-0.01	-0.15	-0.39	

behavioral change is congruent with findings in the brochure and workshop conditions.

2. Observers' Demonstration Ward Enthusiasm, Unilateral Decision Making   This cluster involves two seemingly disparate groups of variables. One group of variables relates to a positive reaction to, and attitudinal acceptance of, the demonstration ward by those who observed it in operation. It was also perceived as an effective educational and demonstration vehicle. Coupled with these variables is a group of variables that reflects what appears to be a superintendent-dominated pattern of decision making. Thus, the initial decision to have a demonstration ward—if made by a single person—was likely to have involved limited consultation with various professional groups. The superintendent felt highly involved in the decision to implement, but did not feel that the entire professional staff was involved.

Table 4.10 shows that this cluster is essentially unrelated to change (0.08), or to most of the other clusters. It is related negatively to the quasi-participative decision-making cluster (- 0.32), which is understandable because of the decision-making variables which the two clusters contain.

3. *Quasi-Participative Decision Making*   This cluster, as indicated above, is shown in Table 4.10 to be related to change (0.33) and is interesting in its own right. It is labeled quasi-participative because the variables included are different from those which were found to be important in the previous analyses. There is a clear cross-disciplinary and lower status involvement in the initial decision to have a demonstration ward and this involvement seems to "narrow" during the implementation decision period. Thus, the implementation decision is seen by the staff as not involving the entire professional staff, but rather as involving a few number of lower status staff persons. In contrast, the contact person saw the implementation decision as involving a number of professional staff persons. Thus, it appears that a relatively small group of lower status staff is heavily involved in decision making, but that in the larger context of the hospital as a whole its participation is limited.

4. *Non-Observers' Demonstration Ward Enthusiasm, General Interest, and the Medical Model*   In many ways this cluster is similar to the second cluster. While generally it is composed of attitudinal variables relative to general hospital satisfaction with the demonstration ward, it also includes behavioral items (attendance at the consultation, questionnaire return rate, etc.) which also portray an enthusiasm of the establishment for the demonstration ward. Coupled with this are items which indicate a considerable acceptance of the medical model of viewing patients.

Table 4.10 shows that this widespread enthusiasm, cooperation, and medical orientation are essentially unrelated to the social change cluster (-0.10). It is also fairly highly negatively related to the next cluster (-0.39), which in turn portrays a much less enthusiastic general acceptance of the demonstration ward.

5. *General Hostility, Hospital Capability, and Decision Making*   A glance at Table 4.10 shows that this cluster is moderately related to change (0.21). It seems to portray a setting in which the hospital at large is indifferent or hostile to the demonstration ward, but in which the staffing, administrative flexibility, and nuts-and-bolts capability relative to the establishment of new programs already exist. A third group of variables hint at a more focused decision-making process reminiscent of the third cluster.

The burden of this chapter has been to explore quantitatively the effectiveness of different experimental conditions upon the persuasion process and, beyond these comparisons, to explore the variables that were associated with this process. The comparative analyses showed that of the four experimental conditions (inaction–action, social status of the contact, geographic locale, state–federal) only the inactive to action dimension yielded a significantly different number of persuaded hospitals. The advantage of action demonstrations and workshops contrasted with written material was highly significant. When workshops were contrasted with active demonstrations it was clear that entry into the organization was much easier to accomplish by "putting on a workshop" for the hospital. But as the process changed the hospital personnel also had to change from being an audience to making a firm commitment to change. As this change occurred (from observers to participants) the advantage of the active demonstration approach became more evident. If a hospital agreed to start a demonstration ward it was far more likely to agree to start a lodge than if it had had the "workshop show." Clearly, the commitment necessary to establish a demonstration project selectively eliminated many disinterested hospitals from the persuasion process while the workshop condition did not.

Beyond the effects of these conditions, the cluster analyses showed several results of importance. They showed that the social change process is much more dependent upon participative decision making in the more inactive approaches (workshop and brochure) than in the more action-oriented approach represented by the demonstration ward. It appears that the response to active intervention is an action response with a minimum amount of discussion while the reaction to verbal intervention is a verbal response culminating in the promotion of discussion within the organization. Equally important is the repeated finding that attitudinal support of persuasion change is not related to behavioral persuasion and that demographic characteristics, such as more money, larger hospitals, better educated staff, to mention a few factors commonly believed to be related to change, were not found to be related or unrelated to persuading mental hospitals to try a new treatment innovation.

CHAPTER 5

The Process of Activating Adoption

This chapter represents a clear transition in the course of the study. It is a shift from striving for verbal compliance from the hospitals and building within hospital models toward the actual process of implementing the lodge program in the community. The purpose of this portion of the study is to compare alternative procedures of assisting those hospitals that had agreed to adopt the lodge. This phase of the study is intended to explore the effects upon activating adoption that different techniques would yield. Essentially, it is aimed at answering the question: how can adoption be facilitated?

The process of *adopting* an innovation by an institution is one that is of the utmost importance to a general understanding of institutional change, particularly as it regards an extension of the innovation-implementation process. The history of social change gives many examples of promises that never get translated into tangible action, or action that destroys the nature of the innovation that is being put into effect. In short, when one is concerned with the adoption of a highly complex innovation, in an organizational context, one cannot assume that adoption will automatically follow from a decision to adopt.

The tangible features of the lodge probably need to be reviewed. The hospital's ostensible commitment was to develop a *community* treatment program emphasizing task-oriented autonomous patient groups, economic self-maintenance, altered staff roles, and a radical movement away from the traditional superordinate–subordinate social status model of curative treatment. To implement such a program, financial support would have to be developed, legal arrangements made, ex-patient employment situations created, decision-making groups formed and developed, staff assignments adjusted, and a lengthy commitment of energy expended.

This was indeed a formidable task confronting the twenty-five hospitals that had volunteered to implement the lodge society. It was also clear that of the twenty-five hospitals that had agreed, a wide variation in enthusiasm and commitment underlined the "yes" decision. Given the magnitude of the task and the uncertain predictability of agreeing to implement programmatic change, the description in this chapter and the data presented in the next chapter, are designed to elaborate the process of moving from verbal acceptance to behavioral adoption.

The activity of approaching the persuading presented in Chapters 3 and 4 can be conceptualized as a process culminating in a decision to adopt. Numerous authors who write about social change seem to assume that such decisions automatically eventuate in the actual implementation of an innovation. Thus, the *decision* to adopt is often treated as synonymous with a behavioral movement toward adoption. In some instances this is true; in others it is not. From a behavioral point of view, there are clear simple bahaviors that one engages in and that can be measured once one has decided to adopt some types of innovations (writing a prescription for a new drug, buying a sample of seed corn, etc.). The description of the advocacy-decision-adoption process found in the literature often assumes a clear continuity between the cognitive and affective aspects of a decision to adopt and its behavioral referent. This model is implicitly used in the academic and professional world where the distribution of written journals, convention activities, etc. are assumed to lead to behavioral change. If the same conceptual framework were applied to this study, we would assume that once a hospital had been convinced of the value of the lodge program and had made a decision to adopt, the motivation necessary for adoption existed and that the adoption behaviors would follow. Thus, the adopter would only need more complete information on the specifics of adopting as be passes through the phases from awareness to adoption. This approach has been translated into an experimental condition (the descriptive manual) in this phase of the project.

An alternative view of the adoption process has its roots in the skepticism of the relationship between verbal behavior and performance, and in a more realistic observation of how social change processes often become stalled. There have been numerous articles and reviews on the minimal empirical relationship between attitudes and behavior (Bandura, 1969; Fairweather *et al.*, 1956, 1964, 1969; Festinger, 1964; and Wicker, 1969) and there are some reasons to expect that this discrepancy might obtain in the current hospital adoption situation. For at least one paramount reason—in contrast to adoption in the medical or agricultural field—the behavioral referent of adoption (the lodge) is a highly complex social phenomenon. Thus, the establishment of a lodge demands completion of numerous sub-tasks and many goals need to be reached which require *drastic changes in professional roles.* Aside from the sheer complexity of this process, we would expect a very limited relationship between the initial verbal and affective positivism and actual adoption unless the initial motivation and attitudinal acceptance could be sustained by social reinforcement. Beyond the difficulties in making the transition from verbal commitment to the actual behavioral steps involved in adoption, there is some serious question about whether or not a group of advocates needs to band together to "pressure for change." Thus, an "enclave" of adopters might be needed within the hospital to achieve full adoption (Leeds, 1969). Such a group of innovators might be able to sustain each other's positive motivation and ameliorate each other's fears about innovating.

From the experimenters' own knowledge gained in helping to implement the first few lodges, it seemed clear that an external consultant could play an important role in aiding the movement from verbal agreement to activating the adoption, particularly in the organization, development, and motivation of a within-hospital "social change" group. This role had many similarities to the advocacy role proposed by Barnett (1953) and LaPiere (1965), and the change agent role proposed by Lippitt *et al.* (1958) and Rogers and Shoemaker (1971). This conceptualization of the adoption process assumes the need for an active external intervention. Thus, an appropriate consultative role would concentrate on resolving uncertainties, building cohesive group process, and strengthening the motivation of the in-hospital innovators. These goals could be met in a face-to-face intensive consultation relationship. The action consultant role would thus emphasize spurring a group to action, and providing a continuous resource for the uncertainties inherent in the adoption process.

Little comparative research has been designed to test the effectiveness of active consultation when contrasted with impersonal information-giving. Therefore, this phase of the research was established to evaluate these two alternative approaches to adoption. The twenty-five volunteer hospitals verbally committed to adoption were offered one of these two types of assistance. They were either given a "do-it-yourself" manual on how to establish a lodge; or were offered action consultant visitations by members of the research team.

OPERATION AND LOGISTICS OF THE EXPERIMENTAL CONDITIONS

The outcome of the previous persuasion phase of the study in terms of a commitment to adopt was a group of twenty-five hospitals. These hospitals were matched by pairs on the following variables: (1) persuasion condition (brochure, workshop, or demonstration ward, (2) urban versus rural location, (3) state or Veterans Administration hospital, and (4) volunteer or non-volunteer for persuasion phase. This matching procedure yielded ten pairs of hospitals perfectly matched on all four variables, two pairs mismatched only on the urban–rural dimension, and one residual unmatched hospital. One hospital of each matched pair was randomly assigned to the *action consultation* condition, and one to the *manual* condition. Further random selection placed the single unmatched hospital in the action consultant condition. Each matched pair of hospitals was then randomly assigned to a consultant team who actually implemented the two conditions.

Procedurally, the action consultant and manual conditions were implemented in the following manner. When a match of two hospitals had been obtained and its experimental condition randomly determined (action consultation or manual) a call was placed to the hospital indicating the type of assistance being offered by the team. If a hospital was in a manual condition the contact person would be informed that the consultant team was mailing copies of a manual to him. He could distribute them to the staff involved in the actual implementation. In addition, it was indicated that two copies of a book describing the initial lodge development and research would be forwarded (Fairweather *et al.*, 1969). The contact was also informed that the team would be calling every ninety days as a follow-up procedure and that he (the contact) could feel free to call the consultant team collect any any time for information and counsel. A similar procedure was followed with the action consultant hospitals. Those institutions were informed of the nature of the consultation and a date was set for an initial consultation visit. As in the manual condition, the contact was informed that he could avail himself of free telephone consultation and that periodic ninety-day follow-ups would be done in any case. In both conditions this initial "implementation call" was a point for gathering data on what progress had been made subsequent to the decision to establish the lodge.

The manual itself was a sixty-five page paperbound publication that intensively and extensively dealt with the procedures of developing a

community lodge. It described the following features of the lodge treatment program: its underlying philosophy, staff roles, guidelines for lodge
operations, ways of financing a lodge, different ways of establishing the
legal identity of a lodge, criteria for selection of patients, how to plan and
develop patient groups, what items to buy for the lodge, information
about real estate searching, how to make the actual move, how to plan the
first day's and first week's operation, what problems to expect, and how to
develop ultimate autonomy of the lodge. The reader may get some feeling
for the instructional manner in which the manual is written from the
following brief excerpts:

I. *Definition of a Lodge*

A lodge is a special kind of social organization in the community for ex-mental patients
with features that make it different from any other kind of place for such patients,
whether it be a family care home, a boarding house, other forms of transitional residence such as a halfway house, or whatever. The essential characteristics are:

A. *The lodge depends on lodge members themselves to keep their members in the
community rather than upon the support of hospital personnel.* Three basic
practices help create this distinguishing feature.
1. *No 'live-in' staff*: Unlike most other community facilities for ex-mental patients, staff persons are kept to a minimum. No staff persons reside on the
lodge premises under any circumstances. Typically, only a single person or a
few hospital personnel will have contact with the lodge during any eight-hour
work day, and this contact will exist only because he or they have been
specifically designated by hospital authorities as the staff for the lodge organization.
2. *Only lodge staff on call*: Unlike most other community facilities, the lodge staff
are the medium through which lodge members contact the hospital. Only these
designated staff members should be used by the members when they feel the
need for assistance. The staff is available to lodge members for all 24-hours of
a day, not for a 'shift' or '8-hour work day.' The resultant minimized contact
with hospital staff should decrease the lodge members' dependence upon hospital staff persons for direction and guidance in everyday life in the
community . . .

V. *How to Prepare for the Move to Your Lodge*

This section is concerned with the actual arrangements necessary for the establishment
of the lodge and the creation within the hospital of a problem-solving group of patients
who can be moved as a unit into their prepared community home at the appropriate
time. Specifically, the financial and legal arrangements necessary for the establishment
of the lodge will be described; the selection of hospitalized patients to comprise the
group that will be moved into the community will be discussed; the manner in which
groups can be trained in the hospital in preparation for their move in the community will
be explained; and the processes required to locate and establish the actual lodge site will
be described.

A. *Financial Arrangements*: A practical approach to the development of a community lodge must be concerned with arranging financial support for the lodge society. Four general sources of support appear to be available. They are: (1) Federal and state (non-hospital), (2) the hospital itself, (3) the community (church, business, volunteer organizations, etc.), and (4) the patient's own monetary resources. Each of these four sources can be utilized separately or two or more of these sources of support can be combined . . .

In addition, as mentioned above, each manual hospital received two copies of the book, *Community Life for the Mentally Ill*, describing the initial lodge research (Fairweather *et al.*, 1969). This supplemented and extended the material in the manual, and provided additional anecdotal information about the lodge as it functioned in the naturalistic setting.

The action consultant program was designed as a series of three visits to each hospital. The first two-day visit was made to all hospitals in the condition. A second two-day visit was arranged if any progress had been made toward lodge establishment subsequent to the first visit. The third visit was of five days duration and was undertaken when, and if, the hospital actually moved a group of patients into a lodge. The consultants were usually accompanied by a graduate research assistant who noted meeting attendance, made ratings, and tape-recorded sessions. His role was essentially an unobtrusive data-gathering one.

The action consultant visits were conducted by three senior members of the research team—all psychologists. The task they were given was basically an open-ended mandate to help the hospital establish a lodge program. The three consultants varied in their experiential knowledge of the lodge program: one had been directly involved in the initial lodge research and development, another had been involved in a more administrative capacity with the development of a lodge in one of the western states, and the third had never participated in a lodge program, but had had community treatment experience.

ADVOCACY BY MANUAL

After the instructional manual was distributed to each of the twelve hospitals participating in that condition, periodic telephone contacts were maintained every ninety days until implementation occurred or until one year passed without movement toward the establishment of the lodge society. More frequent calls were possible at the instigation of the hospital group. In order to "get a feel" for what happened to the hospitals under this condition, both a failure in creating the lodge society and a success are reported from the research journal.

A Failure: Olive State Hospital

At the time that Olive State Hospital decided to establish a community lodge treatment program, their demonstration small group ward had been in operation for approximately nine months; (this hospital had participated in the small group demonstration condition in the approach-persuasion phase). The letter attached to their decision to establish a community program outlines why the decision was made and what the conditions at the hospital were at that time:

Dear ——————————:

I discussed your suggestion about the community treatment program with Dr. Martin, the medical superintendent of the hospital, and we both concur. The answer is a qualified yes. By that I mean, we are impressed with the concept of the community treatment program but we would need a great deal more information before fully committing ourselves. At this point there is, (a) a shortage of funds as usual, (b) a poor staff–patient ratio.

This means that from our best calculations, some kind of special grant or other source of monies would be needed to obtain a dwelling in the community, and also extra full-time staff. It would be impossible to siphon off staff involved in regular work duties for this project, as right now they are stretched so thin. If this was obtained it probably would be possible for me to assist in some way in such a project.

One other point: you state in your letter the small group demonstration project set up in our hospital would be used as a basis for facilitating a decision about the community treatment program. This will be difficult to do because as time has passed it has become increasingly obvious that the program has not worked as intended. Probably the main reason for this is that the ward chosen had too many regressed patients on it. Therefore, self-directed groups have never evolved. This is not to deny though that certain minimal gains have occurred. So in summary, whether the hospital will involve itself hinges on the factors of money and most especially supplemental staff. One final point, after expressing so many reservations, there is another possibility of a positive nature. I have a fairly good relationship with a neighboring university and if there were some way of involving students as helping staff, I would be willing to explore that avenue.

I hope this is not too gloomy a response, but what I stated is, in fact, the situation here.

Sincerely,

On July 18 a letter was sent from the research staff to Olive State Hospital as follows:

Dear ——————————:

This will confirm receipt of your letter stating that your hospital is willing to try to establish a new community treatment program. I will be contacting you in the near future about the particular kind of assistance our research staff will provide you in helping to establish this program. Consequently, one of our research staff will be looking forward to working closely with you within the next few months.

Sincerely,

This was followed by a letter on July 22:

Dear ————————:

Not long ago you were contacted by Dr. David Oplar about starting your community lodge treatment program. He explained that, due to time commitments, the assistance which was promised to you would take the form of a detailed manual to be distributed to each of the persons concerned with developing the program. You will find enclosed ten manuals. Please feel free to request additional manuals for other directly concerned with the development of the lodge program.

Some persons in the program development group may express a special interest in the research study on which the lodge program is based. In order to provide them with background material that supplements the details in the manual with research results, I plan to forward to you two copies of the research report as soon as it becomes available from our publisher in September. It should be clear, however, that the manual itself is entirely sufficient to aid you in creating your lodge in the community. Should you have any questions in this regard, feel free to contact Dr. David Oplar who will be serving you as 'telephone consultant.'

As your consultant, Dr. Oplar plans to contact you on a routine basis every ninety days to see if he can be of service. These arrangements ought to be sufficient to aid you in establishing and operating the lodge program in a relatively short period of time. It is with this goal in mind that we hope to be of continuing service to you.

Sincerely,

On October 6 another letter was sent to the hospital contact enclosing the two books mentioned in the letter of July 22 and expressing the hope that these would aid in establishing the lodge program.

The initial telephone conversation with Olive State Hospital regarding implementation in July had indicated that the contact had talked the problems over with the hospital superintendent, and that they had planned to wait until September, after the holidays, to attempt to establish the lodge. The contact suggested that they might mention it to the education committee at the hospital which was meeting on the next day but that he was the only person other than the hospital superintendent aware of the intention of the hospital to implement such a program. As yet no staff had been assigned to the program and they felt that the financial problem was the one most in need of help from us. At the time of the first ninety-day follow-up on October 27 very little progress had been made toward implementing the lodge program. The hospital contact continued to speak of the difficulty with finances; that he had only met with one group—vocational rehabilitation—to discuss the lodge and that no results were forthcoming. No attempt had been made to establish a planning staff group or to investigate financial arrangements or location. The hospital contact had found the manual which had been sent "boring, matter-of-fact, and elementary."

At the time of the next ninety-day follow-up on January 27, the hospital contact indicated that they were in the process of setting up an in-hospital program with a staff of seven prople. They were to be interviewing fifteen to twenty patients to put in abandoned cottages on the hospital grounds. The in-hospital program was to include a gradual movement toward the community—from a self-help ward to a hospital cottage to a community lodge. The hospital contact had permission to select his patients from two or three wards at this time. He stated that the group had established criteria for patient selection and that they had reread the manual, which made him realize that they did not take only "the cream of the crop." His own personal criteria for selection of patients were: (1) age eighteen to fifty, (2) operating on an open ward, (3) not in seclusion for the past few months, (4) no criminal commitment, (5) not suicidal or homicidal, (6) some work adjustment since leaving school, (7) works well in groups, (8) not overly promiscuous, (9) female—since it is easier to find work for them, and (10) no family obligations.

The hospital contact at this time felt that the selected patients would probably move into the self-help ward in the Spring. He had met with the business office and had gotten money for a stove so that the patients could prepare their own lunch and breakfast. He further indicated that the self-care group might obtain a $4000 donation which was made to the hospital for "innovative purposes" and that he had a slight commitment from the superintendent for that money. He further felt that the shortage of nursing attendants for the program might be taken care of by having local university students come in for a couple of hours a day. However, the patients would be alone in the evening. Medication was to be dispensed at the main hospital. Dr. Oplar (the consultant) suggested that self-medication be instituted. The contact said it sounded good and that he would suggest it to the superintendent.

By this time it was clear that the hospital contact's attitude had become very optimistic. He felt that other staff group meetings were too authoritarian and that his staff meetings were completely democratic with no social status differentiation in role. As a consequence, the staff liked to meet. The hospital contact said further that any planning for the lodge would definitely include the patients and that they could vote on anything. The hospital contact at this point seemed sincere and the consultant felt that he had the proper attitude and idea concerning the establishment of the groups.

On April 20, the consultant received a call from the hospital contact requesting active consultation with the hospital for the establishment of the lodge. The consultant pointed out to him that he was still in the research phase (manual condition) and for this reason he could not visit the hospital for active consultation. The contact then reported that the staff group planned to start a self-care unit on the grounds soon ("already have a cottage for this purpose and are in the process of selecting patients") in which patients would be trained for the move into a community lodge situation. The biggest obstacle for the planning group now was that the self-care unit had no hospital staff. The planning group thought it was sufficient to start the program without any staff at all. The consultant suggested to him that without at least one full-time staff person to help administratively get the program "off the ground" it would probably fail. The contact replied that he might be able to acquire volunteer students from the local university and that possibly some staff could be developed from this pool of volunteers. It also appeared obvious that the staff planning group had not been utilizing the manual or following it very closely. The consultant strongly recommended that in developing the self-care unit and the subsequent lodge that the group *follow* the manual as close to the letter as possible.

Shortly thereafter, on April 29—a second call was received—from a master's level student at the local university. The hospital contact had recruited her and several other students to work on the lodge project. She was interested in replicating, at least in part, the lodge research for her master's thesis. She and the group were excited and stimulated by the lodge idea. They were currently at the stage of selecting patients for the self-care unit (located on the grounds of the hospital) which was to function as the base for developing the lodge. They had begun to follow the manual very closely as recommended by the consultant to the hospital contact. Her call was concerned with the exact method for selection of patients. This was reviewed to both her and the consultant's satisfaction. It was agreed that she could call at any time concerning the project or the research. She understood that the hospital was in the manual condition of the study which did not permit face-to-face action consultation.

The next follow-up call was made on May 18. This was a conference call with the hospital contact, several local university students, and the consultant. It continued to involve the establishment of the self-care unit on the grounds of the hospital. The major problem now seemed to be the definition of the coordinator's role—which the planning group wanted to divide among seven people who would each put in approximately two hours per week. The consultant explained that in his judgment this would not work. Nevertheless, they seemed reluctant to permit anyone to spend more time than that. Some discussion took place about the use of incentives that were not directly related to work. The consultant explained that it was better if the reward system was directly applicable and translatable to community work because there was no evidence that in-hospital rewards resulted in adaptive behavior outside of the hospital. There was some further discussion regarding the volunteering of patients and at what stage this should occur.

Another follow-up was made on September 23. At this time it was reported that the hospital contact had been gone from the hospital for six weeks over the summer so that little had been done toward implementation. The contact also had a new concern—the cottages on the grounds where the self-help unit was to be located had now been scheduled for destruction. However, the contact had talked to the director of the department of mental health for the state who said he would permit the hospital to keep one cottage for their program. A further problem involved determining the administrative status of the patients since they would still be living on the grounds of the hospital. The hospital contact also had a question concerning the role of the university students. How could they obtain academic credit for ten to fifteen hours work in community services? The consultant and the hospital contact discussed various possibilities, such as spending a couple of hours a day, spending one day a week from 7 a.m. to 3 p.m., or working at night. The contact did not discuss the use of professional staff so the consultant was not sure whether the planning group had by now secured anyone for the program. The hospital contact concluded the follow-up by indicating that the staff group hoped to move into the self-care unit in early January.

Further follow-up on December 21 with the hospital contact confirmed that the staff group had started meeting with the patients and doing some selection for the self-care cottage. The hospital contact reported that most of the patients were diagnosed as schizophrenic and a few were diagnosed as character disorders or neurotics. Throughout the conversation, he reiterated that the staff group planned to initiate the cottage program after the first of the year.

In later follow-up with the hospital the consultant learned that the move to the cottage was made in either the latter part of February or the early part of March. Ten women now lived in the cottage on the hospital grounds. The staff soon hoped to expand the residents to twenty. As of March 8, the hospital contact stated that the patients planned to start preparing their own meals within a week, but that there was no professional person on call as recommended in the manual. The students were on call one or two nights per week. Approximately a month later in early April, additional follow-up showed that the patient group was getting along satisfactorily. They had started to make their own breakfasts, but were having trouble finding other activities. The consultant reemphasized to the hospital contact that the staff group should start movement toward the community by choosing a business and exploring the possibility of establishing a nonprofit corporation.

The final communication with the hospital was in mid-April via a call from the hospital contact who had a number of questions concerning the program. The contact indicated that the women wanted to promote themselves, but the staff felt they were not ready. The contact wanted to know what the staff should do and how they should intervene. Furthermore, the women in the cottage were supposed to be having committee meetings and were not doing so, and the staff did not know what to do about that either. The contact felt that if the staff provided an agenda for the meetings and the patients followed through they might begin to rely too much on the staff. It was obvious to the consultant that the staff group had been able to establish only the rudimentary beginnings of a "quarter-way house" or an "exit-ward." They had been unable to move into the community. It was the consultant's opinion that movement toward the community had become permanently stalled in a cottage on the hospital grounds. Further follow-up information confirmed this judgment.

A Partial Success

This federal hospital had established a small group treatment ward while participating in the demonstration ward condition and had been operating that ward successfully for almost eleven months when they volunteered to establish a community lodge. Their decision to opt for lodge implementation was ostensibly based on a desire to develop alternative, post-hospital options, a belief in the lodge concept, and a general dissatisfaction with the status quo. On receiving this decision and the reasons for it, the researchers sent a letter to the contact at the hospital noting that their planning group soon would receive information that would help them establish the community lodge program. On September 30, a second letter was sent from the research staff to the hospital contact stating that the hospital would soon receive the manuals and two copies of the book about the lodge and outlining procedures for the telephone consultation.

In conjunction with this letter, a call was made to the hospital contact to determine how far the hospital had progressed in implementing the lodge program. The contact replied that the program had been "hashed over" by the staff and that they had talked to patients regarding volunteering, but nothing definite had been done about implementing the program. They had established a staff planning group consisting of the ward psychiatrist, psychologist, social worker, the head nurse, two staff nurses, and several nursing assistants. This group had management support as a decision-making body. They were attempting to use the assets of the patients as the financial base for establishing the lodge. At this time they had only tentatively explored possible locations for living quarters.

At the first follow-up, three months later—on January 14, relatively little progress toward implementation had been made. The new hospital director had replaced the ward psychiatrist with another psychiatrist. This new director had put a hold on the program in the latter part of October and the staff group therefore had little time to devote to implementing the program. Thus far, the group had found the manuals we had sent to them very helpful, although their ideas about establishing the lodge had not followed the plan exactly as outlined in the manual.

The next follow-up was made three months later—on April 21. At this time the hospital contact reported that the staff group had moved a four-patient group into the community. The patient group, however, was not working and had no work plans. The four men were living on pensions, were cooking their own meals and doing their own laundry. They were on leave from the hospital and had been out for approximately five weeks. Instead of having a lodge coordinator, they were visited by the ward social worker two or three times a week.

The men were living in a three-bedroom house in a town twenty-seven miles from the hospital. The house was located in a lower middle-class area with homes in the $10,000 to $15,000 class. These men were trained as a group on the demonstration ward, although there had been no special training for their move into the community. Medication came from the hospital. Except for this tie to the hospital the men were almost autonomous. The consultant pointed out to the contact that this independent residential living situation for the four-patient group was not an actual lodge. In discussing this conclusion with the hospital contact, it became apparent that the staff carefully selected from the manual only those instructions about establishing the lodge that they wished to follow. No formal meetings were being held at the lodge and the contact was not sure of what was going on other than that a social worker was checking on the men several times a week. The contact expressed concern about the unemployment of the four men. He felt that the men would have to get work soon. Everyone was beginning to think about employment but no action had been taken. To date there had been no trouble in their relationships with the community. The director of the hospital continued to oppose the program. In fact, the patients had been placed in the community while he was on vacation. The director continued to say that the program took "too much staff time."

At the time of the last follow-up, on August 10, the men were still living in their three-bedroom house. They had worked for two weeks putting up tents for the National Guard. They had not, however, obtained full-time employment and there did not seem to be much push in that direction. The consultant had encouraged the social worker, who had taken over responsibility for the project, to look for full-time employment for the men, but the social worker had not felt like "pushing" the men very much. As a consequence, the men sat around doing very little most of the time. The social worker continued to visit the house once or twice a week. One member had taken over the leadership in the living situation by doing most of the cooking. He had a bachelor of arts degree in accounting and was referred to as the "mother hen" by the social worker. One interesting point about the program was that the men planned it entirely by utilizing the manual originally sent to the staff. However, the men were given little or no guidance from the planning staff.

It is not surprising that the men did not choose to work since they had enough money from their pensions to meet their basic needs. A continuing problem was the hospital director's "all out rejection" of the program. Coincidentally, the hospital director was visiting another hospital when our research group was invited. It may be that he felt his prior contact with the research group had not been satisfactory and he therefore tried to scuttle the program. Although it was not organized along the interpersonal and employment principles set forth in the manual, a "partial lodge" had been established. It turned out to be the closest to a replication of the prototype lodge that could be achieved with advocacy by manual.

ADVOCACY THROUGH FACE-TO-FACE CONSULTATION

The general plan for consultation involved a team visit to each hospital with an agenda of tasks to be accomplished on each visit. The tasks were arranged in a three-visit sequence. The first visit helped to create a planning group and gave this staff group the necessary information to begin work on establishing the lodge. The second visit was aimed at aiding the staff group in movement toward the community. It took place after the hospital planning group had accomplished several of the tasks discussed on the first visit, such as making financial and housing arrangements for the lodge. The third visit was arranged to help the members of the lodge actually move into the lodge setting. As with advocacy by manual, the hospital contacts were permitted as many paid telephone calls to the consultant team as they deemed necessary throughout the consultation period.

A Failure: Little State Hospital

Little State Hospital had been a demonstration ward volunteer which had successfully established and continued a small group demonstration ward. When asked if the hospital was willing to establish a community lodge, the contact said "yes," indicating that although they had a success-ful in-hospital program the staff was acutely aware that their "weakness" lay in the absence of a "halfway house." The contact further stated that the ward group had achieved a concensus among its staff members about the need to establish this type of facility. The hospital staff believed their financial situation was the major stumbling block to the creation of a lodge society, and they wanted the research staff's assistance in establish-ing a lodge, with the understanding that the hospital was not obligated financially in any way.

A letter was sent to the hospital contact on July 9 confirming the receipt of the letter stating that Little State Hospital was willing to establish a new community treatment program and informing him that a consultant's visit was being arranged. A telephone communication was initiated later in July and the first of three visits to Little State Hospital was arranged.

The following information is taken from the consultant's notes after his first visit to Little State Hospital:

> The small group demonstration ward at Little State Hospital had been operating for one year at the time of our first consultation visit. Upon our arrival, we found a rather loose informal planning group for the lodge. It consisted of the demonstration ward staff plus

two people from vocational rehabilitation. The group, however, did not have any members from the administration and through the entire two-day consultation the research consultation group did not meet or see the superintendent of the hospital. Apparently, however, there was some mandate from him although it was not quite clear exactly how strong that mandate was. The planning group, although formed, did not seem quite ready to take the responsibility for actually working on the problems that would be involved in establishing the lodge. Because of this most of the two-day consultation was spent attempting to establish a viable planning group which would commit itself to actually seeking solutions to the problems involved in establishing a lodge. The group was, however, at least ready to discuss all issues involved. Our hospital contact who was the leader of the planning group at first appeared to be extremely motivated towards establishing a lodge or "halfway house" as he called it. This turned out to be one point of contention in the visit since when the contact had an accurate perception of the lodge society he viewed establishing a "halfway house" to be a relatively simple operation as compared to establishing an actual lodge.

The basic difference between this first consultation visit to Little State Hospital and first visits to other hospitals to establish lodges was that the consultative staff did not have to spend time reviewing the lodge conceptually and historically. The hospital had been diligently operating the small group demonstration ward for over a year's time and was convinced that it worked and worked well. They appeared to be at the point of frustration—namely, having cohesive co-ed groups in the hospital with no place to send them. They were aware that patients released on an individual basis were going to fail because they did not have adequate aftercare facilities to which to send them. Prior to our arrival an informal planning group had been discussing the establishment of a lodge for several months and had initially looked into financing and even looked up three prospective houses for the lodge. However, the group really did not have the mandate at that time to follow through so that it could accomplish anything.

The consultant indicated to them that although they had an informal planning group, they did not have a planning group that was committed to taking action. The meetings went relatively smoothly during the first day. Discussions of the essential problems involved in establishing the lodge took place. For two days we hammered away at the absolute necessity for a committed planning group in which the various people had action assignments to solve the problems related to finances, location and housing, choice of business, legal structure of the lodge, staff (selecting a coordinator or coordinators), and selection of a patient group or groups. We maintained that until these six problems were solved or well on the road to solution, they could not really get going with training a group in the hospital and putting it through the necessary steps for community living. We met with the same fifteen to seventeen staff people for two solid days. As indicated previously, the first day went quite well with good interaction and questions. However, the second day was explosive particularly during the latter part of the morning meeting and during the afternoon meeting. Most of the anger stemmed from the anxiety of one of the leaders of the group (the hospital contact) who wanted an explicit outline in step-wise fashion of what was to be done and how the problems were to be solved. He expressed over and over his need for an 'operations manual' demanding one from the research consultation group stating that since we had the experience we did in establishing lodges, then surely something was written down by us that could be given to his group. He seemed to want 'pat' solutions to all of the problems.

It became apparent that the hospital contact was for some reason setting up barriers to the lodge; raising a number of unanswerable questions and continually referring to the lodge as a typical 'halfway house.' In view of this negativism on the part of the hospital contact, the consultant decided to deal directly with the hospital contact's feelings. It soon became clear that the hospital contact was extremely angry because he felt the consultant would not provide him with a blueprint for establishing a lodge. The consultant, with the help of the other members of the research consultation group, made it clear that the problems they would encounter were somewhat specific to the situation in Washington. Eventually, with the help of several members of his staff who agreed that some of these problems were novel and had to be solved by the planning group, the contact verbally stated that he now understood the situation more clearly.

Besides the hospital contact, the social worker on the planning group seemed to be a good organizer and someone who was very motivated. A nurse who also was a member of the planning group seemed to be very motivated as well. But the main concentration of power as related to the lodge's development, was in the hands of the hospital contact. Hopefully, working with him on this first visit would be beneficial in overcoming his doubts.

In regard to some of the problems in establishing the lodge at Little, the planning group felt that financing was going to be its major problem. The vocational rehabilitation person who attended the meeting was unwilling to push or step on anyone's toes to achieve funding for the lodge. The consultants provided the group with a number of suggestions about how to obtain funds but it still seemed to the group that funding would be their major problem. As a follow-up to the funding problem, one of the consultants subsequently made a contact with a representative from the state department of mental health who was very interested in the project. It was suggested to the hospital contact that he get in touch with this person. However, to our best knowledge he did not do it. The planning group had also looked at several houses and felt that they were all satisfactory, but worried about an integrated lodge in this community. They had originally planned to have both men and women in the lodge and were concerned, as one person put it, that the community would look 'poorly' upon a black male living in the same house as a white female. The consultants suggested that a one-sex arrangement in the lodge might make the integration problem easier. There was also a problem with the work situation. The staff felt that work was scarcely available in the Little area, and that placing the lodge in or near a larger city would make it too far from the hospital. Thus, the patients were not being trained for any specific jobs. It was thought that they would try to work at any jobs that might appear. Some indicated that they might link the lodge with a sheltered workshop program which was to begin operation shortly. Even though the small group demonstration ward had been in operation for one year, no group had yet been formed or chosen to go into the community. Since this was a first consultation visit, it was not perceived as a particular problem. What was a problem, however, was how much the staff was willing to allow the patients to do. As an example, a whole kitchen on one of the wards nearby the small group ward was not being used at the time of our visit. The consultants inquired about whether the patients could use this kitchen to learn how to cook for themselves since this would be a survival issue once the group moved into the community. The consultants were told that the staff had not even considered it.

The consultants left Little State Hospital with the knowledge that they had given the planning group a great deal to work on, that a planning group had been formed, that the lodge could be established without too many changes, and that the hospital administration was not seen as a danger to the program. The planning group seemed very proud of the advancements they had made with the patients on the small group ward and they were willing to go further. The major problems seemed to center around the hospital contact, the leader of the group, and around how much commitment to developing the lodge each member of the planning group was willing to make. At this stage of the follow-up it was unclear as to exactly how much problem solving this group would do. The consultant team developed a concensus that somewhere in the system there would be some stalling.

The next contact with the planning group was made three months later—by telephone on January 2. At this point the planning group was having no difficulty locating a house in the community, as they had previously reported. However, their major difficulty seemed to be with financial arrangements. They continued to receive a lack of support from vocational rehabilitation in helping them develop financial plans. To alleviate this situation, the consultant group sent them a copy of the budget for the original lodge in an attempt to stimulate them to make new plans in this area, but the planning group still continued to see the lodge as a "halfway house," and, as a result, little appropriate movement toward the community had occurred.

Subsequently, a further follow-up was made by telephone. On this occasion, both the hospital planning group and the consulting group agreed that sufficient progress toward establishing the lodge had now been made. Accordingly, arrangements were made for the second of the three consultation visits. This consultation visit was cancelled by the hospital planning staff and another was arranged for May 25 and 26. Just prior to the May visit the hospital contact called several times during one day. When the consultant finally was able to talk with him, the contact stated that the lodge planning group at Little, along with several other division chiefs and the superintendent of the hospital, had met several times with citizens from the Little community who were planning a vocational training and job placement project to be located at a phased-out Air Force base nearby. This group consisted of several prominent business men, the chamber of commerce, several city officials, and some of the local politicians. The community planning group was attempting to convert the old base into a lodge training facility where the "students" would be housed temporarily while they were going to school and while efforts were being made to place them in selected jobs in the community. The hospital contact and his planning group had met with the community group in an effort to convince them to incorporate the lodge program into the overall community program. The contact noted that initially the hopes for this type of coordination had run high. However, more recently the community planning group had made it quite clear that they wanted to pursue a more traditional approach to the vocational rehabilitation of poor people in the Little community. This group of poor consisted of individuals who had poverty-level incomes or who were unemployed in a five-county area in and around Little, and who were *not* psychiatric patients at Little State Hospital.

The hope was that the community group would permit a few of the chronic patients to be included in the program, but the hospital planning group ran into resistance when they attempted to integrate the lodge program with the community project. They tried to cooperate with the community planning group; however, the community-based group resisted all attempts at cooperation. Finally, the planning group decided it was impossible for their group to function in this new operation. They also concluded that all other efforts at raising money and getting community support to develop a community lodge program in the Little area would be futile because of the strong political control exercised by the local community group. To use the hospital contact's words, he felt that "we just can't push it (the lodge) anymore."

The consultant inquired about the possibility of developing a community lodge program using resources from another community. The hospital contact responded negatively to this suggestion. The planning group had tentatively checked out the resources in that community and it was their conclusion that this would also be fruitless. The contact and consultant discussed in some detail the processes leading up to this final conclusion. The consultant suggested various alternatives regarding finances and political approaches that might be taken. The hospital contact rejected each in turn, indicating either that the particular approach had been tried or that he was convinced on the basis of his past experience that all such avenues were blind alleys.

The consultant then suggested that he might come on a consultation visit to discuss the matter further. The contact replied that he felt the consultation would not be worthwhile since the planning group had decided (after several recent meetings) not to pursue the development of a community lodge beyond this point. The hospital contact was satisfied that he and the planning group had received the utmost consideration and support from the power structure within the hospital in making their bid to develop a community lodge. However, he said that the "community will not support the lodge project at this time" and that neither the planning group nor the hospital officials were willing to "push it further." After making several suggestions and approaching the topic from various perspectives, it became abundantly clear that the planning group considered that further consultation would be unproductive.

Final contact with Little State Hospital on July 24 confirmed that the planning group there had done nothing more about implementing the lodge. The demonstration ward was still in operation and the plan was to expand it within the hospital operation. The staff was sending some people to a halfway house in a nearby city. An interested community resident had also purchased a large farm and four men from the ward were going to live there as their community aftercare situation. Beyond these two arrangements, no planning had been done for the lodge and it seemed clear that the lodge and its planning group were both dead issues.

A Success: Albon Psychiatric Institute

Albon Psychiatric Institute, initially in the workshop persuasion condition, volunteered on August 28 to establish the lodge. The rather quick decision about implementation was received from the hospital contact who noted its importance in the following way:

> The decision to enter into a community treatment program similar to that presented to us by Dr. Rosen was reached on the basis of three important influences: (1) the fact that we have a counseling grant at the Institute which may be used for rehabilitation of patients in the way deemed most advantageous by our staff; (2) finding a need at the Institute in establishing a type of rehabilitation specifically for the institutionalized and more or less 'chronic' patient problems; (3) the presentation by Dr. Rosen in a clear and forceful manner that inspired us to take advantage of our rehabilitation monies to solve our needs.

The positive response from the psychiatric institute was followed by a confirming letter on April 7. Subsequent to this confirmation from the research staff, several telephone contacts were made with the hospital to establish dates for the first action consultation visit. This resulted in a letter from the research staff to the hospital on May 29 confirming the dates for the first visit.

The following is a description of that visit from the consultant's records:

Upon arrival for the first consultation at Albon Psychiatric Institute, the facility did
indeed impress us as a psychiatric institute rather than a state hospital. It was of new
vintage; its physical plant was well maintained; and its grounds were well kept. The
planning staff at the institute were well prepared for the visit and reacted quite positively to the consultation. The social climate was rehabilitative contrasted to custodial.

The hospital had done a considerable amount of work prior to our arrival on the scene.
The staff of the rehabilitation ward was the planning group for the implementation of
the lodge and at this time they were currently being assisted by a few people from the
state office of vocational rehabilitation in planning the establishment of the lodge. They
had the authority from the superintendent of the hospital to plan the entire operation
and to follow through with it. There were no financial arrangements as yet developed
for establishing a community lodge but the planning group had already talked about
obtaining a grant from the vocational rehabilitation administration or the manpower development training administration. The planning group had not yet found a community
location for a lodge but they had discussed it. No legal arrangements had been established for the lodge although they had discussed the lodge as an extension of the
hospital, as voluntary for the patients, and as a nonprofit corporation. Their discussion
had reached a stage where they were talking about a nonprofit corporation under the
auspices of the office of vocational rehabilitation which it seemed could be used for this
purpose without undue difficulty.

Subsequent to the workshop that had been presented approximately one year prior to
the consultation visit, the ward staff planning group had accomplished more than planning for the community move. They had made considerable in-hospital preparation as
well. The staff had organized five four-man co-educational groups on the ward operating
on a modified token economy program which utilized real money in an attempt to
develop cohesiveness. Apparently the idea had been to make the program as unstruc-
tured as possible in order to allow the groups to develop their own methods of dealing
with problems, etc. However, the consultant pointed out to them that this was not likely
to happen without beginning some structure for the group situation. The staff had some
feeling that any structure would lessen the patients' civil and individual rights. Much of
this first visit, therefore, was spent in discussing the applicability of the current ward
step program to developing cohesive groups that could move quickly and effectively
into the community. The staff planning group agreed that the small group program
would be much more effective in developing groups who could be placed in community
lodges. During this visit little was discussed about actually establishing the lodge, other
than financing, location, and the residents. The main thrust of this first visit was upon
developing groups within the hospital that could move into the community. The staff
planning group consisted of ten people varying in background and training from the
coordinator of the rehabilitation ward who was a vocational rehabilitation counselor,
the administrator of the local regional vocational rehabilitation office, a social worker, a
ward physician, three occupational therapists, another rehabilitation counselor, and the
superintendent himself.

Shortly after the first consultation visit was completed, a letter was received from the hospital superintendent:

Dear _____:

Dr. Watson of your group recently spent two days at the Albon Psychiatric Institute and I received the attached memo describing his activities. Again, we appreciate very much your assistance and look forward to a successful project in rehabilitation.

Sincerely,

The memo referred to in the letter from the superintendent was as follows:

I would like to inform you that the two days with Dr. Watson were very beneficial to the rehabilitation unit's program. The most important things coming out of these meetings were effective ways to apply peer pressure and ways of giving the unit more structure. I feel the staff was very appreciative of his coming and, I believe, is looking forward to implementation of the suggestions he made.

Within one month after the visit, the rehabilitation ward staff instituted the new program on the ward as recommended by the consultant. In less than three months after the visit, a call was received from the hospital contact informing the research staff that they were progressing satisfactorily and that they had decided to make contact with Serto Mechanics, a national janitorial franchise corporation, in an attempt to purchase a franchise and establish a business for the lodge. This call was followed very quickly by a letter from the hospital contact on October 21:

Dear _____:

I am writing to give you information that you will need if it becomes necessary for you to contact the national office of Serto Mechanics. We are working on a plan to purchase a franchise from Serto Mechanics which is, as you probably know, a nation-wide cleaning service which prides itself on its reputation and high standards. Their state representative is interested in selling this contract and has written to the main office in New York to get their permission. I am sure that they will want to know exactly who they are selling the franchise to and this is where you can be of some assistance to us by explaining our program to them. Essentially, we are trying to do the same thing you've done with the other lodges, so I feel you would be able to explain to them what our program is. We also will hire an individual to be responsible for the quality of work done and for keeping up standards that Serto Mechanics might have. Initially, he would provide very close supervision of any team going into a home and would not allow any workers to work in homes that he felt would act in an irresponsible way. We hope to train patient supervisors that will assume this responsibility when the business expands to the degree where one supervisor cannot handle this. I think that this will be the main thing that they will be interested in—whether or not we can give them an assurance that we will not give them a bad name and that we will keep up their cleaning standards.

Serto Mechanics headquarters has your name and address and may be contacting you or they may ask that you contact them. I will write you and let you know if you need to contact them. Hope to see you soon.

Sincerely,

Shortly after receiving this letter, the research consultant contacted Serto Mechanics to confirm our relationship with the psychiatric institute and to establish both their credibility and ours as well as know-how for implementing community lodges and establishing coordinated businesses. The telephone call was well received. This was confirmed by a letter which arrived shortly thereafter, on October 27, from the program development manager in the market expansion services division:

Dear ———————:

It was a pleasure to talk with you on the telephone this morning in regard to the relationship between Serto Mechanics and the Albon Psychiatric Institute.

My plans are to write to Mr. Johansen, our coordinator for that area, to inform him of our conversation. I feel confident that he and Mr. Chalmers will have many pertinent questions for you upon your arrival next month. I have requested a copy of your book from the publisher so that I can become more familiar with your program.

Sincerely,

The three-month follow-up after the first visit took place on October 28. It is significant that the telephone conversation lasted for forty-two minutes. It is interesting to note that the staff planning group at this time had been modified—two of the rehabilitation counselors on the planning group were eliminated and replaced with registered nurses because of the counselors' resistance to the development of the plan. There had been no change in the authority given to the group as to their responsibility and capacity to follow through with the establishment of the lodge. At this time the major problem appeared to be a financial one, as no avenue for the initial financing of a lodge had yet been found, although the hospital rehabilitation program was to be continued for the next fiscal year. It appeared somewhat premature to find a location in the community for the lodge because cohesive groups that would be moved into the community had not yet been created in the hospital. However, progress had occurred in other areas. Arrangements had already been made for potential lodge members who became physically or mentally ill to receive treatment at the psychiatric institute. The hospital was to assign a physician to the lodge who would make the decision as to whether a patient whose symptoms became exacerbated should return to the hospital or remain living in the lodge. As far as legal arrangements for the lodge were concerned, the planning group had decided to develop a nonprofit corporation of some kind but had not progressed far in this direction.

The organization of the small group feeder-ward in the hospital had two groups, one male and one female. It was the planning group's desire to combine these groups and send one coeducational group of twenty patients to live in the lodge. The reason for this decision was mainly programmatic: there was likely to be difficulty in obtaining a lodge location and the housing of both males and females together would simplify the community move. The hospital contact reported that the groups had not yet been fully trained for living and working together. The training to date had emphasized small groups that met once a day to discuss and act on problems. The groups were at the stage of development where they were talking more in fantasy than in reality terms about living in the community. However, some attempt had been made to develop a business. The group had had two jobs for pay outside of the hospital and they apparently had done excellent work.

As far as staffing for the lodge was concerned, the planning group had found a woman to fill the role of coordinator. The contact reported that on moving to the community she would be responsible for the following tasks: providing training for the patient members after she had received training in a course provided by Serto Mechanics, supervision of jobs, transportation, bidding on jobs and training lodge members to do bidding, doing all the business manager paperwork, and being responsible to the employer for the quality of work. The vocational rehabilitation service would pay her salary but the business would eventually take over this responsibility. The hospital contact indicated that currently the coordinator was not a member of the staff planning group because she was not a hospital staff member. However, he planned to bring her into the staff planning group for the second consultation visit and to have the hospital contact, the research consultant, and the prospective coordinator meet for discussions regarding the coordinator's role.

Less than a month after the first follow-up, a letter was sent to Albon Psychiatric Institute attempting to establish the second action consultation visit. The letter follows:

> Dear _____:
>
> I am writing to confirm the dates of December 15 and 16 for the second consultation to establish a community treatment program (lodge) in conjunction with your hospital. As Dr. Watson indicated to Mr. Johansen in their recent telephone conversation, this second visit is the second of a three-part consultation. The third part, as previously indicated, will be a five-day consultation when the hospital is actually prepared to initiate lodge operations.
>
> The consultation will again be conducted by Dr. Watson who plans to have one member of our research staff, Mr. Jeffrey Edwards, accompany him during this visit. Dr. Watson and Mr. Edwards are looking forward to meeting with your lodge planning group.
>
> Sincerely,

A quick response was received from the hospital superintendent reacting to the impending visit:

> Dear _____:
>
> We will look forward to working again with Dr. Watson on December 15 and 16 for his second consultation to establish a community treatment program in conjunction with the Albon Psychiatric Institute.
>
> Sincerely,

Enclosed with the letter was a memorandum to the ward staff from the coordinator of the ward and the hospital contact concerning the agenda for the consultation as follows:

> The following is a rough agenda for the two days Dr. Watson will be with us. I hope that as many as possible of you can attend these sessions. Please bring with you all of the questions you have about any aspect of our program. If necessary, write them down beforehand.
>
> 9:00 a.m. to 10:15 a.m.—Discussion of the janitorial business and the purchase of a Serto Mechanics franchise.
> 10:15 a.m. to 10:30 a.m.—Break.
> 10:30 a.m. to 12:00—Discussion of the lodge, i.e., the hows, whens, wheres of actually moving into the physical structure in the community.
> 12:00 to 1:00 p.m.—Lunch.
> 1:00 p.m. to 4:00 p.m.—Evaluation of our present ward program and things we should begin doing in preparing patients for community living.

The second action consultation visit took place on December 15 and 16 as planned. The staff planning group was changed slightly by the addition of the state director of vocational rehabilitation. This planning group continued to have the authority to plan the entire operation and to implement the lodge. Financial arrangements were by now moving ahead. The planning group was in the process of submitting a proposal for $60,000 to the state vocational rehabilitation administration as support for the lodge. There had been some attempt by the planning group to seek a location but apparently it had not been too serious an attempt because funding was not yet available. The group had agreed to start to look for a location and this situation was discussed in great detail with the research consultant. Several specific places to explore were mentioned.

As far as relationships with the hospital were concerned, the lodge members were to remain on leave from the hospital and would not be discharged. Since the patients would technically still be under hospital jurisdiction, they would be entitled to hospital treatment for physical or mental illness whenever necessary. A hospital physician was to have medical responsibility for the lodge.

The legal arrangements were also moving forward. The lodge was to be a nonprofit corporation accountable to the office of vocational rehabilitation of the state, and lodge members were to be employees of this corporation. As far as the in-hospital preparation of the groups was concerned, they had been meeting daily for several months and they had had some janitorial training. They had also worked as groups on a few jobs in the community. They had not as yet elected their own officials because up to now the staff had not appointed the team leaders for the janitorial crews. But the patients had not yet faced the issue of what their actual roles would be within the community lodge. Furthermore, they had not made clear any decisions about their future in the community. Because of this, the research consultant strongly urged the staff to start facing the groups with the reality of community living, first on a verbal and then on an action level. At this time the planning group anticipated moving into a community lodge in six or seven months. The follow-through on this move was extremely dependent on whether their budget and narrative proposal to the office of vocational rehabilitation were approved.

One month after the second consultation visit a spontaneous letter was received from the hospital contact reporting on the progress of the lodge. It ran:

Dear ———————————:

Things are really swinging up here now and we've made some major strides since your last visit. I thought I would drop you a line and let you know where we are at this point. We have found a lodge which is perfect for us. It's a five-plex, right in the middle of the business district with no homes around it, just commercial establishments. The rent is only $800 a month which is about half of what I thought we would have to pay. We were able to get the money from the vocational rehabilitation for this fiscal year which will pay for the franchise, additional equipment, coordinator's salary, the truck and additional supplies. I'll have to wait until the summer some time to find out if I will get what I want for the next fiscal year.

The janitorial crews are performing 100 percent better than they were and we are getting lots of outside jobs to use as training settings.

You can't imagine how much your visit helped us in terms of getting the nurses on board as to what the program is all about. Our total staff now has stopped being helpers and are now consultants. We have cut the nursing staff down by about a third already and anticipate that by next month we will cut out nursing on one shift completely and by the month following cut out nursing on some days on both of the other shifts. We hope that by May or June we will have nursing cut out of the unit completely. Really, the only reason for maintaining nursing there now, it seems to me, is that we need somebody around to write notes on infractions and to assist in our weekly evaluation. We anticipate moving into the lodge on July 1 and hope that you can make arrangements to be with us then. The way things look now, I don't see any possibility of this being delayed and, in fact, I think we could probably move out right now if we had the money. I hope you will write to me and let me know if you can arrange to be up here on the first of July.

Sincerely,

The research consultant replied on January 21:

Dear _____:

Your letter was a delight; everything you report is of an extremely positive nature which leads me to believe that there must be something negative occurring; in all sincerity I am extremely pleased that you have accomplished all of this in such a short period of time. I certainly appreciate your comments concerning the helpfulness of our latest visit.

July in your state sounds great. Since the third visit entails our being there for a period of five consecutive days, let me suggest the week of June 29 or the week of July 6 rather than July 1 which falls in the middle of the week. Let me take this opportunity to outline the steps we feel are necessary for you to complete the move to the lodge as well as the role of the staff in the lodge situation. You will find this material enclosed.

Let me emphasize, if it is not clear in the enclosed documents, that staff's allegiance must be to the program and to problem solution *rather* than to each individual member's discipline. If this is not done, the program has an excellent chance of *not* accomplishing its goals and aims.

I certainly hope that this information will be of value to you in this final, but crucial step towards establishing the lodge. Please let me know your thoughts concerning the dates of the next visit.

Sincerely.

The hospital contact at the psychiatric institute did not respond until March 27. That letter follows:

Dear _____:

Sorry for taking so long to answer your letter. It will be fine if you can be here for the week beginning June 30.

Everything seems to be running along relatively smoothly. We have purchased the franchise and the equipment is on its way. Also, the truck is on its way. We're to the point now where we're getting jobs every day that we are considering training jobs and feel that, by the first of May, we'll be able to begin practicing under Serto Mechanics. We have trained two cooks and, by next week, they will be cooking all of the meals on the unit in the hospital. Beginning the middle of May, we will have to simulate the lodge experience on the ward, which will mean that we will have no staff on the unit. They will be cooking and buying all of their food outside the hospital. They will be working under Serto Mechanics, etc., etc.

Let me know for sure if you can some on the 30th. Hope to see you soon.

Sincerely,

A reply from the research consultant to the hospital contact informing him that the week of June 30 would not be appropriate but that the week of July 6 would be was sent immediately. This date was soon confirmed for the third and final five-day visit to implement the community lodge. To conform with the consultant's visit, the hospital contact decides that the move to the lodge would be made on July 6.

The second follow-up for the implementation phase was made by telephone on April 3. All of the information concerning their progress, reported in the aforementioned letters from the hospital contact, was reviewed. However, one significant event as of this time was in the process of taking place. Apparently, all the crew chiefs (ex-patients) had gone on strike because the staff had not been satisfied with their groups' actions. The staff had informed the groups of this and enforced it by demoting all the groups—giving them fewer responsibilities and privileges. The day before the follow-up call was made, the hospital contact had come into one of the groups with a job opportunity and was told the groups were going on strike. While this telephone call was in process the patients were in an autonomous group meeting which until then was the longest on record—one and one-half hours. The hospital contact was obviously disturbed but no resolution of this situation had taken place by the time the research consultant's telephone follow-up came through. The follow-up call was completed with the group still "out."

On April 30, a spontaneous telephone call was received by the consultant from the hospital contact. He apparently was in near "panic." This call brought to light that the groups were in actual rebellion. Specifically, the leaders were not responding to any staff leadership. The hospital contact and ward administrator were very concerned that the whole system would fall apart. However, the contact did report that, despite their problems with the hospital staff, the groups were still working in the community and were doing a satisfactory job. All the staff were off the ward. Only a telephone remained as a communication link and the patients used it only to contact the staff in emergencies. The research consultant recommended that the ward now be modeled very closely after the lodge in the following ways:

1. Establishment of a ruling executive committee comprised of the crew chiefs, cooks, and the business manager.
2. That the group now function as a group of the whole rather than in the smaller autonomous groups.
3. That communication through written notes be sent to the executive committee rather than the smaller groups (as it had been in the past) in order to strengthen its new role as the governing body.
4. Elimination of the step-level reward system used in the hospital and replacing it with the distribution of the money from jobs to all members of the ward-lodge on a differential pay basis, the pay scale to be established by the patient group itself.

Another spontaneous call on May 12 from the contact reported on the implementation of the research consultant's recommendations. The contact was very pleased with the results of the recommendations but sounded tired. He said that things looked much better and the introduction of the new recommendations had achieved this. There were six people on the executive board, four of whom were actively involved in governing and making decisions. Communicating through notes to each small group had been eliminated and the notes were now going only to the executive board. The board had instituted the new reward system of differential pay: the poorest workers received one percent of the gross income, average workers two percent, and the members of the executive board three percent. Only thirty percent of the gross income was distributed on this basis. The remaining seventy percent was set aside for future lodge operations. The group would get their new truck on May 13, with a patient already assigned as the driver. The current lodge coordinator, Mrs. Mary Pogue, was pregnant again and would be dropping out as of June 1. However, the hospital contact had already obtained the commitment of a Mr. Joe Michaels, who had a master's degree in counseling psychology, and who was very enthusiastic about the whole project. He was to be hired effective May 1 and would overlap with Mrs. Pogue for a month. Mrs. Pogue had received her janitorial training from Serto Mechanics in Chicago and would try to impart her skills to the new coordinator during their overlapping work period. The hospital contact also was going to attempt to turn over most of his administrative functions relating to the lodge to the incoming lodge coordinator. This action was encouraged by the consultant. The hospital contact also stated that the current lodge premises (owned by a wealthy dentist) were being remodeled to arrange dining facilities and storage space for the janitorial service. They were already planning an extension to the lodge, namely, building a separate dining and storage facility so that they could expand in the summer of the next year to accommodate an additional ten patients, making a total of thirty patients who would reside in the lodge.

The research consultant followed up the spontaneous call from the hospital contact by writing a letter to him on May 13 attempting to give him the needed and necessary support in his endeavors:

Dear _____:

Well, it looks like they had gotten over the last major hurdle prior to moving out into the community—it will be a major accomplishment in and of itself and one not to be underestimated. Let me say that the experience you have recently had was very reminiscent of my experience with the prototype lodge. I received a great deal of vicarious gratification from what you reported on the telephone yesterday.

The major purpose for my writing at this time is to confirm our visit to the psychiatric institute for the move to the community during the week of July 6. As the time approaches, if you find this date to be inappropriate, please let me know. Please continue to keep me informed of the project as we are very, very excited about the impending move.

Sincerely,

A reply received from the hospital contact in early June read:

Dear _____:

This is to confirm our move into the lodge. We are definitely moving on July 6 and will look forward to seeing you then.

I may be in Chicago for the weekend of July 4 and 5 and, if so, would like to ride back on the plane with you. If you could, I would appreciate it if you could let me know what flight you are taking. If I am down there, I'll meet you at the airport.

Sincerely,

The third consultation visit to the psychiatric institute took place between July 6 and 10. A day-by-day report of that action consultant visit as reported in the research journal follows:

Monday, July 6:　The lodge is a gray five-plex in three stories. It is shingle, well constructed and not more than fifteen to twenty years old. The lodge is located in a largely commercial business area with some small apartments nearby. The building was not cleaned up as promised by the landlord nor were the excessive furniture and appliances removed as requested. The lodge members are moving out the unwanted stuff into the driveway before moving in their things. A wall in the front apartment was removed to make a large living room and the same thing was done in the basement apartment in order to make a dining room. Two of the landlord's refrigerators were kept to store food, a new stand-up freezer was bought by the lodge and a large refrigerator came from state surplus. A new dishwasher was purchased from Sears and Roebuck. Most all of the beds, dressers, linens, dishes and kitchen equipment came from state surplus or stores.

The move went well with the research consultants adding a little backwork themselves. The Serto Mechanics truck brought the lodge members' clothing over along with the business equipment. Several trips between the lodge and the hospital were required to accomplish this. No food was cooked during the first day. For lunch the truck driver brought back hamburgers and at night everyone was given $2 to purchase his own dinner. The excess furniture was piled in the driveway. The lodge members unloaded the state surplus truck and brought all the gear in two loads. There was some 'nervousness' when the pins did not come in the first truckload with the bunkbeds, but they arrived in the afternoon. With all the junk piled in the driveway and all the activity around here several people stopped and came in to look figuring that there was a garage sale on. One of Serto Mechanics' competitors stopped by and asked if the lodge wanted its windows washed. He was politely turned away. The women ex-patients did not seem to be working as hard as the men ex-patients. No crews were organized for the move. At times, several people were walking around not contributing to the move. There was so much to do, however, that even the 'nebishes' (poor workers) were pretty busy. It is really neat to see a deserted ward on the hospital grounds.

All in all the moving went well. The beds, bureaus, and chairs were moved upstairs; linens were distributed; the kitchen floors were stripped and waxed. The stove that state surplus sent over had an oven that did not work so two of the old gas ranges were put side by side and hooked up. Some cleanup of the rooms was undertaken but the main part of this effort was scheduled for tomorrow along with the cleanup of the old ward. The patients at the lodge were eighteen strong with ten men and eight women. They ranged from two to twenty years of previous hospitalization with an average of about seven years. The big social thing was sharing, bumming, and smoking cigarettes together. All the people at the lodge smoked—the surgeon general would have a fit.

The business is functioning smoothly. Bud Fisher, the local Serto Mechanics wholesaler, figures they can gross $5000 per month on this lead alone if they can handle the business. They have three crews with about five people on each. Apparently if one or two people are not functioning too well, then two of the others seem to have a good day. They had a job on the second day which I will report on tomorrow.

The office of vocational rehabilitation gave the lodge $27,000 out of case service funds to start and plans to give them about $30,000 next year out of case service funds to continue the lodge. This comes to the lodge in the form of monthly payments of $4400. They bought the truck for cash and paid off the franchise $5000 in two or three payments. The hospital contributed about $15,000 worth of goods out of state surplus. Eight of the lodge members are on social security. This money ($600) goes into the lodge account except for $16 per month to the recipient. They agreed to do this or to leave the lodge. The psychiatric institute costs per patient day are about $37. The lodge without adding in the money made for working, costs about $5 or $6 per day. The lodge business manager called about insurance and said, 'Now this is our setup. We have ten men and eight women moving into the lodge.' The insurance man after a slight pause asked if that might not constitute a moral risk.' The business manager got laughing so hard that he had to hang up and call back later. In the six weeks of May and June, the lodge grossed $1800 and in July alone it grossed $1100. The patients had been in training about six months as of July 1.

Medication was being kept in the cook's room until they could obtain a medicine cabinet. They planned to distribute them in cups like in the hospital and the public health nurse planned to come out about every two weeks to give prolixin to six patients, but the hospital contact suggested that they go off liquid medication and on pills as soon as possible.

Tuesday, July 7:   The research consultants drove to the lodge this morning and all the furniture and debris were cleared from the driveway. Two or three people were cleaning up the lodge; one crew was out on the job, and the rest were on the ward to clean it up at the hospital. Everything was going well and there were no problems at this point. The kitchen was set up and functioning today.

Some of the members got their social security pay and went shopping—purchasing lots of new records, shoes, and one a bright green shirt.

The director of the regional office of vocational rehabilitation came by to take a picture of the lodge. He develops them himself and planned to send us copies since both lodge consultants forgot their cameras. Actually visiting the lodge does the trick in convincing people of its utility. The regional director was never a big advocate of the lodge, but now was consulting in a county in California with the welfare department that is interested in building a lodge.

Wednesday, July 8:   The lodge was operating nicely by this third day. The carpenter had finished with the remodeling and painting. The lodge contracted with the carpenter to pay for materials and his time spent in painting. Some of the labor was donated to the lodge. The place is pretty well cleaned up now except for some of the bedrooms.

Thursday, July 9:   The lodge continued to do well and is more and more autonomous. There was a big drinking party the night before among five of the lodge members. Apparently they had made a lot of ruckus and kept people awake so that the executive committee met and decided that there would be no drinking in the rooms and that one fellow who got in particularly bad shape would not be able to drink at the lodge at all for a period of time. They called this their restricted list.

Some people at this point were talking about wanting to leave the lodge and look for work. The lodge members supported this and offered to let the persons stay and look for work and housing from the lodge. I clued them in: they should not be paid if they did not go to work, and that they ought to set up a sick leave and time off policy. The ideas stressed the fact that the lodge is a business and that members do not just get a work pass anytime they don't feel like going to work.

A testimonial dinner was held for all connected with the lodge tonight. Members of the lodge were not there since they were pushing the 'therapeutic community' concept, i.e., separate lives and autonomy for patients. It was lots of fun and a good experience for all.

Friday, July 10:   The lodge continued to be in good shape. Their training was excellent and the program is running smoothly. No incidents or evidence of extreme anxiety. The hospital contact told me that he was somewhat surprised since they had really gotten frightened as the date to move neared.

The processes involved in advocacy by written manual and action consultation have been reviewed through selected case studies presented in this chapter. Failures occurred and successes were achieved. Which method of advocacy produced the most successes and what the parameters are for success will be pursued in the next chapter from a quantitative perspective.

CHAPTER 6

The Essential Conditions for Activating Adoption

Activating the adoption of the lodge was attempted through randomly assigning *one* of each of twelve matched pairs of volunteer hospitals to either a written manual or face-to-face consultation condition.* The burden of this chapter is to present an evaluative comparison of the outcomes and processes that these two different techniques generated. Under both conditions of advocacy (manual and consultation), the comparative hospitals received follow-up telephone calls every ninety days. These calls served both a data-gathering and consultative function. From these calls, information was obtained on current progress toward lodge establishment, and information was given on how to solve current problems that the in-hospital advocacy group was experiencing. These calls were made by action consultants, who conferred with the hospital staff groups on any problems with which they could not deal. The data in this chapter are largely based on four of the follow-up telephone calls: the initial call, at which time the hospital groups were informed of what assistance (manual versus consulting) the research team would offer; three follow-up calls made at ninety-day intervals subsequent to the receipt of the manual or the initial action consultation visit. In addition to these calls, all hospitals had the option of calling the research team free at any time for more immediate information and counsel.

---

*There were twenty-five hospitals that volunteered to establish the lodge society. One could not be matched on background information and was therefore eliminated from the comparisons that follow.

THE EFFECTS OF ACTION CONSULTATION CONTRASTED WITH WRITTEN MANUALS

The data in this section are concerned with exploring whether the written manual or face-to-face consultation differentially effected task completion by the adopting hospitals. Since the establishment of the lodge was a highly complex series of tasks, the data on how the institutions progressed toward adoption will be presented on various tasks that were an integral part of the "total push." The tasks represent the various "steps" that a hospital had to complete as it moved toward adoption. The following seven tasks constitute the adoption process that had to be completed in order to establish a community lodge:

1. *Business.* The adopted lodge—to be a viable replicate of the model—should have some form of employment activity for the ex-patient members.
2. *Legal.* Each lodge would have to establish some form of legal identity such as incorporation or a clearly defined but separate extension of the hospital.
3. *Finances.* Some source of maintenance funding, either external or internal to the hospital, would be necessary for the basic economic support of the lodge.
4. *Patient Group Development.* The group, or groups, of patients who would be lodge members would have to be developed as a cohesive, task-oriented functioning group, with stable leadership and performance.
5. *Housing.* A community residential facility would have to be located and acquired.
6. *Coordinator and Staff Development.* In-patient staff would have to reallocate time priorities for the development of the patient groups. Some staff person or persons would have to be trained for and assume a coordinator's role.

Taken together, these tasks define virtually all the relevant actions necessary to activate and complete a lodge. An additional task was considered because it appeared to have considerable relevance to the adoption process and intra-institutional social change:

7. *Planning Group Development.* Past experience showed that the six tasks mentioned above would be of such magnitude and diversity that they would have to be completed by a group of in-hospital staff. The seventh task, therefore, was concerned with the parameters of

such a group: whether or not such a group developed and, if so, its viability as a cohesive problem-solving group.

The data for these seven tasks were contained in the information gathered during the initial and follow-up telephone calls to the hospitals. During each telephone call open-ended questions were asked regarding general progress toward lodge adoption and the completion of the specific tasks described above. These data were codified in the following manner: for each telephone call to each hospital a rating of *current task accomplishment* was made on all of the seven tasks. Thus, there were four ratings (including the initial call) made for each task—a total of twenty-eight ratings for an individual hospital. These ratings were in the form of a 1, 2, 3, rating scale with *1* indicating no accomplishment, *2* showing some, and *3* indicating task accomplishment or near-accomplishment. Two judges independently made the twenty-eight ratings for each of the hospitals. Their percentage of agreement ranged from 84 to 100 percent, with a mean agreement of 93.4 percent.

Comparisons between the manual and action conditions were completed on data that did not include information from the initial call. This call was made prior to the experimental intervention in the adoption process and was used to make a check on the matching procedure and the comparability of the two groups of hospitals prior to the treatments. Analysis of the initial call data showed no significant differences between the matched pairs on any of the seven task categories.

Since the progress toward adoption was not significantly different at the start of the adoption phase, analyses were performed on the ratings for each task. The score computed for each task for every hospital consisted of summing the scores for the concerned task for the last three ratings derived from the telephone calls. A sum score was then used to compare the two conditions. For each task the Wilcoxon (Wilcoxon and Wilcox, 1964) Matched Pairs Test was computed.

The results of these comparisons are presented in Table 6.1. It shows that the scores on the Business task yielded a difference favoring the action consultation condition over the manual condition ($p < 0.05$). Legal task accomplishment favored the action consultant condition ($p < 0.005$). Finances task accomplishment indicated a difference favoring the action consultant condition ($p < 0.025$). Comparisons in the Patient Development and Housing tasks yielded no significant differences between the two conditions. The Coordinator and Staff Development comparison was again in favor of the action consultant condition ($p < 0.05$). Finally, Planning Group Development was significantly more effective in the action consultant condition ($p < 0.025$).

The question now arose as to whether the seven separate task categories represented discrete events or were themselves part of a more global process. Intercorrelations among the seven categories were computed and a high degree of interrelatedness was found. Accordingly, the seven scores were summed to provide an omnibus social change index. Table 6.1 shows that the Wilcoxon Matched Pair Analysis comparing the action consultant and manual conditions on this global score yields a highly significant difference in favor of the action consultant intervention ($p < 0.005$).

Table 6.1   Comparison of Mean Task Accomplishment Scores for Action Consultation and Manual Conditions.

Task	Action Consultant	Manual	T
Business	4.58	3.08	0*
Legal	4.79	3.13	0†
Finances	5.17	4.00	1‡
Patient Group Development	4.67	4.17	3
Housing	4.21	3.83	4
Coordinator and Staff Development	4.33	3.58	0*
Planning Group Development	5.96	4.17	7.5†
Mean Omnibus Change Score	33.71	25.96	3‡

*Significant of 0.05 level.
†Significant of 0.025 level.
‡Significant of 0.005 level.

THE EFFECT OF CONSULTANT EXPERIENCE

Imbedded in the initial prediction regarding the effectiveness of the action consultation mode was an hypothesis—not yet reviewed—concerning the consultants themselves. It was believed that a significant positive benefit of face-to-face consultation lay in the consultant's ability to resolve uncertainties and anxieties about implementing the lodge. It was also assumed that the consultant's own experiences in community treatment would assist this effort. The three consultants who carried out the implementation process represented a continuum of experience in handling these interpersonal problems. One had extensive experience with the lodge consultation spanning the time since the establishment of the prototype lodge itself; a second had had community consultation experience with one of the first lodges modeled after the prototype program; a third had no experience whatever with lodge consultation. The central question that arose concerned the effectiveness that these three consultants would have in implementing the lodge. This section details that comparison.

Table 6.2 presents the mean global task scores for each consultant. A Kruskal–Wallis one-way analysis of variance (Siegel, 1956) was performed on these data, yielding no significant effect. These data would tend to disconfirm any simple "experience" differential as it relates to an action consultant's success in the activity leading to lodge adoption.

Table 6.2   Comparison of Consultant Experience in Adoption Activity as Shown on the Mean Omnibus Change Score.

Highly Experienced Consultant	Experienced Consultant	Inexperienced Consultant	H
35.30	36.75	33.25	0.7214

THE PROCESS OF ACTION CONSULTATION

While the comparisons mentioned show the effectiveness of action consultation in inducing lodge adoption, what happened during this process needs to be elaborated. From the exploration presented, the importance of the task expertise of the consultant and his role as an information-giver seems to be an ineffective factor. Perhaps the action consultant's effectiveness lies in building or aiding in the development of some other aspects of the planning groups' processes.

In order to get a better idea of the process involved, an intensive examination of data from the action consultation meetings was conducted. Tape-recordings were available from visits to eleven of the hospitals in the action consultation condition. This included data from fourteen visits, and forty-six planning sessions (i.e., a general discussion meeting, a meeting specifically about moving to the lodge, etc.). A content analysis of this data was performed. Two independent judges assigned content to sixteen selected categories. From each of the forty-six sessions, approximately fourteen two-minute segments ("bits") were selected randomly. Using Tryon's (Tryon, *et al.*, 1941) method of making behavioral ratings and establishing rater reliability, each rater assigned half of the bits to one of the sixteen nominal categories. Six reliability rating checks of twenty bits each were conducted during the process of content analysis with an average percentage of agreement between raters of 83 percent. Each of the hospitals was then assigned a score for each category that reflected the percentage of bits for all meetings that were devoted to each content category. Further inspection of the data indicated some clear redundancies in the original sixteen categories, and they were then redefined into the following nine categories:

Consultant, Planning Group, and Hospital

Refers to conversation concerning the working relationship between the consultant, planning group, and hospital. How the planning group would be organized, what committees it would have, what their leadership was like, what the other roles of the planning group members would be, and how the planning group would relate to the hospital and the consultant.

Finance

All issues which involve financing the lodge: getting funding proposals ready, planning strategies for getting other money, computation of budgets, etc.

Legal

Discussion concerning the legal status of the proposed lodge and the legal status of its members. All references to legislative statutes and/or relevant administrative rulings were included.

Personnel—Group Maintenance

Comments, often of an affective tone, concerning the adequacy, personality, and performance of the planning group and other staff members. Comments concerning intragroup harmony, adequacy of group functioning, etc.

Patient Issues

All comments about patients, treatment programs and patient roles, including a discussion of individual patients, individualistic treatment, peer groups of patients, and the roles of patients in a proposed lodge.

Staff Issues

Included a general discussion of staff roles, statuses, and tasks. Also involved a discussion of staff selection and reallocation, selection and role of the lodge coordinator, and other lodge personnel.

Business

General discussion of issues pertaining to a lodge business. Included selection of a business, possible clientele and equipment needed, lodge roles as they relate specifically to business, insurance, and other such issues.

Lodge Location

Choice of a lodge site and factors in selection. Housing availability, real estate values, rentals, and possible leasing arrangements.

General and Unrelated

Includes agenda setting and general lodge issues not related to any of the above categories, or issues not related to anything discernible.

For purposes of analysis, the eleven hospitals were divided into two groups on the basis of a median split on their omnibus implementation score. This yielded six hospitals which had made relatively little progress toward lodge implementation (low change), and five hospitals that either established lodges or had made significant progress in that direction (high change). Comparisons using the Wilcoxon Rank Sum Test were made between the high change and low change hospitals on the percentage of use of each of the nine context categories. Table 6.3 presents the results.

Inspection of the comparisons presented in Table 6.3 gives a relatively clear picture of the processes that occurred. There are no significant differences between high change and low change hospitals on the amount of time spent on task-oriented items (patients, staffing, finances, legal issues, location, and general issues), but there are clear differences relating to organizational dynamics. Thus, the high change hospitals spent signifi-

Table 6.3 Comparison of Mean Time in Discussion Categories Used by High and Low Change Hospitals.

Category	High Change	Low Change
Consultant, Planning Group		
and Hospital	14.95	26.15*
Finance	7.95	4.14
Legal	2.67	2.78
Personnel-Group maintenance	6.60	1.39†
Patient Issues	38.27	35.51
Staff Issues	13.14	12.41
Business	6.15	7.75
Lodge Location	2.20	1.79
General and Unrelated	8.08	8.09

*Significant at the 0.05 level.
†Significant at the 0.02 level.

cantly *less* time discussing their relationship with the consultant, the legitimacy of their planning group, the roles of planning group members, etc. These are questions in the nature of, "Who are we? What are we doing?" Clearly, the hospitals that change have either resolved these issues previously or do not consider them of importance. There is additional evidence that the high change hospitals have worked out their internal group dynamics. In short, they have a group that is sufficiently cohesive and viable that it exercises one of the major functions of a small group—it rewards and punishes its members. The data indicate that high change hospitals display significantly *more* group maintenance behavior during the action consultation meetings. In contrast, the low change hospitals exhibit little of this behavior which would indicate either that there is insufficient group cohesion to permit reward of task accomplishment or punishment of deviants, or that there is little agreement on task goals from which normative performance or deviance might be judged. From these data it seems clear that a viable functioning small group must exist to enable lodge adoption.

AN OVERVIEW OF THE DATA

So far the data demonstrate that action consultation is more effective in inducing adoption than a detailed do-it-yourself manual; that the previous experience of the action consultant is a negligible factor in adoption; and that high change hospitals rely upon cohesive task groups as their change vehicle. However, the way in which an external intervention interacts with intra-hospital processes needs a finer grain analysis. The experiences that the consultants had with all twenty-five "volunteer" hospitals illuminated the difficulty of obtaining change. While selected examples were presented in Chapter 5, this section presents a brief overview of generalized impressions gained from all the consultants' experiences.

One of the first impressions—obtained from both telephone and face-to-face consultation—was the range of receptiveness to change and enthusiasm for the lodge program. While all the hospitals were ostensibly committed to establishing a lodge, and all had verbally agreed to do so, the "yes" decisions in fact concealed a plethora of intraorganizational politics, public relations image-building, and institutional paranoia. The corollary of all this, of course, was varying *de facto* commitment to establish the program. By way of illustration, some of the correspondence from the hospitals regarding their decision is interesting. At the time of their decision to either adopt or not adopt the lodge, the hospital contacts were asked to reply to an open-ended question concerning why their hospital did or did not want the program. The following was received from an enthusiastic demonstration ward volunteer:

> We like what the program does to the ward... We can't seem to resist the approach—you offer bait which sounds valuable and interesting (has proved so with ward program) and let us hook ourselves...

In marked contrast, is the guarded approach of the following hospital:

> The superintendent will provide his support to the extent that he can. We may be able to get students as volunteer staff, and Dr. Johnson is willing to contribute time. No staff commitments can be made from existing staff. We must be able to 'back out' if not successful!

Aside from these differences in motivation and commitment, it rapidly became clear that hospitals often volunteered for the lodge for reasons divorced from the attractions of its principles, or its innovativeness. As one respondent succinctly put it:

> This is a state hospital with a very limited budget and an exceedingly small professional staff. This three thousand bed hospital has close to three thousand admissions a year. However, there are only three psychiatrists including the superintendent, assistant superintendent, and director of training... The decision to use programs such as this comes out of our basic survival instinct.

While clearly such crisis decision making might impel a hospital to search frantically for programs such as the lodge, the result might be an institution opting for something it knows little about.

Another process that became clear—and had subsequent ramifications for the adoption process—was the different decision-making patterns hospitals used to arrive at a positive decision. These different patterns had serious implications for the ultimate adoption of the lodge. Some decisions were made unilaterally by superintendents who·fancied themselves as "great innovators," but who never bothered to inform their staff about what they had been volunteered for. A quote from the notes of one of the first action consultant visits is illustrative:

> Paragon State Hospital was in the brochure persuasion condition. The consultant, upon arrival at the hospital, found that Dr. Lee, the superintendent, had not distributed the brochure to members of his staff. The staff was therefore both uninformed about the lodge itself, and about the hospital's decision to go ahead with lodge planning. To further complicate matters, Dr. Lee was unavailable throughout most of the meetings.

From another volunteer hospital, a similar picture emerges:

> ... Dr. Williston, our contact (superintendent), had us met by Harry Kline, a methods and procedures advisor from a local mental health clinic who was working in some ways with the hospital, but had little knowledge of the ward program. Mr. Kline was not exactly sure what was supposed to happen, and Dr. Williston was nowhere to be found ... It became clear very quickly that although Dr. Williston had approved the program and asked for the visit, he had not informed the rest of the staff of his approval of the lodge program ...

As a final example of the uncertainty of some hospitals' commitment, and the unpredictable behavior of some hospital superintendents, an additional tale is in order. The hospital in question was in the workshop condition, and the presentation had been well received by staff in attendance. Subsequently, the hospital was volunteered—by the superintendent—for the lodge program, although the accompanying letter was fairly negative and pessimistic. The hospital was eventually assigned to the action consultation condition, and attempts were made to contact the superintendent, with whom the researchers had been communicating, to arrange an initial consultation. Two reactions set in: the superintendent became unavailable; and when he was reached, he continued to put off into the indefinite future the date for the action consultant visit. This continued for a few months until the team was prepared to write off the hospital as a failure. The research team then received a mysterious call from a "community nonprofit corporation" ostensibly interested in working cooperatively with them and the hospital to establish a lodge. A consultant was asked to "come down." The consultant contacted the superintendent and inquired if, indeed, such a cooperative arrangement existed and if it was acceptable to the hospital. He affirmed this and it was suggested that a visit would be in order. The hospital agreed to involve its staff in a joint effort with the consultant and the mysterious nonprofit corporation. The consultants arrived and met informally with the "representatives" from the corporation. It turned out the nonprofit corporation was, in fact, the project of a group of ex-patients, one of whom seemed to be a friend of the hospital superintendent. During the visit the ex-patients-turned-treatment-entrepreneurs spent much of their time organizing wire service press releases and making long distance calls. The behavior of the hospital personnel who participated in the consultation was equally devious. The superintendent sent three "representatives" to the meetings. None of them knew about the lodge program; they had no authority to plan or make commitments, and their instructions were to "report back" to the superintendent. Needless to say, the action consultation visit was less than successful.

From these visits and others, and telephone calls, the qualities of a "good" hospital became readily apparent. It was clear that in those hospitals that moved toward adoption a group of staff existed which was reasonably cohesive, committed to the lodge, had some leadership, and had at least some authority to plan and work toward establishing the lodge. This was more likely to occur in a hospital in which the staff group had participated in the decision to accept the lodge, and had been involved in decision making throughout.

This descriptive overview derives mainly from the experiences and research journals of the research team. It now seems important to take a more quantitative overview of the adoption process to see if the generalizations emanating from these sources of information are confirmed. To accomplish this task, a key cluster analysis was performed on all data collected from all twenty-five hospitals that volunteered to establish the lodge program (Tryon and Bailey, 1970).

The cluster analysis was similar to that reported in Chapter 4 for the persuasion phase. The variables considered in the analysis included all the persuasion phase data plus the data gathered during the implementation phase of the study. In order to obtain all possible data on these twenty-five hospitals, all previous experimental conditions (brochure, workshop, demonstration; action consultation, manual; state, V.A.; urban, rural; initial contact status) were treated as variables in this analysis. A "change" cluster was obtained by use of the BC TRY preset analysis. Since the analysis only could be done with the twenty-five hospitals that volunteered to adopt the lodge, the cluster analysis should be interpreted with some caution. Because of the small sample size it was decided that no residual clusters would be computed as they were in the persuasion phase where each cluster analysis was completed on a sample of eighty-five hospitals.

The change cluster is presented in Table 6.4.

A glance at Table 6.4 shows that twenty-six items are associated with

Table 6.4   The Change Cluster.

Variable	Loading
A. Pre-Adoption Communication and Decision Making	
1. Greater number of professional staff involved in decision to implement the lodge.	0.55
2. Greater personal satisfaction among the hospital staff about the decision to implement.	0.45
3. Greater number of persons talked to, and talked to more often, at time of initial contact with the hospital.	0.44
B. Communication with the Consultant	
1. Greater number of calls and letters during implementation period.	0.88
2. Greater number of spontaneous calls to consultant during implementation period.	0.78
3. Greater number of letters to the consultant during implementation period.	0.56
4. Longer telephone conversations with consultant at time of second follow-up during adoption.	0.54
C. Reduced Status and Prestige Hierarchy	
1. Greater likelihood that hospital superintendent will be a non-specialist M.D. or public health person, than a psychiatrist.	0.55
2. State salaries for psychiatrists are relatively low.	0.49
3. Hospital perceives less difference in prestige between superintendent and other staff members.	0.43
D. Superintendent Characteristics	
1. Superintendent agrees that patients are in many ways like children.	0.51
2. Greater career geographic mobility for the hospital superintendent.	0.48
3. Greater number of career job moves for the hospital superintendent.	0.44
4. Superintendent feels that ex-patients are no more dangerous than the average citizen.	0.43
E. Hospital Effectiveness and Capability	
1. Quick turnover of patients in the hospital.	0.53
2. More favorable staff–patient ratio throughout the state.	0.52
3. More favorable staff–patient ratio in the hospital.	0.52
4. Decision to implement (as perceived by the contact) was not affected by availability of funds.	0.46

Table 6.4 *Continued.*

Variable	Loading
F. Delegation of Authority	
1. Greater number of people attending first action consultation meeting.	0.57
2. Lower status person is the contact at time of first follow-up during implementation.	0.46
3. Lower status person is the contact at time of third follow-up during implementation.	0.43
G. Demonstration Ward Development	
1. Starting the demonstration ward later than the second follow-up after the consultation.	0.74
2. Starting the demonstration ward later than the first follow-up after the consultation.	0.50
3. Starting the demonstration ward later than the third follow-up after the consultation.	0.49
4. Starting the demonstration ward later than the fourth follow-up after the consultation.	0.49
5. Having a demonstration ward.	0.43

institutional adoption. For purposes of clarity, the twenty-six items have been assigned to seven conceptual categories. They are: (a) pre-adoption communication and decision making, (b) communication with the consultant, (c) reduced status and prestige hierarchy, (d) superintendent characteristics, (e) general hospital effectiveness and capability, (f) delegation of authority, and (g) demonstration ward development. A discussion of each of these categories is presented below.

Pre-Adoption Communication and Decision Making

Once again a group of variables centering about discussion and participation enters into the social change process. In those hospitals that exhibited more actual change there is a greater degree of discussion among the staff, a sharing of interchange with the research team and hospital personnel, and a greater resultant satisfaction with the decision reached. It should be emphasized that the continuous importance of these variables through contact-persuasion-adoption is a strong indication of the importance of an "open" organization in effecting change. Some of the rationale for this was discussed in Chapter 2, but it might bear reemphasis. To make a decision for innovation, and to carry out that decision, involves a great deal of clarification, the resolving of personal and institutional uncertainties, the modifying of institutional roles and values, etc. It appears that this process does not occur without communication aimed specifically at resolving these problems.

Communication with the Consultant

This group of items is especially difficult to interpret in terms of cause-effect directionality. It is clear that those hospitals that change tend to communicate with the consultant more; it is not clear whether this means that they are "using" the expertise of the consultant about the task at hand; whether this communication is a symptom of high motivation and performance that are produced by other processes; or whether the communication with the consultant is part of the cohesion-building or uncertainty-resolving function served by intra-hospital communication. These explanations are not, of course, mutually exclusive.

Reduced Status and Prestige Hierarchy

This group of variables fits nicely with the group of items concerning organizational openness. Thus, it is reasonable to expect that a more "open" hospital would also be a less hierarchical one. This group of items appears to bear this out. It should also be pointed out that reduced hierarchy was actual and perceived. The staff in the high change hospitals tended to the superintendent as having less status, and, in fact, he was more likely to be less than a fully accredited psychiatrist. Similarly, the hospitals that changed were likely to be in states where psychiatrist salaries were low relative to national norms.

Superintendent Characteristics

This is a group of items that is interesting in two ways. For one, the items tend to reinforce the notions of Rogers and Shoemaker (1971) concerning cosmopoliteness and change, and concerning value congruity and change. Those hospitals that showed more complete adoption of the lodge were likely to have directors who were more geographically and occupationally mobile. In addition, their superintendents must apparently have a value system that is congruent with the lodge: they must be somewhat paternalistic and realistically skeptical about patients ("patients are in many ways like children"), and they must also be trusting of discharged patients ("ex-patients are no more dangerous than the average citizen"). These beliefs are consistent with the lodge innovation. The lodge idea does not assume that chronic patients will likely make a return to complete independence immediately upon discharge. But it does assume, and implement, the notion that self-determination, responsibility, and autonomy are feasible even at that time.

General Hospital Effectiveness and Capability

This might be called a group of "nuts and bolts" items. All of them pertain to hospital capability and performance (staff–patient ratio, a perceived funding cushion, demonstrated ability to turn over patients). It should be pointed out that these variables did not figure significantly in the persuasion phase of the experiment. Apparently in the persuasion phase, when decision making and discussion are paramount, these processes are essentially symbolic and verbal. However, during implementation, when actual behavioral change on an individual and organizational level is needed, such things as staff–patient ratio are important. This clearly reflects the difference between talking and doing.

Delegation of Authority

These items probably reflect action on the part of the hospital to invest responsibility for implementation to a group of line staff. Thus, changing hospitals were more likely to have a lower status person as the "contact." Since the contact's role was typically one of managing the adoption effort, the fact that a lower status person had assumed this role would indicate that project activity had moved from an administrative level to an operational one, often a ward team. Also related to change was the involvement of more people in the action consultation meeting. Once again, this probably reflects an assumption of responsibility by an operational staff group, probably on the ward level. This would also be congruent with the findings reported earlier concerning the action consultation meetings where group cohesiveness and viability were related to change.

Demonstration Ward Development

This group of items—with some qualification—is consistent with the findings of the persuasion phase. Not only does establishing a demonstration ward lead to a positive decision regarding lodge adoption, but apparently that decision will be more likely translated into *actual* adoption and change behavior if the hospital has its own demonstration ward. There is also an indication that how one sets up a demonstration ward has implications for ultimate lodge adoption. Not all hospitals that established demonstration wards set up lodges, regardless of their verbal commitment to do so. It was only those hospitals that took their time and set up a better—a more replicative—demonstration ward that went on to successful lodge adoption. This might be interpreted in terms of the initial rationale for the demonstration ward condition. The idea was that such a ward would demonstrate the principles of patient responsibility, peer group decision making, task-oriented groups, and other features of the lodge in a concrete observable way so that the personnel of these hospitals would be persuaded to take the step of establishing a lodge in which these principles were implemented in the community. The data indicate that this description of the process probably is accurate for those hospitals that replicated these processes exactly. However, those hospitals that hurriedly established a poor replica of the small group ward did not do well in lodge adoption, perhaps because the principles were never demonstrated in a clearly observable behavioral fashion.

Community Involvement

It is not surprising that greater movement toward development of a community program like the lodge would be associated with the hospitals that involved community persons, and sought advice from other community lodge programs. Nothing further need be said.

Family Stability

This group of items might also be labeled "mom and apple pie" and is one of the most unexpected findings in this study. It should be pointed out that there is a certain amount of consistency between the persuasion and implementation phases of the experiment in that these variables seem to be related to both the persuasion and adoption aspects of change. Change seems to be found in those states in which there is a greater percentage of large, intact family units and non-working wives. How such demographic data are related to change needs to be spelled out. It may, of course, be idiosyncratic to the lodge project, and may have nothing to do with other social innovations. For example, the traditional family structure described may suggest an underlying regional idealogy that is congruent with the lodge innovation. The relationship needs further elaboration and clarification.

THE EFFECTS OF ADOPTION

An often neglected question in diffusion-of-innovation work is how the adoption affects the adopters. Applied to the adoption of the lodge, this question becomes: how did the adoption of the lodge affect the patients, staffs, and the adopting institutions? Since the effects of lodge living on patients have been described in great detail elsewhere (Fairweather *et al.* 1969), this inquiry will concentrate on the latter two groups affected: the staff who developed the lodge, and the hospital itself.

Although we have no quantitative data on this matter, the observations of the consultants when dealing with the adopting hospitals have yielded a rich supply of anecdotal material. Consider first the staffs who were directly involved in lodge adoption in various hospitals. The most drastic alteration that occurred was a change in how these staffs perceived their roles as professionals. Before the lodge projects, most of the affected staff had a fair degree of personal investment in their professional role, as traditionally defined. Psychologists and psychiatrists considered themselves as dispensers or assessors of therapeutic expertise, whether it was in the area of drugs, diagnostic testing, psychotherapy, or whatever their traditional roles had been. Social workers did casework. Nurses, by and large, assumed the traditional role of their profession—dispensing TLC, drugs, etc. Performing as a traditional ward "team" often reinforced the rigidity of the role structure and its accompanying status differentials and led to the usual degree of professional rivalry and chauvinism.

What the lodge project often did was to disrupt radically these patterns of behavior. Behavior became oriented toward a new set of task demands, often at odds with anything the staff has previously done as mental health workers. This had two implications. One was that the former status hierarchy became at least partially disrupted, in that the implementing staff groups became more egalitarian and organized themselves in terms of lodge tasks rather than professional statuses. In other words, the staff persons who hustled money, found real estate, explored business opportunities, etc., became more valuable team members than the ones who kept the in-hospital operation in order. Staffs did organize along these dimensions: some concentrated on in-hospital tasks, such as developing the patient task groups; others became more involved in tasks whose locus was in the community itself. There was a clear difference in who successfully completed what the researchers had come to call the "truck test."*

*The "truck test" was a way the consultants used to assess the commitment of hospital staff. It was developed from previous experience with the prototype lodge and concentrated on the difference between verbal behavior and performance. For example, some staff talked freely of changing roles, etc., but when challenged to go in the community, look at real estate, learn to run a buffer, or in fact *drive a truck*, their enthusiasm would cool. They had failed the truck test!

Affecting all staff who participated in lodge planning and development was a certain amount of change in self-perception. Gradually, they began to perceive themselves as "innovators" and social "change agents" in their own right. The adopting staff groups came to think of themselves as the "stars" of their particular hospital. There was a great deal of in-group–out-group dyanmics going on, in that the lodge adopting group came to think of themselves as somewhat deviant from the rest of the "do-nothing" system.

Perhaps as a result—and certainly a corollary—there is little evidence that the rest of the hospital was affected by the adoption of a lodge by one unit within it. While there was often some awareness that something different was going on, or that a small group or lodge program was being implemented, there was little desire to learn more, or to change their own behavior. Although enthusiastic members of the lodge planning group would occasionally try to "sell" the program to other staff members, the response usually ranged from indifference to hostility.

The picture that emerges is of a somewhat lonely group of innovators, highly cohesive, often at odds with the rest of the hospital, but pushing ahead with the lodge because "in their hearts they knew it was right." To complete the picture and to give the reader a better "flavor" of the successful lodge adopters, a conference telephone call was arranged between the adopting groups in seven of the more successful hospitals. It was tape-recorded. That call in its entirety is presented below.

INTERVIEWER: What was the nature, size, and composition of the group that developed your community program in the hospital? Did it have formal legitimacy and status? Was it a spontaneously generated group or was it formally established. I am talking about your staff group there, the group that actually but the program together.

ALBON: The staff group was a group that was the planning group for the rehabilitation unit prior to our taking on a lodge program, so it had existed approximately two and one-half years with the result of a cooperative agreement between (hospital) and vocational rehabilitation and consisted of the traditional kind of thing; the social worker, the occupational therapist, the psychologist, etc.

INTERVIEWER: OK, how large was this group?

ALBON: A group of about, counting the nurses, it was about twelve.

INTERVIEWER: OK, somebody else want to pick up from there?

HARLINGTON: Ours was more spontaneous, a smaller staff group. The head of the unit and two other people, that's described as young Turks, picked up on the idea and avidly developed something in the community. On the second effort it was one caseworker sort of spear-heading and trying to get enthusiasm from anybody else who would pitch in, like some volunteer students who seemed to have a lot of resources and helpfulness.

INTERVIEWER: OK, does anyone else want to pick up from here?

HARMSVILLE: Our staff group is exactly the same staff group that we have on our regular rehabilitation unit. Our chronic group was housed in an adjacent building and was handled through different techniques than our regular rehabilitation and evaluation unit. The group was . . . the staff group was the same.

BIG JUNCTION: I did not hear the question but judging from the answers maybe I can get close to it. Our program was more or less imposed on an existing ward of long-time chronic patients. We started with the staff that was already in that building.

ALTON: We started with a staff of a standard ward but the program was optional; no one forced it upon us, it was voluntarily agreed upon by the group. Twelve of us I'd say.

LEWISVILLE: We went into the lodge program off the small group ward program that we had for approximately two years prior. It was a staff that had worked on that ward, which was a sixty-bed ward with a nurse, psychiatrist, social worker, and probably eight aides who were all involved in the planning. The patients did their own planning. There were four of them that were in one lodge.

INTERVIEWER: What we are really interested in is the staff group that put together the community program, that made that push. What was its composition, its history, its legitimacy, how was it established, that sort of thing. (*Telephone connection disrupted at this point.*)

INTERVIEWER: OK, let's try again gang. OK, let me throw in another question at this point. Does everybody hear me now? OK, once again focusing on the group that developed the community program. We talked somewhat about the size, and nature, and composition and so on. Now what I want to get at is to what extent authority was delegated to the group and important decisions were made by them regarding the development of a lodge or community program. In other words, what degree of power and authority did the group that developed your community program have?

ALTON: We were given permission because of a written memo which we sent to the administration. In it we outlined the program, what the lodge was. Given that information we were given permission to develop the lodge and thereafter no one paid a great deal of attention to what we were doing. We had a lot of communication back and forth with the administration. Nobody put any blocks in our way and we got quite a bit of cooperation from the hospital. I would say we were free to develop as we wanted to.

LEWISVILLE: We ran into a little bit of static. We had a change of hospital administrators in the midst of the planning who wrote us a memo saying that we should stop planning for the lodge pending an increase in staff throughout the hospital. We changed the name of the lodge into something else, I don't remember what we called it, and we planned and got the patients out. We had a little bit of difficulty because of this, but I think the administration now is for us. So in a sense, we were legitimate, turned illegitimate, back to legitimate.

ALBON: We had almost total freedom to do with the lodge program anything we wanted. The superintendent is a very open-minded guy that just let us do, even when things were really disastrous, just let us do whatever we wanted to do.

BIG JUNCTION: We had three changes in our chief of staff within two months. We lost the chief of staff we had when we started our ward program and we roughed along with the assistant or fill-in, you might say, for several months and then we got in another man. We had little static but we had difficulty in communicating. This has been our problem here all along. Our current chief of staff, who has been here about three months now, is giving us some support. Our big problem in the community has been finding employment. Our (ex-patient) group has a great deal of autonomy, as much as we could give them. We could not get it set up so that they could pay many of their bills; their utilities, rent, and so on. Beyond that the group has considerable autonomy. The staff also has considerable autonomy at this point. What static we have had seems to have pretty well died down right now. The treatment team which is composed of the psychologist, a nurse, a social worker... I would say we have pretty complete autonomy as to what we do in the community.

HARLINGTON: Fairly strong degree of autonomy is invested in each unit director. Since one of the directors himself led the program the only authority problem was a check back with the administration to make sure that the first trial was a success. The second try was completely autonomous. The administration knew about it afterwards.

OKKENER: When we went for our funding it was required of us as a nonprofit corporation to get a letter from our superintendent giving us complete autonomy. He wrote a letter saying that he agreed to pay the wages for our staff (the nonprofit corporation).

FARMSVILLE: Of course our program was altogether different. The lodge program was attempted, I attempted the lodge program, and it was carried along with other things. I had a vocational rehabilitation caseload of sixty plus psychiatric patients that I was working with on top of the lodge program. When I got ready to place people in the lodge I started with sixteen. Through a six-month period my group dwindled to twelve for various reasons. When I got ready to place them I ran into so many barriers regarding hospital policy, regarding vocational rehabilitation policy, that I split my group, made placement of three, placement of two, eventually made a placement of five in an apartment setting in a room-and-board rooming house. Individual rehabilitation plans were written for all. I think out of the group there has only been two that have been rehospitalized. But I found the attempt at lodge placement to be an excellent evaluative tool for placing small groups in the type of surroundings that are conducive for them to relate to each other and to get along in the environment. (It should be pointed out that this hospital established a marginal community program, with considerably less emphasis on autonomous group process and decision making.)

INTERVIEWER: OK, let me focus on something else. All of you did establish some form of community program whether it was a lodge, or something similar or something not so similar, and all of you did have some group that worked together, a staff group, that spent many months trying to do this. Now, if you could sort of reflect on what were the factors that enabled your planning group or staff group just to hang together and remain cohesive for all those months that it took. In other words, what kind of rewards did you and group get from developing community programs over this long haul? You may have to reflect on this one a little bit.

OKKENER: Our program, as it started did die as you said after one year, and all interest was lost in it and we hired—the hospital hired—two new persons with weird job descriptions to take over the program and at that point they were given total responsibility for the program. And there were only two persons involved in the actual planning and the implementation of the program aside from the staff of the ward itself, who were aides alone and only assisted in the small group program. Their only binding force was just guts, I guess.

BIG JUNCTION: We had a number of personnel who just could not fit into the concept and they asked to be removed, so we wound up with a very congenial group on the whole, and we stayed together for a year. That was the case until about two months ago. Our social worker resigned and went to a state agency. Our nurse reassigned. But one of the nurses who had been on the ward for the full length of our program took her place. We do have a new social worker and so far we have gotten along just fine. I think the enthusiasm generated on the ward program is what has held us together. The morale among the men and the morale in staff is the highest that I have ever seen at this hospital.

ALBON: Our group, as I said before, had been really together for about two and one-half years before we started the ward program and was a very close, cohesive group. We had a lot of communication groups or sensitivity groups that went on for at least a year prior to our starting the lodge thing. And then although it was a little difficult to change the total concept of our treatment, everybody cooperated. We lost one or two nurses but other than that the group just really stuck together and the transition was relatively easy.

ALTON: Our team had a nucleus of about four or five members who had been together for a year or more prior to our introduction to the ward program. In addition to that I would say that we were very determined to do it. Probably we got some pleasure from offending the system a little bit. We really want to change the system; we want to do it and I think that that is probably what it was.

FARMSVILLE: Our staff was exactly the same as the staff on our regular rehabilitation unit except that our chronic group was given an identity. A special program was worked out for the chronic group through our home economics department, through our social worker, through our industrial therapist. Our activity therapist organized special activities for the group; a special part of the dormitory was given for group living; our group ate at one table in the dining hall every night and the program went along synonomously with our regular rehabilitation program, within the same setting.

LEWISVILLE: We had, when the small group program got going on the ward, I'd say we had excellent feedback from top administration. They were concerned and they liked the idea, and I guess we were the only ward that had a program, to tell you the truth. So that made us somewhat special. Then probably at the end of the first year we noticed that we were having a great deal of trouble trying to get referrals, appropriate people from the other wards. Either they ran out of them, which I doubt . . . which I know not to be a fact, or they thought, well we don't want to give them the better patients; we could make our own placement plans for this fellow, you know. So we kind of fell into disuse; we did kind of. We got a lot of staff backing, or I should say administration backing at first. Then we had to undergo a change in the ward; we had a doctor switch. We lost a psychologist who was a very strong supporter and then they made us an admission ward in rehabilitation. This caused us some problems, particularly keeping the small group program alive. But I'd say, all in all, we have had some pretty good support. It's been hot and cold. The idea of people going out of the hospital and living independently in a community group home or a lodge has scared everybody but the staff team. We had a lot of fears to work through there and a lot of regulations in the hospital that said it couldn't be done. We had to kind of circumvent them. Now most of the top administration is for us. But we are having trouble keeping our staff on the ward in line with the small group program because of the new admissions.

BIG JUNCTION: I would like to say that in the beginning we had very little administrative support. I think our administrative support is stronger right now that it has ever been before. But we are having problems and have had all the time with getting the appropriate referrals. I would be interested in knowing if this is difficult in all of the programs.

OKKENER: We have. The only time that we ever got referrals was when we got the lodge open, and everybody thought it was a nice place.

FARMSVILLE: Referrals for the lodge program has not been a problem here. We've had an increase in admissions over the past two years and most of the psychistrists' loads are so heavy they look at it with the attitude of just go through my wards and take anyone you like.

ALBON: The referral for the lodge was never any problem. We had a lot of difficulty when we were running a kind of traditional rehabilitation program, a ward program, getting referrals. We were asking them really for people that, you know, were pretty well-knit together and could function at a pretty high level. For that reason we had difficulty getting referrals. But once we changed the program and started taking chronic patients they just gave, you know, gave us everybody, or all the chronics.

INTERVIEWER: Look, let me throw this one out here. All of you were involved in a consultative relationship with either myself, or Dr. Watson, or Dr. Smith. Some of you were visited and some of you we talked to on the phone over a period of months. Now what I would like to get is, how did you see the role that we played as consultants and how might this role have helped you more or have been different? This will give you your chance now.

ALTON: I think that without a site visit the enthusiasm that was generated by the two people who came would not have occurred, and that the personal visit was very important. The written material, the first book, was very impressive. Whether I would have pushed and gone after that book without a site visit, I'm not sure. I think that the personal visit was very important and I was very impressed with the two persons who came at different times.

INTERVIEWER: Well, thank you, Nancy.

ALTON: Right-o.

ALBON: I feel the same way. I doubt if we would have gotten anything going. Oh, that's not quite true. We were working on some kind of chronic program. We would not have gotten the staff enthusiasm that we did without Dr. Watson coming up here. But his visit really turned our staff on to getting with the lodge thing and I'm sure that without his coming we would not have gone anyplace.

BIG JUNCTION: I think that we would have gone ahead even without the visit from the consultant because we were geared that way. But I think the visit of Dr. Smith and his assistant was a great deal of help to us in giving us some suggestions, alerting us to some of the problems that we would run into in the community so it smoothed the way for us, but I think we would have gone ahead anyway.

OKKENER: Yeh, we found that the consultation was of immeasurable help in suggestions, although I'd like to feel that the consultations to our staff were more in the lines of an ace in the hole when we were in trouble. The several letters you wrote for us in support of our efforts or for additional information were invaluable and I think helped our funding process.

LEWISVILLE: I'll kind of combine the answers. First of all, as far as the consultation. The site consultant for us was Dr. Smith. I wasn't here at the time when he came, I think he was probably the only thing that got the program going because it gave it some outside status.

INTERVIEWER: Let me clarify that situation. After the hospitals agreed that they wanted to establish a lodge, they were put in either an active consultation condition or a manual.

LEWISVILLE: Oh, you mean after the lodge.

INTERVIEWER: After you decided to go ahead with the lodge.

LEWISVILLE: OK, yeh.

INTERVIEWER: So you received those manuals, remember?

LEWISVILLE: Manuals, yes.

INTERVIEWER: Right. And the other hospitals got visits.

LEWISVILLE: The manual we found to be somewhat a useful tool to start planning, you know, how do you attack the problem? It gave us some ideas. To tell you the truth, we had to throw the manual away. There seemed to be no outside funding at all. We were not able to get any money out of vocational rehabilitation; they were busted that time we approached them on it. No one else would take a gamble on it at all. So the veterans went out on their non-service connected pension. Basically they were able to get $110 a month and that's what they . . . that's what they did. They had to buy all of their own furniture and so forth and rent their house and furnish it on $110 a month. They have done it and done very well. So, I guess that's the only way I can answer that.

FARMSVILLE: Our group was funded entirely on an individual basis through (state) vocational rehabilitation. The group itself, it was not given any special grant or special funds. It had to be handled simply on a single case basis. But there was no problem of money other than it had to be a written, individual, organized, rehabilitation grant and then the funds were made available for each individual.

INTERVIEWER: Harlington?

HARLINGTON: Yeh, I was trying to think back.

INTERVIEWER: In terms of the consultation, now you were in the manual condition, so this is what you got.

HARLINGTON: I think the manuals have been seen by many units here. But, by and large, they sit on shelves and I think what's happening is the bootstrap effect. Going back to your first question, what are the goodies the staff gets out of a project like this. It seems to be the opportunity to demonstrate their own ideas. They are a fairly young, new staff involved. There is no funding other than what local volunteer groups can come up with in terms of furnishings, church groups or public welfare, cash grants for the individual. The employment opportunities are not reliable. They are not sufficiently reliable to carry any sizable portion of the program.

INTERVIEWER: Let me throw out one last question that you can hash over a bit more among yourselves and this is: knowing what you do now, what would you do if you wanted to establish a lodge in another hospital. In other words, if you had the role that we've tried to assume for the last couple of years of trying to help people set up programs, how would you go about it?

BIG JUNCTION: I think on the basis of my experience I'd bring in top administrative people to the very first meeting.

ALBON: I think, although you did to some degree the first time you visited our hospital, you brought some slides and things, but I would initially come in and present programs that have been successful either on a film or on videotape or even slides and try to capture the whole essence of the process. I think that once personnel and administrators get the idea that it's possible, you know, like it's such a drastic change in traditional concepts. Like I say, my stress would be on demonstrating or showing that programs have worked and worked well.

FARMSVILLE: From our experience here, I do not feel that an in-hospital program needs a tremendous amount of support and assistance. But, of course, the support and assistance, everything that can be mustered, is needed at move-out time. And if there were an experienced team available in our country to be utilized from one facility to another at move-out time, that this would be the greatest asset we would have. [*It should be noted that this hospital was in a manual condition, did not receive site visits during implementation.*]

HARLINGTON: Along those lines I would think that an area to start, we're experiencing some need to focus on, is the community groups. Some of the groups are chaffing at the bits and picking up projects, to get involved, to support community things. The hospital, however, is in the role of picking or choosing or guiding certain projects according to the in-house priorities. It seems to be working with community mental health centers as they look at their priorities for what goes on in the community, may be in the long-run a way to start. We are seeing now some evidence of community groups that want to be involved.

ALTON: I think it would have been helpful at the beginning to have some sessions on fund raising as it has been one of our problems. I didn't question the approach, it was a good approach, but videotape maybe would have helped, I don't know, but I think sparking the individuals on the team is the best and first step. And then beyond that I think some additional help with fund raising and maybe some more talk on how to get together with community agencies. We are doing this now, and I think it is going to be helpful.

OKKENER: I think Mr. Mayer's idea of the videotape would have been a more inspiring idea for say the gut level staff involved on the ward. To them this always seemed to be some kind of a fairytale, that something physical would come out of this hospital. This is, I'm sure, a new experience for many of our hospitals to actually build a halfway house or something physical that can be looked at and explained. I think physical takes away from the magic connotations that everybody seemed to think of as we went trudging through the program. People never thought that it would really happen. If people honestly saw that it could happen it would provide a great deal more spark to go on. On the other hand, I think the funding idea is good. I think the majority of our time was lost in preparing our funding. We spent nine months getting the funding for our program. Mostly because neither of the persons involved knew anything at all about how to get money from anybody. We did, you know, just feel around. We went to every agency in the city. At first, everybody said, well you know, it was a bad time of the year and things like that. If we had made our approach with the proper language we would have succeeded earlier. We found the secret to our funding was the language we used. If there was some kind of information bank of that sort I think it would make it far easier in many other states. I don't know about other states, but I suspect other states are like ours. In our state it would be easier to get funding because the money is there, and you just have to know how to get to it. Now I don't know if we would have got some money if we had done something like that, but I think that would be something I'd like to see tried.

LEWISVILLE: If I were going to enter a new hospital and try to start this idea I think I'd try, especially as a social worker, I would attempt to sell the team on it at the ward level. I think most of this could be done by pictures and the like. Basically, some kind of information that would say, "look, this is what's happening, you know, all throughout the country and these are working." And if it is a federal hospital the big hangup we ran into was—"how in the world are you going to supervise these patients? If something happens and they get in trouble the whole world is going to come down on our neck." And I think I would work a little heavier in getting at least one community type involved, if nothing more than a public health person, to stop in and see them, to diffuse this away from the top administration so they wouldn't feel that if something happened they could say, "well other people in the community were looking in on these fellows." We did have them about thirty miles away from the hospital. But funding, yeh, we could use all the help that way we could get. We don't have a great number of philanthropists out here in our state. So we didn't have much to go on except the veteran's pension which is a real good deal, so funding wasn't really our main problem. I think getting the community to share the responsibility for the patients is important also.

INTERVIEWER: OK, look, I am going to have to cut this off in about one minute since we're going broke. Has anybody got anything else to say real quick?

There was a miscellaneous exchange of addresses and telephone numbers before termination of the telephone conference.

CHAPTER 7

Follow-Up Diffusion of the Community Lodge

Reference to Fig. 2.2 shows that the diffusion of an innovation is the final step in the change process. Diffusion is the "process by which an innovation spreads among members of a social system" (Rogers and Shoemaker, 1971). The diffusion aspect of the experiment had two goals: to determine the degree of adoption of the lodge program that occurred after all attempts to create change by active intervention had ended, and to discover the factors that are involved in the diffusing process. The specific questions that the study sought to answer were: Is there an actual spread of lodge adoption after the active phase of the experiment is over? Is there any information spread? If so, how is it spread? Is the pattern of decision making in the hospital as important to diffusion as it is in persuading and activating? What happens when there is a crisis or change in leadership in the organization? Are there any attitude or goal orientations which affect diffusion? Is a "systemic" perspective as important as Katz and Kahn (1966) believe? Do "proud" organizations diffuse less? Or more? This follow-up study attempted to answer these specific and some additional questions about the diffusion process mentioned below.

DESIGN OF THE DIFFUSION PHASE STUDY

Of the 255 hospitals in the original sample, 244 were contacted for this phase of the research. These included 102 hospitals that did not permit a persuasion attempt (turned-down-cold), 117 of the hospitals that permitted the persuasion attempt but refused to adopt the lodge (foot-in-the-door), and all 25 of the volunteer hospitals (all-the-way).

Three sources of information were used to evaluate the diffusion process: a telephone questionnaire, hospital data from the previous implementation study presented in Chapters 4 and 6, and demographic information available from the *American Hospital Association Journal.* Ninety variables were investigated in this study.

Since all interviewing was completed by telephone, a hierarchy of possible respondents at each hospital was established so that some knowledgeable person there could be interviewed. It was decided that the first choice in each hospital would be the administrator who had made the implementation decision. If this person was not available, other administrative contacts or the present superintendent could be interviewed. In most cases, this procedure provided the necessary interview research information. Respondents were generally cooperative, if not friendly. Even though interviews averaged about forty minutes, there were few complaints or criticisms about the interview process from the interviewees. One interviewee actually requested the interviewer to apply for a job at the respondent hospital.

The basic outcome criterion (the diffusion score) was the degree to which each hospital had moved toward adopting the lodge since the implementation decision date of the persuasion phase. For those hospitals that had decided not to adopt the lodge (turned-down-cold and foot-in-the-door) this score concerned progress toward adoption that had been made as measured by the stages of the adoption process (knowledge, persuasion, decision, communication, and action confirmation) as defined by Rogers and Shoemaker (1971). However, a different diffusion score was necessary for the twenty-five all-the-way hospitals since several had already implemented one lodge. For this group of hospitals, the diffusion score measured the degree of movement toward adoption that had occurred after implementation attempts were ended. It therefore includes a measure of continued movement toward adoption by those hospitals that had already started this process, or movement toward the adoption of a second lodge by those hospitals that had already adopted one. In order to assess completely all aspects of diffusion and its processes, some concepts proposed by other researchers as important in this procedure were also measured. They are:

1. Type of subunit designed to search for new programs. (Havelock, 1969; Katz and Kahn, 1966)
2. Types of activities funded by the hospital. (Havelock, 1969; Katz and Kahn, 1966; Rogers and Shoemaker, 1971)

3. Goals expressed by the hospital. (Havelock, 1969)
4. Change of administration in the hospital. (Carlson, 1965; Griffiths, 1964; Marrow et al., 1967)
5. Crisis situations in the hospital. (Havelock, 1969; Schon, 1967; Watson, 1966)
6. Power and type of influence in developing new programs. (Griffiths, 1964)
7. Subjective assessment of the hospital's treatment facilities. (Havelock, 1969)
8. Systemic research approaches by the hospital staff. (Katz and Kahn, 1966)
9. Types of programs started at the hospital since the last experimental contact. This score includes the number of community programs, the degree of autonomy afforded patients, and the degree of community orientation given patients in the programs.

EVALUATION OF THE DIFFUSION PHASE

Two basic techniques were employed to evaluate the diffusion of the lodge. First, a comparison about the amount of diffusion in the three different types of adoption hospitals (turned-down-cold, foot-in-the-door, all-the-way) was made. Second, a correlative analysis revealed the associative data related to diffusion.

Table 7.1 presents the chi-square comparing the amount of diffusion that occurred in the three types of hospitals. The most striking result is the lack of diffusion. Only twenty-three hospitals of the 244 investigated actually proceeded beyond discussion of the lodge concept. Of these

Table 7.1   Amount of Diffusion by Hospitals Showing a Differential Responsiveness to Adoption During the Preceding Phases of the Experiment.

	Stage of Adoption Reached During Diffusion Phase Follow-up					
Willingness to Adopt Lodge in Original Experiment	Knowledge		Persuasion		Decision and/or Confirmation	
	(N)	(%)	(N)	(%)	(N)	(%)
1. Turned-Down-Cold	36	84	14	14	2	2
2. Foot-in-the-Door	79	68	32	27	6	5
3. All-the-Way	5	20	5	20	15	60
$\chi^2 = 115.70^*$ (4 df)						

*Significant at 0.001 level.

twenty-three, fifteen were volunteers (all-the-way hospitals) that had regularly received input from the research team in the activating phase of the experiment. For the turned-down-cold hospitals, little diffusion occurred; for the foot-in-the-door hospitals, diffusion is somewhat greater; and for the volunteer group, it is considerably greater than for both these groups. Table 7.1 shows that diffusion is directly related to the initial willingness of a hospital to become involved in the change process.

The diffusion score clearly shows that diffusion did go on during the follow-up period, particularly among the volunteer hospitals. Within that group of twenty-five hospitals, diffusion was the greatest among those hospitals that adopted the first lodge during the activating phase. Several of these hospitals continued this adoption activity into the follow-up diffusion period. This finding emphasizes the importance that initial adoption has upon later diffusion. An inspection of the diffusion data shows that only one hospital that had *not* previously adopted the lodge continued with action toward adoption after the last experimental contact. On the other hand, five of the eight adopters continued to develop new lodges and spread the innovation. Beyond this comparative information which shows again that a hospital in a state of change tends to remain in change, what was discovered about the diffusion process itself? Information about this process is presented in summary form through a cluster analyses of the data.

The correlative data that formed the basic associative information for the diffusion phase are presented in three separate cluster analyses. A separate cluster analysis was carried out for each of the three groups of hospitals since the comparative data presented in Table 7.1 showed significant differences among the three categories of hospitals on the amount of diffusion generated.

"Turned-Down-Cold" Hospitals

The ten clusters obtained from those hospitals that indicated *no willing-ness to adopt the lodge* are presented in Table 7.2.
Ten clusters were found when data from these hospitals were analyzed. They are described as follows:

1. *Diffusion*   This cluster is entitled "diffusion" because the diffusion score was preset to appear in it (Tyron and Bailey, 1970). Recalling the lack of diffusion reported in Table 7.1, it is not surprising that this cluster contains only four variables whose highest loading is 0.63.
There is a relationship between this cluster and other cluster domains,

Table 7.2   The Ten Clusters for the Turned-Down-Cold Hospitals.

Cluster	Loading
Cluster 1 *Diffusion*	
1. Low status head of group looking for new programs	0.63
2. More funds for workshops	0.50
3. More diffusion	0.46
4. Hospital has little concern for community needs	0.44
Cluster 2 *"Middle" discipline total influence on new programs*	
1. Social work	
(a) Greater total influence	0.88
(b) Greater breadth of influence	0.85
2. Psychology	
(a) Greater breadth of influence	0.88
(b) Greater total influence	0.86
(c) Greater amount of influence	0.60
3. Nursing	
(a) Greater breadth of influence	0.66
4. Vocational rehabilitation	
(a) Greater breadth of influence	0.68
(b) Greater total influence	0.66
5. Higher mean breadth of influence for hospital	0.86
Cluster 3 *Hospital census data*	
1. Greater increase in census (less decrease in census)	1.00
2. Less absolute difference in census, 1969–1970.	0.84
3. Less decrease in occupancy, 1969–1970	0.76
Cluster 4 *Superintendent influence on new programs*	
1. Superintendent	
(a) Greater total influence	1.00
(b) Greater breadth of influence	0.87
(c) Greater amount of influence	0.70
2. The most influential discipline is a high status position	0.54
Cluster 5 *Hospital expenses*	
1. Greater increase in expenses, 1969–1970	0.96
2. Greater absolute difference in expenses, 1969–1970	0.93
Cluster 6 *Adoptiveness*	
1. New Programs	
(a) Greater total number	1.00
(b) More in-hospital programs	0.81
(c) Higher community locus score	0.53
(d) More community programs	0.45

Table 7.2 *Continued.*

Cluster		Loading
Cluster 7	*Psychiatrist influence on new programs*	
	1. Psychiatrist	
	(a) Greater breadth of influence	0.95
	(b) Greater total influence	0.84
	2. Greater resistance in hospital	0.51
Cluster 8	*Crises*	
	1. A crisis has occured in the hospital since our last contact	0.93
	2. More crises have occurred since our last contact	0.92
Cluster 9	*Amount of influence on new programs*	
	1. Greater mean amount of influence across all disciplines	0.89
	2. Greater amount of influence	
	(a) Social work	0.79
	(b) Nursing	0.73
	(c) Vocational rehabilitation	0.61
	(d) Psychiatry	0.41
	3. Greater total influence:	
	(a) Nursing	0.65
	4. Lower variance of the amount of influence	0.53
Cluster 10	*Committee to find new programs*	
	1. More people on the committee	0.92
	2. More disciplines represented on committee	0.73
	3. Superintendent came to position from outside the hospital	0.57
	4. Superintendent is interested in public relations	0.48
	5. Less time spent in this function by head of the group	0.42

adoptiveness (0.42), hospital expenses (-0.41), and superintendent influence (-0.26) as shown in Table 7.3. It shows that the little diffusion that did occur was related to general hospital adoptiveness, poorer hospitals, and those with weaker superintendents.

2. *Middle Discipline Influence* This cluster is essentially a group of variables measuring the breadth and total influence of social work, psychology, nursing, and vocational rehabilitation in the hospital. The high relationship, as revealed in Table 7.3, between this cluster, psychiatric influence (0.53) and amount of influence (0.44) reveals several groups who have influence. Interestingly enough, they do not include the superintendent.

Table 7.3 Correlations Between Oblique Cluster Domains for the Turned-Down-Cold Hospitals.

Clusters	1	2	3	4	5	6	7	8	9	10
1. Diffusion	—	0.08	0.22	−0.26	−0.41	0.42	0.08	0.15	−0.02	−0.16
2. Middle discipline total influence	0.08	—	−0.07	0.23	0.04	0.00	0.53	−0.15	0.44	−0.20
3. Hospital census data	0.22	−0.07	—	0.29	−0.01	−0.22	−0.06	−0.13	0.10	−0.11
4. Superintendent influence	−0.26	0.23	0.29	—	0.11	−0.15	0.34	−0.16	0.19	−0.01
5. Hospital expenses	−0.41	0.04	−0.01	0.11	—	−0.05	0.02	−0.12	−0.11	−0.09
6. Adoptiveness	0.42	0.00	−0.22	−0.15	−0.05	—	−0.01	0.10	−0.13	0.14
7. Psychiatrist influence	0.08	0.53	−0.06	0.34	0.02	−0.01	—	0.00	0.23	−0.12
8. Crises	0.15	−0.15	−0.13	−0.16	−0.12	0.10	0.00	—	−0.19	0.03
9. Amount of influence	−0.02	0.44	0.10	0.19	−0.11	−0.13	0.23	−0.19	—	−0.17
10. New program committee	−0.16	−0.20	−0.11	−0.01	−0.09	0.14	−0.12	0.03	−0.17	—

3. *Hospital Census Data*   This cluster is a group of demographic variables descriptive of hospital census information. Mildly related to the census data are two staff variables. This cluster is only marginally related to two other clusters, superintendent influence (0.29) and adoptiveness (-0.22) (Table 7.3).

4. *Superintendent Influence*   This cluster includes the variables which measure the superintendent's breadth, amount of, and total influence in the hospital. It is interesting that this cluster is only mildly related to middle discipline influence (0.23) and moderately related to psychiatrist influence (0.34). There appear to be three levels of influence in the hospitals that would not permit any kind of entry: superintendent, psychiatry, and "others." This cluster is also mildly related to hospital census (0.29), as shown in Table 7.3.

5. *Hospital Expenses*   This cluster consists of two variables which indicate an increase in expenses from 1969 to 1970. Its relationship with other clusters is negligible (Table 7.3).

6. *Adoptiveness*   This cluster includes all variables looking at the programming which exists in the hospitals. It demonstrates that hospitals with more programs are likely to have both community and hospital programs. Unlike the cluster for all-the-way hospitals shown in Table 7.6, however, these hospitals do not show a high degree of patient autonomy in their programs—an essential "role change" element. This cluster is relatively independent of the other clusters, mildly negatively related to hospital census (-0.22), and strongly related to the diffusion cluster (0.42) (Table 7.3). This seems to indicate that for non-changing hospitals greater diffusers also create more programs.

7. *Psychiatrist Influence*   This cluster includes breadth and total influence of psychiatry in the hospital. It is interesting that it also includes the measure of greater resistance to new programs in the hospital. It would appear that greater influence of psychiatry is associated with greater resistance to change. The psychiatrist's influence appears to be related to being a good "status-quo" doctor. The high relationship between this cluster and middle discipline influence (0.53) has been mentioned above. In addition, this cluster shows a moderate relationship with the superintendent influence cluster (0.34) (Table 7.3).

8. *Crises*   This cluster of two variables indicates the occurrence of a crisis in the hospital as reported by the respondent. Table 7.3 shows that its relationships with other clusters are negligible.

9. Amount of Influence   This cluster contains information descriptive of the amount of influence accorded social work, nursing, vocational rehabilitation, and psychiatry which are all related to greater mean influence for new programs across all disciplines. In addition, it includes the variable indicating lower variance of influence scores—a flatness of the power structure. Table 7.3 shows this cluster is related to middle discipline influence (0.44) and psychiatrist influence (0.23) as discussed above.

10. *New Program Committee*   This cluster includes variables which describe the committee for new programs. It also contains two superintendent variables. The variables indicate a larger committee, a superintendent who is interested in public relations and who came from outside the hospital. This cluster is essentially unrelated to other clusters, as shown in Table 7.3.

"Foot-in-the-Door" Hospitals

This cluster analysis was obtained from the hospitals that indicated *a willingness to receive a brochure, attend a workshop, or develop a demonstration ward, but would not volunteer to implement the lodge.* Table 7.4 presents the nine clusters generated by this analysis.

Table 7.4   The Nine Clusters for the "Foot-in-the-Door" Hospitals.

Cluster	Loading
Cluster 1 *Diffusion*	
1. Diffusion score	0.52
2. Experimental conditions	
(a) More active persuasion condition	0.70
(b) Lower status respondent	0.41
3. Other	
(a) More money for rewards	0.83
(b) Higher status head of group looking for new programs	0.44
Cluster 2 *Total influence of all disciplines below superintendent*	
1. Social work	
(a) Greater breadth of influence	0.95
(b) Greater total influence	0.88
2. Psychology	
(a) Greater breadth of influence	0.80
(b) Greater total influence	0.73
3. Nursing	
(a) Greater breadth of influence	0.75
(b) Greater total influence	0.70

Table 7.4   *Continued.*

Cluster		Loading
	4. Vocational Rehabilitation	
	(a) Greater breadth of influence	0.69
	(b) Greater total influence	0.61
	5. Psychiatry	
	(a) Greater breadth of influence	0.68
	(b) Greater total influence	0.53
	6. Greater resistance to new programs	0.51
	7. Greater mean amount of influence	0.92
Cluster 3	*Hospital size*	
	1. Larger staff	0.96
	2. Larger budget	0.96
	3. Greater difference in census, 1969–1970	0.66
	4. Greater difference in staff, 1969–1970	0.42
Cluster 4	*Adoptiveness*	
	1. New Programs	
	(a) Greater total number	1.00
	(b) More in-hospital programs	0.81
	(c) High community locus score	0.44
	2. Committee to find new programs	
	(a) Meets rarely	0.52
	(b) Greater diffusion of its information	0.40
Cluster 5	*Hospital expenses*	
	1. Greater increase in expenses	1.00
	2. Greater absolute difference in expenses	0.91
Cluster 6	*Superintendent influence on new programs*	
	1. Superintendent	
	(a) Greater amount of influence	0.88
	(b) Greater breadth of influence	0.66
	(c) Greater total influence	0.69
	2. The most influential discipline is a high status position	0.74
Cluster 7	*Amount of influence on new programs*	
	1. Greater mean amount of influence across all disciplines	0.97
	2. Greater amount of influence	
	(a) Social work	0.79
	(b) Nursing	0.69
	(c) Psychology	0.61
	(d) Vocational rehabilitation	0.60
	(e) Psychiatry	0.35
	3. Low variance of the amount of influence	0.62

Table 7.4   *Continued.*

Cluster	Loading
Cluster 8 *Crises*	
1. A crisis has occurred in the hospital since our last contact	0.90
2. More crises have occurred since the last contact	0.92
Cluster 9 *Hospital census data*	
1. Greater increase in census (less decrease in census)	0.90
2. Less decrease in occupancy, 1969–1970	0.80
3. Superintendent is interested in community programs	0.86
4. Informal source of new programs has low status	0.42

1. *Diffusion*   The variable leading the diffusion score loadings is only 0.52. In this analysis the previous experimental conditions (Chapters 4 and 6) become variables in the cluster, including active to inactive persuasion conditions, interviewer and respondent variables. The cluster shows that the respondent in the greater diffusion hospitals was of lower status. The other experimental variables indicate that the more active the persuasion condition the more diffusion occurred. Apparently, the more active the process of involvement, the more intense will be future activity after the experiment is over (diffusion). It is also of interest that, unlike the turned-down-cold diffusion cluster, this cluster is virtually unrelated to other cluster domains (Table 7.5).

2. *Total influence*   This cluster is identical to the middle discipline influence cluster of the turned-down-cold hospitals with the addition of the psychiatrist influence cluster (Table 7.2). It includes the breadth and total influence of all disciplines below superintendent as well as their related measure—the resistance measure. It is moderately related to both amount of influence (0.47) and hospital census (0.32). This cluster shows a clear distinction between the superintendent and other disciplines since the correlation between this cluster and the superintendent influence cluster is only 0.11 (Table 7.5).

3. *Hospital Size*   This cluster did not appear in the turned-down-cold hospital clusters, though it is moderately related to the hospital census cluster (0.46) and somewhat related to influence of disciplines below the level of the superintendent. The cluster is described by variables indicating a large hospital in terms of staff, budget, and differences in census and staff. It is interesting to note that hospital size is virtually unrelated to measures other than the two just mentioned (Table 7.5)

4. *Adoptiveness*   This cluster is similar to the adoptiveness cluster presented previously (Table 7.2). It includes new programs, more in-hospital programs, and the community locus score. It does not include more community programs or the autonomy of patient score. The addition of two variables concerned with the new program committee is interesting. Table 7.5 shows that this cluster's correlations with all other clusters are negligible, thus for these hospitals adopting programs does not mean adopting "innovative" programs.

5. *Hospital Expenses*   This cluster is identical to the hospital expenses cluster reported earlier. Its relationship with other clusters is negligible (Table 7.5).

6. *Superintendent Influence*   This cluster, once again, is identical to the superintendent influence cluster generated by the turned-down-cold hospitals; however, the moderate relationship between this cluster and the psychiatrist influence cluster and middle discipline influence cluster found in Table 7.3 does not appear for these hospitals. Apparently the superintendent is seen as less a part of the other disciplines than in the turned-down-cold hospitals. Only with hospital census (0.27) does the correlation with another cluster show even a mild relationship (Table 7.5).

Table 7.5   Correlations Between Oblique Cluster Domains for the "Foot-in-the-Door" Hospitals.

Clusters	1	2	3	4	5	6	7	8	9
1. Diffusion	—	0.17	0.08	0.12	−0.01	0.01	0.22	0.16	0.04
2. Total influence	0.17	—	0.21	0.03	0.19	0.11	0.47	−0.07	0.32
3. Hospital size	0.08	0.21	—	0.14	−0.03	0.03	0.11	0.02	0.46
4. Adoptiveness	0.12	0.03	0.14	—	−0.08	0.04	−0.15	0.04	−0.04
5. Hospital expenses	−0.01	0.19	−0.03	−0.08	—	0.05	0.13	−0.19	0.07
6. Superintendent influence	0.01	0.11	0.03	0.04	0.05	—	−0.10	−0.03	0.27
7. Amount of influence	0.22	0.47	0.11	−0.15	0.13	−0.10	—	−0.06	0.13
8. Crises	0.16	−0.07	0.02	0.04	−0.19	−0.03	−0.06	—	0.01
9. Hospital census data	0.04	0.32	0.46	−0.04	0.07	0.27	0.13	0.01	—

7. *Amount of Influence*   This cluster is another which is virtually identical to a cluster presented in Table 7.2. It includes the amount of influence variables of all disciplines except superintendent. As shown in Table 7.5 it is moderately related (0.47) to the total influence cluster.

8. *Crises*   This cluster is identical to the crises cluster in Table 7.2. It is, once again, virtually unrelated to all other clusters (Table 7.5).

9. *Hospital Census Data*   This cluster is similar to the hospital census cluster in Table 7.2 though it is not as consistent. It includes only two census variables, and adds one superintendent and one new program source variable. Its relationship to the total influence (0.32), hospital size (0.46), and superintendent influence (0.27) clusters have been mentioned previously (Table 7.5).

"All-the-Way" Hospitals (Volunteers)

The clusters obtained from the twenty-five *hospitals that indicated a willingness to implement the lodge* are presented in Table 7.6.

Table 7.6   The Three Clusters for the Implementation Volunteer Hospitals.

Cluster	Loading
Cluster 1 *Diffusion*	
1. Diffusion-adoption	
(a) More diffusion since last implementation attempt	0.88
(b) Greater degree of adoption	0.80
2. Hospital power structure	
(a) Less amount of influence by the superintendent	0.65
(b) Less amount of influence by psychiatry	0.61
(c) Lower mean amount of influence	0.54
3. Hospital is not generally for new programs	0.45
Cluster 2 *Information gathering—Stability*	
1. Positive information gathering	
(a) More funds for workshops	0.98
(b) More funds for travel	0.92
(c) Hospital actively looks for new programs	0.75
(d) More disciplines on the new program committee	0.51
(e) Funds exist to reward staff for new ideas	0.49
(f) There is a committee to look for new programs	0.45
(g) More people on the new program committee	0.48
2. Crisis	
(a) Few crises occurred	0.69

Table 7.6 *Continued.*

Cluster	Loading
(b) Little change due to crisis	0.56
(c) A crisis did occur	0.43
3. Present programming	
(a) All programs approved were implemented	0.65
(b) Programs are seen as fine the way they are	0.49
4. Staff, expenses	
(a) Small change in staff, 1969–1970	0.71
(b) More staff, 1969–1970	0.67
(c) Small numbers of total staff	0.54
(d) Small budget	0.45
(e) Low staff–patient ratio	0.41
5. "Middle" discipline influence	
(a) Greater amount of influence—psychology	0.61
(b) Greater breadth of influence—social work	0.61
(c) Greater amount of influence—nursing	0.50
(d) Greater breadth of influence—psychology	0.49
(e) Greater breadth of influence—vocational rehabilitation	0.48
(f) Greater total influence—social work	0.58
(g) Greater total influence—psychology	0.52
(h) Higher mean breadth of influence	0.56
6. Experimental conditions	
(a) Interviewer was B.P.	0.52
(b) More active persuasion condition	0.49
Cluster 3 *Adoptiveness*	
1. Innovative programming	
(a) Greater total number of new programs	1.00
(b) Greater number of in-hospital programs	0.85
(c) Greater number of community programs	0.55
(d) Higher autonomy score	0.53
(e) Higher community-locus score	0.52
(f) Less resistance to new programs	0.43
2. Superintendent role	
(a) Superintendent seen as innovative	0.55
(b) Superintendent came to hospital from inside the hospital	0.48
3. Search for new programming	
(a) New program committee does little with their information	0.82
(b) New program committee meets rarely	0.71
(c) Informal source for new programs is a low status person	0.71
(d) Less money for the library	0.42

1. *Diffusion*   The diffusion variable in this cluster has a loading of 0.88. There was some diffusion beyond mere discussion in contrast to our finding in the turned-down-cold and foot-in-the-door hospitals. While only four percent (six of the 219 hospitals) of the hospitals in those two conditions did anything but discuss the lodge, twenty percent (five of twenty-five) of the implementation volunteer hospitals made actual new movement toward adoption.

The power structure variables included in this cluster are interesting—less amount of influence for both superintendent and psychiatry and a lower mean amount of influence for the hospital. It appears that lessened traditional hierarchical power is related to diffusion and adoption. Yet the final variable included indicates that *verbally* the hospital does *not* encourage new programs. This cluster is virtually unrelated to either of the other two clusters as shown in Table 7.7.

Table 7.7   Correlations Between Oblique Cluster Domains for the Implementation Volunteer Hospitals.

Clusters	1	2	3
1. Diffusion	—	0.04	− 0.11
2. Information gathering— Stability	0.04	—	0.11
3. Adoptiveness	− 0.11	0.11	—

2. *Information Gathering—Stability*   This cluster includes several variables which seem to express a feeling of stability in the hospital. These include variables descriptive of few crises, satisfaction with present programming, small changes in staff numbers, and generally equal influence across psychology, nursing, social work, and vocational rehabilitation.

A second aspect of this cluster is the variables that demonstrate a positive approach to information gathering. These include more funds for workshops, travel, and rewards for innovative ideas as well as variables indicating a large committee to look for new programs. Finally, experimental condition variables are also included. Table 7.7 shows that this cluster is unrelated to the other two clusters.

3. *Adoptiveness*   This cluster differs from the adoptiveness clusters in the two previous analyses in that it includes programming variables and

autonomy variables as well as variables describing the superintendent's role and general information-seeking. In addition to these innovative programming variables, we find information describing the superintendent as innovative and as coming from within the hospital structure. It is interesting that the information-gathering variables are negative ones; the new program committee meets rarely and does little with their information. The positive variables of information gathering are found in Cluster 2, and appear to be a part of a stable, not an innovative system. As indicated previously, this cluster is unrelated to the other two clusters.

The major question asked in this follow-up period was how much diffusion actually occurred in our sample after active experimental intervention had ended. This afforded the researchers a unique opportunity to look at unplanned diffusion (turned-down-cold hospitals), partially planned diffusion (foot-in-the-door hospitals), and planned diffusion (all-the-way hospitals) in the same study. Other writers have warned that innovations do not spread in an unplanned way (Glaser, et al., 1967). Our data would indicate a confirmation of such warnings. It appears that anything less than full-scale implementation attempts (as with the all-the-way hospitals) results in little or no significant diffusion, at least of a complex social innovation. Over half of the respondents in the turned-down-cold and foot-in-the-door hospitals revealed little awareness of the lodge program. Of those aware, only eight indicated any movement beyond discussion. Little lodge diffusion occurred automatically; and it occured only rarely in those hospitals even when they had been exposed to persuasion attempts in the past (foot-in-the-door hospitals).

On the other hand, discernible diffusion did occur in the all-the-way hospitals. For the most part, the diffusion which occurred was among those hospitals that had already established one lodge and continued to develop new lodges without direct outside intervention. Those who stopped short of adopting the lodge during the active implementation effort, described in Chapters 4 and 6, did *not* complete adoption once those efforts were discontinued. *It is the hospitals that are actively involved in a program, and that have behaviorally committed themselves to it, that con-tinue to diffuse the innovation.* Even the more actively approached foot-in-the-door hospitals diffused more than those that permitted no entry even for discussion purposes.

Of equal interest is the relationship between the diffusion cluster and the other cluster domains shown in Tables 7.3, 7.5, and 7.7. Only in the turned-down-cold hospitals, which refused all attempts at intervention, is diffusion related to other clusters, and here only to hospital expenses, superintendent influence, and adoptiveness. Apparently, completely un-planned diffusion *is* related to more general hospital characteristics. But once intervention is introduced into the system, the intervention itself becomes the *most* important diffusion factor. Therefore, it appears that un-planned diffusion may be related to general hospital characteristics, but only before intervention activities begin. The intervention attempt seems to alter those relationships.

It is important to pursue for a moment a corollary of this finding in order to answer those theoreticians and researchers interested in the relationships between "innovativeness," "adoptiveness," and "diffusion." From the perspective of most hospital personnel, the adoption of *any* "new" program is defined as an innovative act. However, viewed from the perspective of change in social role and status this may not be the case. From this perspective it is not innovative to adopt a program which does not *change* the normal functioning of that institution—particularly social role and status changes or other actual organizational changes. In the present study, the derived cluster concept of adoptiveness is related to diffusion only in the turned-down-cold hospitals. it is unrelated to any other concepts in the foot-in-the-door and all-the-way hospitals. This finding suggests that once intervention begins in a hospital, actual diffusion of the lodge itself is unrelated to the adoption of any *other* new program. It would thus appear that diffusion of a complex social process like that of the lodge is only related (0.42—Table 7.3) to high adoption rates by a hospital when innovation is unplanned. The notion that innovative hospitals are those that adopt more new programs is *not* well supported by the evidence in this study. A glance at the adoptiveness cluster generated by the turned-down-cold hospitals (Table 7.2) shows that autonomy of patient functioning does not appear there. Since autonomy of patient functioning is the central issue in role change in the lodge society, it appears obvious that when innovation is diffused through inaction, the adoption of new programs is more likely than not to include programs that do not feature role change which is often the *mark* of social innovativeness. On the other hand, a high loading for patient autonomy does occur in the adoptiveness cluster of the all-the-way hospitals (0.53—Table 7.7). This comparative finding suggests that patient autonomy, which was the central feature embodied in the lodge society, was diffused to new programs in the adopting hospitals as a spin-off from the activities involved in this process. It seems clear, therefore, that institutions that adopt innovations requiring role changes are *not* the same institutions that adopt many "new" traditional programs. Adopting hospitals tend to be innovative hospitals when active intervention is occurring in them. Without such active change efforts high adopters probably will adopt only traditional programs and under these conditions, they actually are status-quo hospitals.

The adoptiveness cluster shown for the all-the-way hospitals (Table 7.7) reveals another interesting organizational fact about those institutions that are actively involved in adopting a new social program. The variables involved in the search for other new programs that the hospital might adopt are related to innovativeness in a curious way. The adoptiveness cluster includes variables describing a committee which meets rarely, does little with the information gathered, and in which the source of information is seen as a fluid, less-structured new-program committee. Thus, most structured information-gathering variables which appear in Cluster 2 are not associated with diffusion (Cluster 1) or adoptiveness (Cluster 3), but with stability. More funds for workshops and travel and a large new-program committee are associated with variables which describe a stable, established hospital experiencing few crises, having satisfaction with its programs, and showing little turnover of staff, and with a great amount of influence among persons from the middle disciplines. It seems that once such a committee is formally established and becomes part of the hospital's organizational routine, it tends to reinforce the traditional norms of the hospital. Thus, programs are often discussed and reviewed by such well-structured committees, but innovating new programs is placed in much less well-established hands.

It is also important to note that in all three cluster analyses (Tables 7.3, 7.5, and 7.7), the same results obtain as in the activating adopting process described in Chapter 6: there is little relationship between hospital organization (committee for new program) and the diffusion of the lodge innovation. Thus, follow-up diffusion such as the processes of approaching, persuading, and adopting are empirically related to an active thrust toward adoption, not to the "often-cited" theoretically derived variables of political influence and abundant resources.

In terms of the questions asked at the outset of this chapter, what has this study revealed about the diffusion process? Generally, the results of both comparative and correlative analyses may be summarized as follows:

1. As with approaching, persuading, and activating adoption, more active implementation attempts led to greater diffusion of the lodge.
2. Diffusion of a complex social innovation is relatively unrelated to other organizational, attitudinal, and demographic variables.
3. There is little correlative evidence to indicate that the nine concepts

discussed at the beginning of the chapter—goals, issues, etc.—had any bearing upon diffusion of the lodge.

4. Little diffusion actually occurred except in those hospitals which adopted the lodge during previous implementation attempts.

The fact that diffusion did occur in those hospitals where active implementation attempts *were* made is further evidence that active intervention has a long-term pay-off. One additional piece of empirical evidence shows this quite clearly. As a direct consequence of implementing the lodge, several members of one hospital's planning group continued to spread the lodge concept throughout their home state. Specifically, they presented information about it to state psychological, social work and vocational rehabilitation meetings. The psychologist member of the team visited other state hospitals and even brought staff members from these hospitals to view the lodge. Thus, active intervention in the approach, persuasion and activation phases helped create a "diffusion center," located within an adopting institution. The experiences of the planning group in this adopting hospital highlight the importance of an active change agent. This information indicates that a linkage should exist among all the processes involved in the adoption of an innovation from approaching to diffusing. What these relationships might be is explored in the next chapter.

CHAPTER 8

Principles for Creating Change in Mental Health Organizations

It seems obvious that a mechanism for creating continuous change in mental health organizations is necessary if new programs are to be incorporated into existing health practices. This study has shown that organizational change does not occur unless a specific set of techniques is established to create that change. Historically, much of the effort in the mental health area has been devoted to creating new treatment programs, yet little attention has been paid to the adoption of beneficial programs by mental health organizations. This study has disclosed a number of findings that provide some guidelines to help mental hospitals change when new, beneficial treatments are found. These principles may be applicable to other institutions as well, but the degree to which they are generalizable must itself be established·by additional researches with these selected institutions.

This study was designed to seek answers to a number of specific questions about the social change process in mental institutions. The series of questions asked in Chapter 2 were oriented around some key notions about organizational change that currently are central issues in the developing field of social change. They included concerns about the effectiveness in creating change of several crucial variables: of the written or spoken word when contrasted with action; of the geographic location of the hospital; of the use of administrative power; of the effects of task orientation; of the urbaneness and cosmopoliteness of the leaders; of the resources available to the organization; of the bureaucratic nature of the organization; of the need for outside change agents; of the communication processes within the organization; and other similar variables.

Answers to these questions emanating from this study incorporate information from statistical analyses (both comparative and associative), personal experiences, and observations. They can probably be most clearly presented as a set of summarizing principles about the social change process itself that has emerged from the experimental results presented in the preceding chapters.

A final note is in order before we proceed. We have labeled the subsequent suggestions as principles. All have varying degrees of empirical support from the study, either experimental-comparative or correlative. In a strict scientific sense some might better be considered as working hypotheses or empirically based hunches, but we have chosen not to make these distinctions. We trust the reader will digest these principles in the spirit of cautious optimism with which they are given.

THE PRINCIPLE OF PERSEVERANCE

The first principle of social change that seems of major importance is the principle of hard work and tolerance for confusion. If there is a single general notion from our data and experiences that we would like to impart to the reader it is that effecting institutional innovation is a highly complex multivariate phenomenon; that it takes a long time to achieve; and that the payoff is often minimal when weighed against the effort expended. Looking back over the five years of effort that this action research program has involved we are left with perceptions of both positive and negative accomplishments. On the plus side, it was possible to establish the lodge in other locales, and in this sense the program was successful both in effecting change, and in demonstrating that a social innovation developed through an action research program could be replicated. On a more negative note, those who were members of the research team will also remember meetings that came to naught, letters that stimulated nothing, telephone calls unreturned, and promises unkept. The intent here is not to sound the horn of alarm about institutional resistance to change, but to introduce reality to the prospective change experimentalists. While in this chapter we hope to impart some guidelines and principles that will assist in innovation implementation, the reader should be forewarned that the procedure is not easy nor is there any guarantee that the principles will work all the time, or even most of the time. We do feel that they might help others in avoiding many of our mistakes and wasted motion. At least, this is our hope.

THE PRINCIPLE OF DISCONTINUITY AND INDEPENDENCE

This principle might best be considered as a de-mythologizing one. It incorporates several sub-principles which deflate some of the contemporary folklore on social change. In the terms normally used to report research results, we are essentially talking about a group of negative findings. However, these negative findings are not uninformative when considered in light of the volumes that have been written or spoken about change. We are concerned with those variables we found *not* to be related to change, and that we—and others—had expected to be related to change.

Resources and Change

It will be recalled that one group of variables measured and included in the cluster analyses were indicators of financial and institutional input to the hospital. They included salaries, budgets, physical facilities, staff size, etc. These were the "raw material" from which these institutions were to render therapeutic services. We found little, if any, evidence that these resource variables were related to change in the persuasion and implementation phases of the experimental study, or to the degree of lodge-specific or general innovation adoption of hospitals studied in the diffusion follow-up. The two exceptions to this generalization were found in the implementation cluster in which a more favorable staff–patient ratio was found to be related to adoption and in a negative relationship between unplanned diffusion and hospital expenses.

The relative lack of relationship between these variables and change is of considerable importance. Since much current discussion about social problems tends to focus on the reallocation of resources (priorities, money, people, etc.), a cautioning note is in order. Most of these variables are traditionally in the province of legislative action. The upshot of our findings is that there probably is at best a questionable relationship between the allocation of more resources and the effecting of tangible institutional change. In short: you can pay for progress but you cannot buy it. The similarities between these findings and those of the Coleman Report on Education are obvious (Coleman *et al.* 1966).

Social Climate and Change

A number of variables also gathered were primarily demographic indicators of the social climate of the states, and locales, in which the hospitals were located. The variables consisted of a number of indicators of social, economic, and political development. In addition, it will be recalled that a specific urban–rural dimension was built into the experimental design as an experimental condition. The rationale for including these variables has been discussed elsewhere, and generally is related to concepts of cosmopoliteness, social and political conservatism, urbaneness, and the like, as they relate to change. The assumption, of course, is that highly developed, urbane, and "modern" social systems will be more conducive to change.

We found virtually no relationship between change and these indicators of the social climate in which the hospital was located. This was true with the experimental-comparative results, and the cluster analyses of the approach-persuasion phase, the activating-adoption phase, and the diffusion follow-up. The only exceptions were in the adoption clusters where there was an inexplicable relationship between lodge adoption and some aspects of family structure in the state. The overwhelming impression is one of independence between change in the hospital and the social, political, and economic climate of the surrounding community.

There might be two explanations for this. One is that the nature of a mental hospital as a "total institution" might make it relatively impervious to the input of the surrounding social climate. If this is true, then we might *not* find these low relationships if we examined the change process in other institutions, such as schools, industries, etc. This finding also suggests that subsequent experiments on social change in an institutional context should measure the degree of interchange with the surrounding locale that the target institutions have. The other explanation, of course, would be that there is, in fact, *no* relationship between the process of innovation in an institution and the social environment in which it resides. If this is true, it probably means that the social change process is considerably more fragmented and situation-specific than it has been considered to be heretofore.

Attitudes and Change/Continuity of Change

The usual description of the change process often conceptualizes it as involving several steps leading to ultimate adoption. Thus, Rogers and Shoemaker (1971) have described it as awareness leading to evaluation leading to a decision to adopt leading to adoption. This seems simple enough, but it is not what we found empirically. In general, we found a number of fairly independent steps that are necessary but not sufficient to create the actual adoption. For example, in the approach-persuasion phase we obtained clearly defined clusters of variables indicating attitudinal acceptance of the lodge innovation, which were *unrelated* to whether the institution verbally agreed to implement the lodge, and independent of its success in actually implementing. Clearly, although persuasion and awareness are necessary (or else how could an institution agree to do something it does not know about), they seem to be useful primarily as a way of stimulating other processes that are more directly related to change. In other words, all of the efforts prior to actual implementation might merely be developing "brand awareness."

In a similar vein, we found a high degree of dissimilarity between the variables that were related to change during persuasion, and those that were related during adoption. The social change clusters obtained in the persuasion phase tended to place a much greater emphasis on discussion and verbal activity than the change cluster obtained in actual adoption. Thus, the adoption cluster is more highly weighted with items that are behavioral, and indices of tangible action. Clearly, change is not as continuous as one would surmise and involves a number of overlapping but different processes. The diffusion study also suggests that there is a very deep chasm between awareness and actual action leading to adoption. This finding is shown again in the approaching-persuading phase of the study that reveals the relative ineffectiveness of verbal and written media in creating action leading to adoption.

Thus, there appear to be two relatively separate and unrelated stages that must be achieved prior to the adoption of an innovation. A cognitive stage which includes awareness, accumulation of knowledge, and the like, as mentioned by Rogers, and a series of specific behaviors that activate the adoption, such as the creation of a committee whose goal is to arrange for the adoption, the rental of a lodge property, the movement of patients from the hospital into the community, to name a few actions pertinent to activating the lodge. It is this gap between the cognitive and performance aspects of adoption that needs to be bridged by a concentrated effort to move from cognition to action.

THE PRINCIPLE OF OUTSIDE INTERVENTION

In many aspects, the data confirm the concept that outside intervention is essential for change to occur in the mental hospital. There is no evidence from the diffusion follow-up study that any appreciable degree of spontaneous adoption of innovation occurs in the absence of external stimulation somewhere in the process. The experimental data from the implementation phase also indicate that the outside intervention must be active, personal, and often. From other data it is also clear that outside intervention does not directly result in change, but rather activates a chain of processes which may result in change. In this sense, the outside change intervention serves as a catalyst for the subsequent change process. For example, the persuasion intervention resulted in some attitudinal acceptance which may or may not have stimulated discussion which may or may not have resulted in a decision to adopt. In turn, the action consultation visit contributed more directly to adoption by stimulating group cohesion and task orientation among the adopting staff.

By far the most important aspect of the outside change agent's role was the leadership he could give to the hospital change group, particularly his sensitivity to the interpersonal and organizational problems that the group faced. More often than not he found himself not only the giver of technical information, which was an important aspect of his role, but also helping to keep up the morale of the change groups in the face of organizational resistance to change, often manifested by a lack of concern for the group or refusal to give the group the resources they needed to develop a community lodge. And what do we know of the role itself?—an issue that was mentioned earlier. The different change agents represented a continuum of role styles that varied from the rather authoritarian to non-directive leadership and experience. Although past experience and different role styles led to clear differences in the group processes that developed, no differences in outcome occurred. None of the change agents was more or less effective than the others in inducing change. Thus, it appears that an individual change agent's style is far less important in aiding the change group's functioning than the perception of the group that he is a concerned leader who is willing to deal not only with the informational processes required but also with their personal and group needs.

Two aspects of the outside change agent role are difficult to achieve and sometimes seem incompatible with each other. *One* involves maximizing the apparent need for persons involved in the change to perceive the innovation as their own. This perception seems necessary in building the morale of the group so that continuous movement toward adoption occurs. To do this, the change agent was often requested by the planning group to change the innovation so it would "fit" better into the organization's practices. But permitting these changes in the innovation would affect its results. The *second* aspect of the change agent's role thus becomes keeping the innovation intact so its results will be the same as those found in the prototype model. An example of this incompatibility comes quickly to mind. One of the foremost difficulties in establishing the lodge was placing into action the principle of ex-patient autonomy. Staff members had been trained for so many years in a superordinate role in their relations with patients that it was almost an automatic response for them to "do things" for the patients. However, previous experimental work had shown that when this basic dimension of the lodge society was lost, the ex-patient group itself lost its decision-making powers and momentum (Fairweather, 1964). For this reason, the role of the change agent involves keeping a complex balance between serving as a "social therapist" for the innovative group and, simultaneously, preventing them from destroying the outcomes of the model by excessive modification.

THE PRINCIPLE OF ACTION-ORIENTED INTERVENTION

The results from the persuasion and implementation phases indicate that intervention strategies oriented primarily toward cognitive awareness and attitudinal acceptance will be less effective than those oriented toward behavioral compliance and task accomplishment. Thus, in the persuasion phase, the demonstration ward condition—which demanded a considerable behavioral commitment—was more effective than the workshop or the brochure conditions in producing change. Agreeing to adopt the lodge innovation was more often followed by actual adoption when the hospitals had first established a demonstration ward, as shown in the adoption chapter. And the action consultation condition was more effective than the relatively passive manual in producing change, especially when the hospitals had previously been subjected to the more active persuasion technique (demonstration project). In other words, the behavioral commitment demanded in establishing a demonstration program resulted in greater behavioral carry-through and action during implementation.

There is much evidence in the approach-persuasion clusters to indicate that the type of organizational intervention affects the type of institutional reaction that occurs as a response to the intervention. Thus, distributing brochures and holding workshops tend to induce verbal discussion, whereas demonstration programs tend to induce action. Simply stated: action begets action; inaction begets inaction. This is not meant to imply that attitudes did not change, or that cognitive understanding did not occur. It does point out that a change criterion that is performance based is likely to be related to other antecedent variables from a similar domain (i.e., action).

THE FOOT-IN-THE-DOOR PRINCIPLE

The above principle of action-oriented intervention also involves a reciprocal phenomenon: action produces resistance. This was most clearly demonstrated in the persuasion phase. The persuasion conditions which turned out to be the least effective in producing change (brochure and workshop) were the ones that were the easiest to "sell" to the organization in order to gain initial entrance into the hospital. In turn, a proposed demonstration program was turned down at the initial entry level a good portion of the time. It is possible that this early initial loss simply eliminates those organizations that wish to "talk" about innovation but that do not want to "do" anything about it. If such is the case, initial losses should be expected and even sanctioned because one simply eliminates from further advocating endeavors those hospitals that only want to "talk" about change. The organizations that remain interested—the residual organizations—are good risks for change. The change agent can thus focus his attention and energies on institutions that have a high probability of change.

On the other hand, it could be that the initial demand for a commitment of staff and space required for the demonstration program was asking more than the organization could give at the moment. Only further research can resolve this issue, but as an operating hypothesis it seems important to reduce the possible losses by entering the organization in a less demanding manner. What is needed, it appears, is a strategy of gradually moving from discussion to more active interventions directed at an institution. In other words, a relatively innocuous and ineffective intervention would be followed by a stronger and more effective one, etc. The analogy between the salesman's "foot-in-the-door" technique is obvious.

THE LIMITATIONS OF FORMAL POWER PRINCIPLE

It has been nearly axiomatic in the folklore of social change that the way to effect change is to control, convince, or coerce the formal power structure of the target social system. We found very little empirical support for that notion. Rather we found a much more complex and limited role of formal authority *vis-à-vis* change. It will be recalled that the comparative analysis of the persuasion phase data showed that entering the hospital organization at different levels in the status hierarchy yielded no significant differences in the number of hospitals that were persuaded to adopt the lodge. In turn, there is no evidence in any of the persuasion clusters that having an advocate of a high status in the hospital is of any advantage. We found some evidence in the implementation cluster to support the notion that having a lower status hospital director was related to greater implementation and that having a lower status contact during implementation was related to greater implementation.

Thus, the social status of the person who is contacted by the change agent appears to be relatively unrelated to whether or not actual change will occur. While there is no direct empirical evidence testing the notion that this result occurs because the successful contact finds the change notion compatible with his own and is thus motivated to change the organization, there was much observational feedback to this effect. If this is the case, it appears that change will not necessarily result because a person in top management is approached. Rather, it seems far more important that an individual be interested in changing the organization as a precondition to actively promoting change. Although it is undoubtedly true that the superintendent is eventually contacted by the individual or a group he has formed, it still remains an empirical fact that persons lower in the social status hierarchy are often just as adequate social change agents as are those higher in the hierarchy. Furthermore, this finding indicates that changes do not always start at the top, a significant conclusion itself in view of the bureaucratic nature of the mental hospital.

Therefore, it appears essential that persons within organizations who are motivated to change be approached because they can act as "internal change agents." Apparently, such persons are found as often in high and middle status positions as they are in low status positions; however, lower status persons tend to stick with the effort longer. Thus, the finding that although initial entry was promoted equally by persons in the different social statuses (superintendent, psychiatrist, psychologist, social worker, and nurse), the adoption of the lodge was more prevalent in hospitals where lower status directors and contacts were located.

Taken together, these findings shed considerable doubt on a simple conception relating power and status to change. This is not to deny that higher status positions and persons were important, but their importance was in the context of other variables which will be discussed below. Though it may be unsafe to generalize beyond these data, the implications for the larger society are important. A social change strategy aimed at gaining the levers of power and authority might fail to produce any actual tangible social change.

THE PRINCIPLE OF PARTICIPATION

The clearest and most consistent finding throughout the persuasion and, to a lesser but still important extent, implementation phases is the degree to which *involvement* across disciplines, across social status levels, and with more groups, produced greater change. In the persuasion phase, the degree and broadness varied as a function of the experimental condition, with participation much more apparent in the brochure and workshop conditions. In turn, in the demonstration program persuasion cluster few of the communication and participative variables were as important. Also of particular interest is the extent to which the role and perception of the superintendent is much more apparent and important when brochures and workshops were used than when one established a demonstration program. In contrast, the analyses of the persuasion aspect of the demonstration program seem to imply that when this type of intervention is used, discussion and decision making are focused on a group that usually does not include the superintendent.

While it is clear that the pattern of participation may change depending upon the intervention technique, the importance of some degree of broad participation cannot be stressed sufficiently. From our data, it is abundantly clear that change does *not* emanate from unilateral decisions—even though they might emanate from the top.

THE PRINCIPLE OF GROUP ACTION AND IMPLEMENTATION

The crucial importance of having a group within the hospital to spearhead the change effort is clearly related to the constrained participative decision making that occurred in the more active demonstration program condition. It is apparent more fully when we consider the results from the adoption phase. From the implementation cluster, it seems clear that a certain delegation of communication authority to lower status contacts is related to adoption. In the development of the adoption phase, we found that planning for group development was highly related to all other aspects of lodge adoption. Finally, in the content analysis of tapes from the action consultation visits we found effective and ineffective hospitals differed on the degree of "groupness" manifested in these meetings.

Thus, it appears that a small *social change group* within the organization that promotes the change effort is necessary to provide leadership in the change process. It further appears from our results that change is more often possible if the small group is established by the management of the organization. On the other hand, it is not entirely clear whether or not such change might occur even if it does not have the sanction of the organizational leaders. It further appears that this group needs a leader who continuously pushes for change and attempts to keep the group organized and its morale high. Such an individual can come from any disciplinary group, but it appears quite clear that most such individuals do not emerge from the physician group. The reason for this is unclear, but it probably stems from the training which may so inculcate them into an inactive role politically that they are not interested in leading reform movements.

This is another indication that the adoption of social innovation is much more complex than the analogous process related to hula hoops and hybrid corn. Since an innovation such as the lodge is so highly complex it takes a group of people continually working for adoption if adoption is to occur. The data also indicate that the group must be a group, and not merely a collection of people. In other words, the adopting unit must be a cohesive group of interacting and committed people.

THE PRINCIPLE THAT RESISTANCE TO CHANGE IS DIRECTLY PROPORTIONAL TO THE SOCIAL STATUS AND ROLE CHANGE REQUIRED BY INNOVATION

Rogers and Shoemaker (1971) have remarked about the difficulty in assimilating into the cultural practices a complex innovation when contrasted with a simple one. Thus, for example, the diffusion of a drug that fits neatly into existing medical practice diffuses much more quickly than a more complex medical innovation. And this investigation showed that the difficulty increases when social status and role changes are involved. For example, in the diffusion study, it was clearly evident that hospitals were able to move in a community direction with day hospitals, community mental health centers, etc., that were not as innovative as the lodge. These programs did not alter the superordinate social status of the professional mental health worker and the subordinate status of the patient. However, much more resistance was encountered with the lodge program since it required some basic role changes (from helper to consultant) on the part of the professional persons involved. It was also clear that such changes required retraining of the professional group. Thus, it is highly likely that when social change requires role changes resistance will occur. It can be partially ameliorated if such changes are accompanied with a retraining program for the involved professional personnel who are often frightened of role change both because of its economic implications (loss of job) and because of the occasional perceived loss in social status (who is the boss?). As the society moves toward more rapid social change, it seems imperative that training for the newly required roles will have to be a necessary accompaniment of such change in order to overcome the resistence that will inevitably occur.

THE PRINCIPLE OF CONTINUOUS EXPERIMENTAL INPUT

One of the most generic findings of this study was the relative situational specificity of social change and the need for information upon which to act. A review of the three cluster analyses in the persuasion-approach phase (brochure, workshop, demonstration program) shows that different variables entered into the change process in different combinations when the intervention varied with the particular organization involved. Thus, participation of the lower status people in the decision-making process appeared much more important in the written and verbal approaches than it did with the more active demonstration. It also seems highly probable from these results that innovations in different institutions, such as educational, political, etc., will have some variables in common with mental health organizations and some that are unique to the institution involved. It therefore seems essential that attempts to implement new programs be accompanied by a major research effort.

Unlike this research which was simply evaluative, however, it appears that future researches could productively use information from preliminary research phases to help them in movement toward activating the adoption. Thus, experimental techniques can be used to help determine the next step in activating adoption. In the current study, for example, after the initial approaches were tried and it was found that the demonstration program led to a reasonably high percentage of persuasion and that hospitals persuaded in this fashion were much more likely to adopt the innovation than those exposed to written and verbal approaches, it would have been possible to try to persuade the brochure and workshop hospitals' failures with a second attempt, a demonstration program. If several of the brochure and workshop hospitals accepted this second offer and were moved toward adoption, it would then be possible to take the residual pool of hospital failures and approach them with a different technique and with a new experiment aimed at persuading these remaining failures to adopt the lodge. Additional experiments could continue to be conducted with this dwindling group of failures until only the "hard core" were left. Even these might be persuaded to change as the original innovation became the "fad." Thus, experimentation can be used to create new information which can then be used to focus the attention of the change agents on those aspects of social change that seem to "work" for a specific innovation. This immediate type of information feedback that can be used to create change is especially important as time passes because techniques that were effective in the past will probably not be effective much longer. Only continuous experimentation in implementation can clearly show changes as they occur so that change agents will not pursue "blind alley" approaches.

Another aspect of an experimental approach should not be overlooked. This study clearly demonstrated that a few motivated researchers can attempt to implement a new social model through experimental means on a national scale. With jet aircraft and computer processing of data, it is obvious that even international implementation studies can be carried out. The researchers' experimental activity during the course of this five-year experiment shows behaviorally that persons who have created and carefully evaluated small scale models as a solution to a pressing human problem need not restrict their attempts at implementation simply to surrounding geographical areas. Thus, not only can experimentation be used to give information feedback that can determine what additional implementation activities might be productive, but it is also clear that such experiments are possible over extensive geographical areas with a limited number of personnel and amount of research funds.

THE PRINCIPLE OF ACTIVATING DIFFUSION CENTERS

A few hospitals in the study became so involved in the process of establishing their own lodge that they became centers for visiting persons to come to see the program. Involved personnel from these hospitals also began to distribute information about the program to other hospitals in their area and, in this way, the hospitals served as centers that, after they adopted the lodge, became advocates of the new program to others. It seems clear that full advantage should be taken of those institutions whose staff is interested in serving as unpaid "change agents." Thus, considerable time and effort should be spent in receiving follow-up information about the activities of the adopters so that such "diffusion units" can be located and their activities encouraged. With the spontaneously emerging diffusion centers in this study, the continuous interest and follow-through by the social action consultant seemed to have accomplished this result quite well.

THOUGHTS FOR THE CHANGE AGENT

We will now attempt to distill from the previous principles some more specific rules and guidelines for the change-agent-to-be. To effect the adoption of an innovation in an organization such as the mental hospital, you should consider the following:

1. Don't worry about where the organization is. Cleveland is likely as good as San Francisco to the limited extent that location effects internal change.
2. Don't worry about how much money the institution has. If change is possible, money will be found; if change isn't coming, then money is irrelevant.
3. Don't expect anything to be too systematic, predictable, or organized.
4. Be very skeptical of verbal promises. Verbal change is *not* the same as institutional social role and status change.
5. If you (or someone like you) don't change the organization, it likely won't change by itself.
6. Make your initial forays into the organization limited in intensity and scope, and then gradually increase the action and commitment required.
7. Don't worry excessively about seducing the powers-that-be in the organization. You may, or may not, need their support, but don't focus exclusively on them.
8. Try to get a number of people and power blocks involved in discussion and consideration of the innovation. Maximize participation and then gradually focus toward concrete action.
9. Work to develop an adopting group, or focus attention on a pre-existing group that could become the adopting group. Concentrate on their viability as a group.
10. Your change activities will probably arouse the anxieties of some persons within the organization. Try to alleviate this condition. Where their jobs might be affected, a retraining program is a must.
11. While trying to ameliorate undue anxieties, do *not* yield to pressure to modify the major dimensions of the innovation so that the end product will be so watered-down it will not work well.

12. Develop a technique to quickly and effortlessly "pick yourself up off the floor" when knocked down. Perseverance may not pay off but change cannot occur without it.
13. Learn to lose gracefully.
14. Hope.

THOUGHTS FOR GOVERNMENT PEOPLE WITH MONEY

If we assume that change agentry is not strictly an entrepreneurial venture, and that the government is really interested in improving society, we might take a brief critical look at current federal research policy in view of our principles of change. Clearly, federal research programs as they are currently structured are *not* likely to produce the development and diffusion of innovation. Consider the few glaring violations of our principles of social change.

For one, most federally funded program research *never* gets communicated to those who could put it into operation (the adopting units). More often than not, the research effort is only communicated to other researchers, those who funded the project, or high status people who can give prestige and rewards to the researchers.

Beyond the limited audience, the modes of communicating the output of the research results are typically those which are empirically ineffective in producing change in the recipients or the recipient organizations. Thus, it is easy to write books and scholarly articles which are ineffective in producing any change other than in the author's and publisher's bank balance.

The governmental research effort falls victim to the next malady, but is clearly not alone. What we speak of is a contemporary fixation on talking and posturing about change, and doing very little. This has been accompanied by a doublethink that equates verbal behavior with performance, and pronouncements about the need for change with actual change. We may seminar ourselves into oblivion before we realize this crucial distinction.

Another mistake that is correlated with the previous one is an assumption that more equals better. In crass words, a twofold increase in research spending will produce twice as much social innovation. Unfortunately, as we have discussed, social innovation is a much more complex process than the development and diffusion of hardware innovations.

The federal research effort is also essentially one oriented toward the formal power structure of involved institutions, with limited degrees of participation of lower status members of those institutions. In view of our data, both of these practices are likely to lessen the development and spread of social innovations.

Finally, because of historical precedents, political considerations, etc., there is limited commitment to intervention in the research effort as it is currently structured. Explicitly, there is no corps of change agents whose function would be to focus on institutional targets of opportunity.

Although the above picture may be moderately discouraging as a critique, it does not imply that an alternative could not be created. It could. We will attempt to sketch out some of the features of such a model. These would be:

1. A mixture of centralized and decentralized disbursing of research funds and establishment of research priorities. In other words, the federal research program should be a total program. Centralization will enhance degree and control of diffusion. Decentralization will enhance participation and lower level involvement. We should be clear about the degree of decentralization we are talking about. Using the mental health system as the prototype of the new system, we would envision regional federal research centers (perhaps turning the V.A. system into this), federal demonstration wards in each state hospital, and federal units in each community mental health center.

2. The diffusion of research information should not be haphazardly entrusted to the academic world, nor to conferences and high-level meetings of administrators. Using the previously described decentralized research apparatus as a vehicle, program information should become part of the continuous in-service training of staff. Specifically, this in-service training should be directed toward organizational units which are potentially adopting units of the programmatic innovation involved.

3. Participation in federal research programs for personnel in target institutions should be maximized. A number of vehicles could serve this purpose. Staff could rotate on and off the federal research unit; research policy advisory boards could be established in target institutions, etc.

4. Change agentry should be legitimized and built into the system. Even with the previously discussed organizational supports for research activities at the regional, state, and institutional level, there is a missing ingredient. Each level must work to influence innovations

at the other levels. Thus, the federal demonstration ward should have a change agent to influence other adopting units within the hospital. The regional research center would need one or more change agents to influence institution-based and/or state level research units, and so on. While this concept might seem excessively novel, there are many similarities between this and the agricultural extension agent model.

5. Finally, there needs to be developed a norm and enforceable policy that funds will be contingent upon empirically demonstrated results. Only if the research apparatus—and individual research projects—are rewarded on the basis of the change and innovation *produced* will the aforementioned organizational changes occur. This, of course, is a decision that cannot be reached on empirical grounds. A moral commitment is necessary.

CHAPTER 9

Social Policy Decisions Aimed at Solving Human Problems

Contemporary societies are faced with a number of survival problems that must be solved if the quality of man's life is to be improved or even maintained. Daily, we read of the catastrophic consequences that will accrue if excessive population growth is not stopped, if environmental degradation is not ended, and if unjust human relations continue. Problems like these require for their solution social policy decisions specifically aimed at alleviating the conditions causing them. Ameliorative action cannot be taken unless a solution to the particular problem is known and that solution is incorporated into social practice. Decisions about such serious survival issues clearly require basic social change in American society.

Some examples from current events clearly show this lack and suggest some of the barriers that prevent needed social reform. A recent newspaper article presented an excellent example of the contradictory values often called into play when a public official makes a decision. Officials in a small rural town were portrayed as being much interested in having an old mine on the edge of town filled with radioactive substance since the federal government was willing to pay the community to create the first radioactive waste dump in the nation (Howard, 1971). The proponents of this scheme argued that the radioactive dump would create new jobs for the local townspeople, and it was viewed positively by many of the city planners, the risk to life that such radioactive material might cause being minimized by both the government and interested local persons because of the anticipated employment gains. A second example is the recent SST controversy. The discussion in the United States Congress about developing the SST was based on the real problem of providing employment for workers as well as company profit as contrasted with the insults to the environment from the production of the aircraft (Shurcliff, 1970). Another example of the developing conflict between economic and ecological interests is the Alaskan oil pipeline. Ecologists testify that laying of the oil pipeline across the length of Alaska could result in an ecological disaster. People in the area reply that they are becoming increasingly poor and that the new pipeline would be an economic bonanza for them. These conflicts raise a more crucial general issue. It concerns whether a society whose social processes are organized around economic profit can also achieve long-term ecological survival. The difficulties inherent in making such decisions suggest in microcosm a major dilemma that American society will increasingly have to face when concerned with solving human and ecological issues. Making survival decisions in a democratic society demands farsighted concern about the future of society on the part of both the people and the politicians. It is very difficult to obtain such decisions from political processes not aimed at survival. This is particularly true when the power groups themselves usually represent various *economic interests* that have already chosen short-term profit rather than the quality of life as their primary value. Many of the long-range decisions that must be made today, however, concern preserving the physical environment and creating a livable social environment for present and future generations, despite the inconveniences and loss of immediate financial gain that will undoubtedly result from the necessary postponement of pleasure.

There are other difficulties with the decision-making processes in American society, not the least of which is that solutions to problems are often determined by pressure from special interest groups. An example of how such decisions are made is given in a recent publication from *Science Magazine* (Eipper, 1970). The article presented a discussion about how a decision to implant a new nuclear energy source for the manufacture of electricity in upper New York State was effected by *special interest groups.* The author drew the following conclusions from a study of the decision-making process:

> The special-interest groups promoting such developments may be industries that wish to use the water or other resources in a way that will yield them maximum profit, or they may be persons whose welfare or sympathies are more indirectly tied to an industry's success. The latter category includes groups of citizenry primarily concerned with immediate industrial benefits to the local economy, and persons in state or federal agencies who are much concerned with promoting the development of industrial technology. (Unfortunately, many of these agencies are assigned the dual role of promoting *and* regulating an industry.) Technological interest groups often make irrational assertions

(based on questionable assumptions) to support programs that will exploit public natural resources. These assertions—or implications—include the following:

The program—as proposed—*has* to be enacted *now*.

The program will be enacted in any event. You can't stop progress.

The program is needed to fill the demand that will be created by the program.

No one opposes the program. It will benefit the majority, and harm no one.

Data used to estimate effects of the program are the only valid, pertinent data available.

Since there is no proof that the development will damage the environment, we can safely assume it will not.

All effects of the program have been considered.

The program, as presented, represents the sum total of the development contemplated for this particular resource.

All applicable alternatives have been considered.

Not only should such assumptions be questioned when they appear in discussions of pollution issues, but other questions should be asked, such as the following:

Who participated in formulating the assumptions and conclusions about this program's desirability?

What lasting social benefits—and costs—will this program produce? Who will derive these benefits?

What environmental problems will, or may, be created?

What alternatives exist? Has the relative desirability of not enacting the program been evaluated?''

This is one example of the issues considered when decisions are based on political compromise among competing power groups.

Equally disastrous are the groups with *no* political and economic power to push their cause. These can be found among many minority groups in American society. One example is the manner in which decisions are made about the pressing human problems resulting from poverty as exemplified in the plight of the migrant farm workers. Hearings on the deplorable living conditions provided for migrant farm workers by growers have been held since the turn of the century. On each occasion living and working conditions of the migrant farmers have been described as grievous. Nonetheless, little has been done about the situation. When these deplorable conditions were recently described to a Senate committee, Senator Walter F. Mondale, its chairman, is reported to have said,

"If history is a guide, we won't do much about them."

And at another point in the hearings, he is quoted as saying,

"We have been through this before. The nation was outraged and then forgot it."

He specifically noted that migrant farm workers are helpless because they

"are without political and economic power and without enough friends to get the legislation needed for a decent life." (Associated Press, 1970)

The problem of lack of power is often confounded with *verbal* discussion that does not lead to corrective action. Endless congressional hearings illustrate this aspect of the decision-making processes of American society in the late 20th century, which makes it difficult to approach in a meaningful way those survival problems that demand an immediate reaction from the society. Verbal and written reports are thus often substituted for action, particularly when the offended parties have no political power. In American decision making, economic and political power, not humanism or survival, appears to be the name of the game.

Another aspect of the American decision-making process that promotes its ineffectiveness is the *lack of emphasis on scientific verification* of adopted policies. The obvious need for population regulation may serve as an example of this lack. A great deal of money is being invested in establishing family planning centers. The family planning unit has been *uncritically* accepted by governmental planners as a means through which population can be regulated. Unfortunately, family planning has not yet demonstrated by comparative experiments that its application will result in reducing birth rates. Nonetheless, if the created family planning centers follow the usual bureaucratic procedures for acceptance as a societal institution the following events are likely to occur. First, the units will be established as a national policy with a large investment of federal money. Second, there will eventually be some inquiry by the Congress about whether or not these units are, in fact, reducing the birth rates. At that point, research money will become available (notice, it will not be available until after the governmentally sponsored units are almost unchangeable institutions). Voluminous data will show interested members of Congress that, indeed, these units are being dramatically effective in reducing fertility rates. However, a close scientific scrutiny of that data would probably reveal that *no* definitive scientific information validating family planning in direct experimental contrast with other forms of population regulation will be presented. Since the researchers evaluating the family planning program will usually be hired by the agency itself, their continued employment may depend on a positive evaluation of it. It is highly unlikely under these circumstances that any negative information will get to the congressmen. Current research is often aimed at supporting existing governmental programs whatever they might be. Comparative experiments that question the program or the social policy from which it emanates are typically not funded.

Thus, a cycle of action is established that results in the creation of information which corroborates the initial social decision. The generic process goes something like this: An agency establishes a program designed to implement a particular social policy. Once having established the program there is some question by the Congress or the administration about whether or not it has accomplished the purpose for which it was established. The program is the *evaluated* by researchers who usually collect *selected* kinds of information. This information often supports the notion that the program is accomplishing its goal. Because of these reassurances, more money is appropriated to the program and more evaluations positive to the program are forthcoming. Thus, a vicious circle is created in which a particular governmental policy is supported by *"scientific"* evidence which results in the creation of a bigger and bigger bureaucratic organization with more and more funds at its disposal. *The basic question about whether the governmental program is better or worse than other programs the government might have adopted to solve the problem is never raised.* In the example just given, no one has raised the issue as to whether or not the family planning model itself is valid.

Thus, in America, decisions about solving survival problems are ineffective because policy decisions are influenced by special interest groups, social marginality, verbal solutions, and scientifically unsound evaluations. This often results in a flurry of activity that gives the appearance of solving a problem without actually solving it. Arms instead of food are sent to foreign countries; medical research money is more often than not channeled into politically "safe" laboratory research rather than survival-oriented research that has social, political, religious, and other complicating features, such as providing clean air and water and population regulation; industrial manufacture is sustained that does not consider the ecology of the environment, etc. Such actions yield short-term gains and long-term losses. The disaster of this type of decision making, particularly in contemporary societies, is that it is often not aimed at improving or maintaining the quality of life or the biosphere on which we live.

Thus, human problems, even the survival issues, receive very little problem-solving attention. America's institutions have developed an ineptness for creating the social changes required for living in our century. Industry with its profit motive, political parties with their constant search for power, governmental agencies with their unbridled bureaucracies, and educational institutions with their perpetuation of inaction and "ivory-tower" approaches to problems are veritable blockades to creating the beneficial type of change required for man's continued existence on this planet. And at this historical moment such resistance to change can have tragic consequences because *if society waits until population and ecological crises occur before change is instituted it may be too late, for the destructive processes may then be irreversible* (Borgstrom, 1969; National Academy of Sciences, 1969).

What can be done about it? Do the findings in this study give any hints about change processes that might be helpful in creating the needed change? The major implication from this study is that social change requires active and continuing effort to achieve the needed modifications. It appears obvious that to create the changes needed now and that will be increasingly necessary for man's survival in the future, an immediate change of the social policy practices of American society must be accomplished. The social change process *must* involve continuous feedback to decision makers based upon scientific inquiry. *Thus, the scientist himself must help society improve its decision-making processes so that needed problem-solving change can occur in an orderly and systematic manner as problems arise.* This means the creation of a new more socially responsible role for the scientist because he must become involved in societal activities that he has long avoided.

A SOCIAL POLICY ALTERNATIVE

New programs could, however, be established in a problem-solving manner. Accepting the governmental policy of population stabilization as desirable, the following sequence of events might occur. *First,* a set of model programs would be established on a small scale basis and compared for their effectiveness in reducing the fertility rate. Only *one* of such programs would be a family planning program. Others might be tax incentives for fewer births, change in sex roles (more high-salaried jobs for women), townhall discussion meetings, and even cash bonuses for vasectomies, or some combination of these five alternatives. Their effectiveness could be directly compared and determined prior to accepting one solution as governmental policy and *before* the government invests a great deal of money and thereby creates a new unchangeable tradition.

Such comparative information would be available to a society's decision makers who could then plan for society on a more rational basis. Furthermore, through continuous model building and *comparison* the techniques for population stabilization could be modified to meet new needs as they arose. Thus, it appears that carefully planned model building and evaluation is an essential *first* step in making realistic decisions upon which problem-solving social policy can legitimately be based.

But the models found to be successful need to be implemented on a national scale. So a necessary *second* step would involve researches similar to that presented in this book. Such implementation experiments would have to be used by social policy creators whenever a new problem-solving model was discovered. Whatever solution is found, whether it is a new educational program, a new health delivery system, a new method for purifying water, a further experiment attempting to discover the "handles to press" in order to facilitate its implementation would have to be carried out. The continuous experimental processes—model building evaluative research and implementation research—form the two basic processes for establishing a continuous problem-solving mechanism that contemporary societies need, for it is inherently a self-correcting mechanism. When old practices do not solve the selected problem, information from a continuous research effort shows this lack very clearly. At the same time it provides valid answers for new techniques that will show the social planners what "levers to press" to implement the new problem-solving practice.

The experimental social innovative (ESI) processes described (model building and implementation evaluative research) can sharpen the decision-making processes in a democratic society. The manner in which this could occur is described elsewhere in the following manner:

> The experimental problem-solving mechanism described here proposes a problem-solving approach to human survival issues. By using it, one can answer beforehand, in probabilistic terms, questions about what the outcomes will be when definite public policy steps are taken. It will give information to decision makers about the outcomes of new programs as an alternative procedure to verbal discussion and parliamentary debate. Decisions based upon extensive debate may make the parties feel better and may even create a high degree of group cohesion, but the innovations growing out of such debates are new and untried practices nonetheless and are, therefore, subjected to all the uncertainties of any outcome from an untried invention. The hoped-for outcomes growing out of debate are as unpredictable as the outcomes of any innovation developed by one person. Surely the failure of such legislation as the 18th Amendment should tell us this, and other examples are near at hand. The outcomes of bussing or not bussing children to schools, about whether or not an SST would cause climatic changes,

about what new educational programs would meet society's needs, about what the ecological effects of a new type of nuclear generator might be, could all be ascertained before changes in national policy that implement a particular course of action were adopted. It is these kinds of decisions, where the outcomes of alternative are known before policy is formed, that would create a segment of a problem-solving device. Under such conditions, the job of the legislators would be to decide among alternatives whose outcomes were already known, at least in probabilistic terms. For example, if an individual should argue that bussing has a deleterious effect upon black and white students, there could be outcome results from an evaluative experiment that would show directly what such social innovations would probably do. Or, if one wished to determine whether the SST should be built on a large scale or not, there could be direct evidence from a few prototypes which would have been flown as models so that the measurement of change in the upper stratosphere could be recorded. Or, as another example, if the members of Congress wished to underwrite a new medical program, such as Medicare, its outcomes could be known on the basis of trial models established specifically for their evaluation before expensive and often ineffective national legislation was passed.

Such a decision-making apparatus would have many advantages over those currently used in political processes. It could, in subtle but realistic ways, reduce bigotry and individual bias about particular programs because it would render arguments that a particular social or physical model would produce certain results ridiculous if actual experimental programs had already shown that different results would be produced. Furthermore, it would reduce political pressure for decision making advantageous to only one power group because the results of any trial model could easily be ascertained. Such a program would, thus, enhance the rational problem-solving decisions of governmental bodies. In this way science and humanitarian concerns could become an accepted part of the political process. (Fairweather, 1972)

Immediate steps could be taken to integrate this new problem-solving social change mechanism into the contemporary political scene. As a first step, it would be necessary to establish centers for experimental social innovation throughout the nation. This could be done in several ways. One way would be to establish nonprofit corporations that would contract with the federal, state, and local governments or agencies to establish models for comparative purposes and to aid in implementing their results. This approach to experimental social innovation would reduce excessive dependence upon the government and thus permit the experimenters to more readily question governmental policies and decisions.

The independence of the research organization from influence by any contracting agent, whether it was federal, state, or local government, or private party could be maintained. Furthermore, such private research centers would need to contract with many different organizations to prevent domination by a particular agency or branch of government. For example, it is well known in scientific circles that certain private research organizations have contracted mainly with the defense department or other agencies, and have become dependent upon them for their funds. It places these centers in an awkward position when trying to evaluate new social models objectively. It is for this reason that the contracts for social innovative research should be distributed among groups representing a diversity of interests. Such a distribution of financial support would help insure the freedom to raise serious questions about the implementation of particular policy decisions and, to some extent, the policies themselves.

Another course of action might involve the universities themselves. They could also become homes for such experimental centers. If this should be the case, a strong link could be formed by the legislators, colleges and universities, and the public. This course of action would have some advantages not readily available through cooperative work with other organizations. It would provide a means of bringing together interested scientists, students, legislators, and the public so that they could work together on human problems of mutual interest, particularly those of survival value. There are other advantages in this approach. One is that the universities historically have been as free from political influence as any organization in our society and they have jealously guarded their independence from governmental domination. This is an important aspect of experimental social innovation. Professors could choose to contract for such research and would thus not have to engage in any research that they did not wish to be involved in with the government or the public. On the other hand, it would permit such a relationship for those who wished to work actively on the solution of human problems. This is also an appealing situation because it would create a new mission for the contemporary university, particularly one that has always had a public service orientation. It is just such a role that is mandatory in attempting to solve the survival issues of our time. An additional advantage of centers being located in universities is the potential for training.

Thus, a center for experimental social innovation would be particularly valuable if located in an educational institution. In addition to promoting research on many other human problems, it could serve as the place for educational innovation. New academic programs could continuously be created and contrasted with existing educational practices. This is exceedingly important since the needs of the society are constantly changing and these changes should be reflected in educating persons for contemporary living in the society. Continuous experimentation with educational innovation and implementation could serve as a constant source of renewal for the schools.

Since a new generation of experimental social innovators needs to be educated, if the centers were located in universities it would be possible to train these individuals more easily. They could enroll in courses or internships in such centers. Because of the central role the university plays in higher education in America, the training of change agents and experimenters would be accomplished much more easily if such an education program were located there. It is, of course, highly doubtful that problem-solving centers *could actually* be established in the typical university setting. Most such institutions have not had a history of public service and historically they have been isolated from society.

However, social innovative centers could be established in other important organizations that might aid in creating a meaningful social change mechanism. Despite the fear of governmental domination, this problem-solving system could be integrated directly into the political process. Nationally, it would be most effective and helpful if it were established as an evaluative arm by the Congress itself. In such a case, the Senate and House members would need to have money to establish their own centers so that the results would come directly to them or their committees rather than to the administration. This is important because, in a democratic society with a legislative system such as ours, the House and Senate members need to have direct access to information about alternative outcomes so that, from such information they can resolve conflicts within their own organizations. Furthermore, the Congress needs access to its own experimental social innovative results because it may wish to try its own alternative solutions to problems that may be in opposition to administration policies. It is obvious that under conditions where the administration alone could contract for model establishment and evaluation it might not permit the testing of alternatives in opposition to its own policies, a possibility mentioned above. If the researchers could not contract with the Congress but only with the administration, they would probably eventually become agents of the administrative arm of the government because of this economic control. On the other hand, if Congress had its own budget to support such research centers, the diversity of opinion in Congress could provide an opportunity for the creation and evaluation of many new models spanning the political spectrum whose implementation could be essential for progress. Furthermore, the Congress could use such centers to bring about a resolution of the difficulties that periodically arise in the course of debate. Suppose that two alternative courses of action were possible with regard to racial policy. Take police relations as an example. One course of action might involve the creation of racially homogeneous police forces—a black police force in the black area and a white police force in the white area of the city. Each separate force would be controlled by the local people, a model proposed by many black persons. A second model might involve an integrated force of black and white policemen who would work closely with a grievance committee comprised of members from the local communities (black and white). These two programs could be established as models and their outcomes, upon evaluation, could be given to House and Senate members for their review. Such information could be crucial to the writing and funding of new problem-solving legislation. To provide adequate legislative direction in inquiry, budgets for such information centers would have to be given to the Senate and House members themselves so that the Congress could control the expenditure of the research funds on matters they thought pertinent. It would also restore to the Congress the mechanism to gain information upon which to base legislation, a course of action not available now with the administrative branch controlling almost all research expenditures through its departments and related agencies. This would not, of course, prevent the experimenters from attempting to persuade the congressmen of potential problems that might arise in order that attention could be focused on them as well as the contemporary problems with which the legislators would be properly preoccupied.

In addition, agencies could establish experimental centers within their own organizations. The Veterans Administration Hospital system is one example of such an agency. Here is a vast system of medical facilities, including hospitals, outpatient clinics, rehabilitative centers, domicilaries, etc. that have historically been used to provide complete medical service for veterans. One hospital in this system could be designated as a research hospital to create new programs of health delivery and to evaluate them so that treatment success could be determined. These beneficial treatment programs could then be adopted by all hospitals within the system. This would create a method of generating innovative programs which would continuously create new models, and evaluate and implement them as its *primary* concern. Such action would consistently place the federal hospitals at the forefront of medical knowledge since they would serve as generators of new health delivery systems that could benefit all the persons within our society. This same procedure could be followed by other agencies, such as the Department of Labor, the Department of Health, Education, and Welfare, the Department of Interior, etc. Each could have its own experimental center, either in conjunction with a major university, such as the colleges described, or within its own agency, with scientists from universities as consultants and researchers.

These would not be the only possible locations for experimental social innovation (ESI) centers. Aside from whether universities were involved in this problem-solving effort, it is possible that each city could establish an experimental center; so could governments for states and counties. It is especially important in this day of urban unrest, with deep-seated racial hatreds extant in society, that new and cooperative innovative programs be established to alleviate these crises. As with the federal government agencies mentioned, experimental social innovative centers for the cities could be used by the mayors, planning commissions, boards of education, and city councils, to create, evaluate, and implement new programs.

Beyond their national significance, however, centers for experimental social innovation could have international importance. The United Nations could establish its own human problem research center. Scientists from different countries could come together with politicians and other persons from the various cultures to create and evaluate social and physical models that would have problem-solving significance for several nations simultaneously. This cooperative approach to problem solution is essential to a resolution of such problems as air, and water pollution, racism, and war. Beyond the problem-solving contribution that such a research group could make, the understanding of other cultures and persons that should emanate might help ameliorate international conflict. The center could establish a practical working basis for the solution to international strife. One giant stride in this direction could come from improved communication resulting from the exchange of research information about problem solving. It could make further progress toward international cooperation by serving as a training center for young social innovators from around the world, and providing a new avenue for creating world peace—a necessary condition for any international research effort.

But such centers cannot be successful unless the need for reeducating the public and for providing information about human survival and humanitarian concerns to all persons is recognized. A new educational effort would certainly need to be aimed at preparing all of society, including future legislators, for a collaborative effort to improve the quality of life. Training in law, which is the basic background for many legislators, prepares an individual to discuss and find compromise solutions to complex issues. It does not prepare him to solve survival issues in any other way. Thus, the solution of contemporary social problems and the increasing need for such solutions in the future require a new orientation for contemporary legislators. It is for this reason that training in scientific methodology as a means of looking at the solutions to human problems needs to be incorporated into the educational program of future decision makers, although it must be done with a humanitarian emphasis. *It is therefore exceedingly important that decision makers understand the weakness of decisions arrived at through political compromise when the future of man is at stake.* An ecology for a society aimed at survival cannot be compromised away. There is no point in a legislator agreeing that an electrical generating system that dumps nuclear wastes into a particular river can be traded for an underground atomic explosion plant located in some unpopulated area of the United States. Both threaten man's survival. Such a trade is not permissible when one is concerned about future generations. And it is even more important that this new generation of legislators who will be educated for living in the latter part of the 20th century and in the 21st century be aware that the answer to complex problems can only be found through adequate research and evaluation. A scientist who is accredited by his society with expert knowledge in a particular field must most often answer serious questions about his field by saying, "I don't know." The legislator, without such training, surely must find himself in no better position. But what the scientist can do in cooperation with the public and the legislator is to find the answer through experimental means. Legislators, the public, and scientists must learn to collaborate in searching for such answers. It is this sort of collaborative effort that can serve as a background for resolving arguments about how to solve the survival issues of each generation.

One action that should occur immediately is that each research project funded by the federal government and private foundations should have in its budget the money to implement any new program that the research shows would be beneficial to man. Most research today is done in a vacuum. The research project is carried out and no provision is made by the researchers or the granting agencies to implement the results. The research itself has nothing to do with social change. Because of this practice, when a better school program is found, a more adequate health treatment system discovered, or a new smog device invented, there is no way that the researcher can see to it that these beneficial innovations are placed in action. To correct this inadequacy, governmental agencies and private foundations that finance such researches should appropriate with each innovative grant the money needed to implement the beneficial model, if one is found. Thus, there would be a "built-in" implementation for each social innovative study that was supported by federal or private funds. This would have additional value, too, because it would become the researcher's responsibility, as a condition for accepting the grant, to make plans for implementing his findings—at least to establish an experiment in its implementation. Such a change of policy in awarding research grants would prevent the inaction of the typical scientist from taking precedence over his need to act for humanitarian reasons.

In the future, man will probably continue to create crises before problem solutions are attempted. But unlike crises in the past, the new ecological crises may be irreversible. For example, if we wait until the SST fills the upper stratosphere with jet engine wastes there will be no way, now known, that man can prevent the dimming of the sun's rays and all the problems that would follow. The continuous fashioning of garbage disposals out of our rivers will eventually result in impure water and a decrease in oxygen that will inevitably bring about man's demise. Man can no longer afford the luxury of crises as an antecedent condition to problem solution. It is, however, probable that he will continue to have crises. Certainly the current increasing crises created by the internal combustion engine must serve as a classic example of man's unwillingness to change. For even though man is aware that smog will increase annually because of the increase in population and attendant car usage that inevitably occurs, he does not diminish his use of the car. Faced with the obvious adjustment that must be made—the elimination of the internal combustion engine—man has found himself totally helpless. It is just such crises that make it clear how difficult it is for a society to change its norms, and people their ways of behaving.

Will a social change process like that described be adopted by our society and placed in action as a blueprint for survival? Probably not. It is highly doubtful that persons in positions of authority would be willing to change their method of decision making, which often insures their own power and omnipotence, for a method that insures nothing except problem solution and a good life for most of the persons in a society. However, it is important that the public be aware that unless such a problem-solving system is established there may be no future society at all.

Thus, there is both optimism and pessimism about man's future. The optimism is about the future man is capable of creating. The pessimism is about the future he is likely to create. Optimism, because man is in possession of scientific methods at this very moment that would permit him to make problem-solving decisions that would bring about the continuous change required to maintain a high quality of life for the indefinite future. There is pessimism that his greed and insecurity will lead him to cling to decision-making patterns of behavior that, while they may have been helpful in the past, will most certainly lead to his destruction in the future. Like the errant child of well-educated parents who never lives up to his potential, man may not pass the survival test. The parents always wait, hoping that their underachieving child will blossom to full maturity. Usually, he does not. So it is generally with man. Like the errant child, he has the capacity to create the "good life" but his history of destroying those elements in nature that supports him and his fellow man create for the thoughtful person many doubts about his future existence on this planet. New, more scientific and humane decision making would create a future with hope and optimism. Contemporary decision making creates another, filled with grief and despair.

References

Agryris, C. *Intervention theory and method: A behavioral science view.* Reading, Mass.: Addison-Wesley, 1970.

Associated Press, *State Journal,* Lansing, Michigan, July 25, 1970.

Bandura, A. *Principles of behavior modification.* New York: Holt, Rinehart, and Winston, 1969.

Barnett, H. D. *Innovation: The basis of cultural change.* New York: McGraw-Hill, 1953.

Bennis, W. G. *Changing organizations.* New York: McGraw-Hill, 1966.

Bienen, H. *Violence and social change: A review of current literature.* Chicago: University of Chicago Press, 1968.

Blake, R. R. and Mouton, Jane S. *Building a dynamic corporation through grid organization development.* Reading, Mass.: Addison-Wesley, 1969.

Borgstrom, G. A. *Too many.* New York: Macmillan, 1969.

Bowers, D. and Seashore, S. Predicting organizational effectiveness with a four-factor theory of leadership. *Administrative Science Quarterly,* 1966, 238–263.

Carlson, R. *Adoption of educational innovations.* Eugene, Oreg.: University of Oregon Press, 1965.

Clark, D. L. and Guba, E. G. "An examination of potential change roles in education," paper presented at the symposium on Innovation in Planning School Curricula, Airlie House, Virginia, October, 1965.

Clark, D. L. and Hopkins, J. E. Roles for research, development, and diffusion: Personnel in education: Project Memo #1, *A Logical Structure for Viewing Research, Development and Diffusion Roles in Education.* CRP Project No. X-022, April 1966.

Coleman, J. S., Campbell, E. Q., Hobson, C. J., McPartland, J., Mood, A. M., Weinfeld, F. D., and York, R. L. *Equality of educational opportunity.* Report from Office of Education, Washington, D.C.: U.S. Government Printing Office, 1966.

Eipper, A. W. Pollution problems, resource policy, and the scientist. *Science,* 1970, **169**, 11–15. Copyright 1970 by the American Association for the Advancement of Science.

Fairweather, G. W. (Ed.) *Social psychology in treating mental illness: An experimental approach.* New York: Wiley, 1964.

Fairweather, G. W. *Methods for experimental social innovation.* New York: Wiley, 1967.

213

Fairweather, G. W. *Social change: The challenge to survival.* New Jersey: General Learning Press, 1972.

Fairweather, G. W., Sanders, D. H., Maynard, H., and Cressler, D. L. *Community life for the mentally ill.* Chicago: Aldine, 1969.

Fairweather, G. W., and Simon, R. A further follow-up comparison of psychotherapeutic programs. *J. Consult. Psychol.,* 1963, **27**, 186.

Fairweather, G. W., Moran, L. J. and Morton, R. B. Efficiency of attitudes, fantasies, and life history data in predicting observed behavior. *J. Consult. Psychol.,* 1956, **20**, 58.

Fairweather, G. W., Simon, R., Gebhard, M. E., Weingarten, E., Holland, J. L., Sanders, R., Stone, G. B., and Reahl, G. E. Relative effectiveness of psychotherapeutic programs: A multicriteria comparison of four programs for three different groups. *Psychol. Monogr.,* 1960, **74**, No. 5 (whole no. 492).

Festinger, L. Behavioral support for opinion change. *Public Opinion Quarterly,* 1964, **28**, 404–417.

Forsyth, R. P. and Fairweather, G. W. Psychotherapeutic and other hospital treatment criteria: The dilemma. *J. Abnorm. Soc. Psychol.,* 1961, **62**, 598–604.

Glaser, E. M. and Wrenn, G. C. *Putting research, experimental and demonstration findings to use.* (Report of a multi-agency seminar; Office of Manpower policy, evaluation and research, U.S. Department of Labor): Los Angeles Human Interaction Research Institute, 1966.

Glaser, E. M., Coffey, H. S., Marks, J. B., and Sarason, I. B. *Utilization of applicable research and demonstration results.* (Final report to Vocational Rehabilitation Administration, Department of Health, Education and Welfare): Los Angeles Human Interaction Research Institute, 1967.

Goffman, E. *Asylums* (essays on the social situation of mental patients and other inmates). Chicago: Aldine, 1962.

Griffiths, D. Administrative theory and change in organizations. In Miles, M. (Ed.) *Innovation in Education.* New York: Bureau of Publications, Teachers College, Columbia University, 1964.

Havelock, R. *Planning for innovation through dissemination and utilization of knowledge.* Ann Arbor: Institute for Social Research, 1969.

Havelock, R., and Benne, K. "An exploratory study of knowledge utilization." In Watson, G. (Ed.) *Concepts for Social Change.* Baltimore, Md.: Moran Printing Service, Published by N.T.L., NEA for COPED, March, 1967.

Howard, W. E. Of the Newhouse news dispatch, appearing in the Detroit *Free Press,* February 24, 1971.

Katz, R. and Kahn, R. *The social psychology of organizations.* New York: Wiley, 1966.

LaPiere, R. T. *Social Change.* New York: McGraw-Hill, 1965.

Leeds, R. The absorption of protest: A working paper, In Benis, W. S., Benne, K. D., and Chin, R. (Eds.) *The Planning of Change.* New York: Holt, Rinehart, and Winston, 1969.

Lippitt, R., Watson, J., and Westley, B. *The dynamics of planned change,* New York: Harcourt, Brace, 1958.

Mann, F. C. Studying and creating change: A means to understanding social organization. In Arensberg, C. M. (Ed.) *Industrial relations research association: Research in industrial human relations.* New York: Harper, 1957.

Marrow, A., Bowers, D., and Seashore, S. *Management by participation: Creating a climate for personal and organizational development.* New York: Harper and Row, 1967.

Miles, Mathew B. Innovation in education: Some generalizations. In Miles, Mathew B. (Ed.) *Innovation in Education*. New York: Bureau of Publications, Teachers College, Columbia University, 1964, 631–662.

Mishler, E. G. and Tropp, A. Status and interaction in a psychiatric hospital. *Human Relations*, 1956, **9**, 187–205.

National Academy of Sciences. Committee on resources and man of the division of earth sciences, National Research Council, *Resources and Man*: A study and recommendations. W. H. Freeman, 1969.

Roethlisberger, F. J. and Dickson, W. J. *Management and the worker.* Cambridge, Mass.: Harvard University Press, 1964.

Rogers, E. M. and Shoemaker, F. F. *Communication of innovations: A cross cultural approach.* New York: The Free Press, 1971.

Schon, D. *Technology and change.* New York: Delacorte Press, 1967.

Selznick, Philip. Foundations of the theory of organizations. In Etzioni, Amitzi (Ed.) *Complex organizations.* New York: Holt, Rinehart, and Winston, 1964.

Shurcliff, W. A. *Stand sonic boom handbook.* New York: Ballantine Books, 1970.

Siegel, S. *Non-parametric statistics for the behavioral sciences.* New York: McGraw-Hill, 1956.

Stanton, A. H. and Schwartz, M. S. *The mental hospital.* New York: Basic Books, 1954.

Tryon, R. C. and Bailey, D. E. *Cluster analysis.* New York: McGraw-Hill, 1970.

Tryon, R. C., Tryon, Caroline M., and Kuznets, G. Studies in individual differences in maze ability. IX. Ratings of hiding, avoidance, escape, and vocalization responses. *J. comp. Psychology*, 1941a, **32**, 407–435.

Tryon, R. C., Tryon, Caroline M., and Kuznets, G. Studies in individual differences in maze ability. X. Ratings and other measures of initial emotional responses of rats to novel inanimate objects. *J. comp. Psychology*, 1941b, **32**, 447–473.

Watson, G. *Social psychology: Issues and insights.* Philadelphia, Pennsylvania: Lippincott, 1966.

Weber, M. (translated by Parsons, T.) *The protestant ethic and the spirit of capitalism.* New York: Scribner's, 1958.

Whyte, William F. Human relations: A progress report. In Etzioni, Amitzi (Ed.) *Complex Organizations.* New York: Holt, Rinehart, and Winston, 1964.

Wicker, A. J. Attitudes and action: The relationship of verbal and overt behavioral responses to attitude objects. *J. of Social Issues*, 1969, **25**, 41–78.

Wilcoxon, F. W. and Wilcox, Roberta A. *Some rapid approximate statistical procedures.* New York: Published by Lederle Laboratories, 1964.

Wright, P. Technology transfer and utilization: Active promotion of passive dissemination? Research/Development, November 1966.

Index

TITLES IN THE PERGAMON GENERAL PSYCHOLOGY SERIES